The Films of Audie Murphy

THE FILMS OF AUDIE MURPHY

by Bob Larkins
and Boyd Magers

with forewords by
David Stratton and Michael Pate

McFarland & Company, Inc., Publishers
Jefferson, North Carolina, and London

> *The present work is a reprint of the illustrated case bound edition of* The Films of Audie Murphy, *first published in 2004 by McFarland.*

LIBRARY OF CONGRESS CATALOGUING-IN-PUBLICATION DATA

Larkins, Bob.
The films of Audie Murphy / by Bob Larkins and Boyd Magers ;
with forewords by David Stratton and Michael Pate.
p. cm.
Includes bibliographical references and index.

ISBN 978-0-7864-4508-0
softcover : 50# alkaline paper ∞

1. Murphy, Audie, 1924–1971.
I. Magers, Boyd, 1940– .
II. Title.

PN2287.M814L37   2009   791.4302'8'092 — dc22   2004002813

British Library cataloguing data are available

©2004 Deidre Lassau and Boyd Magers. All rights reserved

No part of this book may be reproduced or transmitted in any form or by any means, electronic or mechanical, including photocopying or recording, or by any information storage and retrieval system, without permission in writing from the publisher.

Cover photograph: Audie Murphy in *To Hell and Back,* 1955 (Universal Pictures)

Manufactured in the United States of America

McFarland & Company, Inc., Publishers
Box 611, Jefferson, North Carolina 28640
www.mcfarlandpub.com

To the memory of Audie Murphy

ACKNOWLEDGMENTS

This book could not have been completed without the assistance of many people — some of whom I called on many times over. To their credit, they always proved unrelentingly helpful. In particular, I want to thank actor Michael Pate, who, after I learned of Bob Larkins' basic Audie Murphy film analyses, put me in touch with Deidre Lassau, Bob's widow. It was Michael who put Deidre and me together to complete Bob's initial work. Much credit goes to Rolla Mires, whose knowledge of Audie Murphy is vast beyond words. If this charming, intelligent lady doesn't know the answer, she knows where to find it. Author Robert Nott was gracious in sharing material he had gathered over the years, and you will find his research mentioned often. Ned Comstock at the University of Southern California pulled together their extensive files from Universal-International and allowed me to go through them for several long, rainy days. The manuscript itself would still be in longhand if not for the tireless efforts of my wife Donna Magers. Credit must also go to her for a most complete index.

Also sincere thanks goes to Jan Merlin, G. D. Hamann, Barbara Hall, Michael Fitzgerald, Tom Weaver, Bobby Copeland, Tom and Jim Goldrup, Tinsley Yarbrough, Jack Williams, David Chierichetti, Gene Blottner, Ken Stier, Francis Nevins, Dr. William Russo, Chuck Thagard, John C. Tibbetts, Tommy Farrell, Earl Bellamy, Ken Jones, Les Adams, Chuck Anderson, Dale Crawford, Jim Sorenson, William Russell, Richard Smith III, Joe Copeland, Lance Copeland, Greta Nareau, Don Graham, Jack Bennett, Jeff Raymond, David Macklin, Larry Jensen. I'm quite sure some of these people are unaware they played an important part in making this book a reality; but whether their contributions were large or small, they all helped in some way. For that I am appreciative.

Thanks also to all of Audie's co-workers that I interviewed for sharing their remembrances and insight into a complex individual.

— Boyd Magers

Table of Contents

Acknowledgments — vi
Foreword by David Stratton — 1
Foreword by Michael Pate — 3
Preface — 5
Introduction — 7

The Films

Beyond Glory	21
Texas, Brooklyn and Heaven	24
Bad Boy	26
The Kid from Texas	31
Sierra	36
Kansas Raiders	40
The Red Badge of Courage	45
The Cimarron Kid	55
The Duel at Silver Creek	60
Gunsmoke	64
Column South	67
Tumbleweed	73
Ride Clear of Diablo	76
Drums Across the River	81
Destry	84
To Hell and Back	88
World in My Corner	96
Walk the Proud Land	100
The Guns of Fort Petticoat	104
Joe Butterfly	107
Night Passage	111
Suspicion: "The Flight"	118
G. E. Theatre: "Incident"	119
The Quiet American	120
Ride a Crooked Trail	124
The Gun Runners	127
No Name on the Bullet	130
The Wild and the Innocent	135
Cast a Long Shadow	138
Ford Startime: "The Man"	142
Hell Bent for Leather	143
The Unforgiven	148

Table of Contents

Seven Ways from Sundown	152	*Bullet for a Badman*	187
Posse from Hell	158	*Apache Rifles*	191
Whispering Smith (TV Series)	162	*Arizona Raiders*	196
Battle at Bloody Beach	169	*Gunpoint*	201
6 Black Horses	172	*The Texican*	208
Showdown	175	*Trunk to Cairo*	212
War Is Hell	179	*40 Guns to Apache Pass*	214
Gunfight at Comanche Creek	180	*A Time for Dying*	216
The Quick Gun	184		

Epilogue	221
Bibliography	223
Index	225

FOREWORD
BY DAVID STRATTON

The first Audie Murphy film I saw was *The Kid from Texas*. It was the summer of 1951, and I watched it on a Saturday afternoon with a couple of friends. Already a keen film buff at the age of eleven, I was thrilled by the movie and by Murphy's performance (I know, because I still have a copy of the notes I wrote at the time). Of course, I had no idea then of the baby-faced actor's background; to me he was simply a very youthful western hero who was fast on the draw and whose innocent face masked a steely character. This very affectionate book by Bob Larkins and Boyd Magers brought back vivid memories of that Saturday afternoon more than a half century ago, and of the other Audie Murphy films, some good, some bad, I've seen over the years. Both Bob and Boyd loved the cinema of Hollywood's golden era, and especially westerns. They are as saddened as I am that the western is no longer a staple of American cinema, and that people who should know better reject the genre out of hand. But, in the age of video and DVD, we can re-live the films of the past, not just the acknowledged classics but the minor pleasures, the unselfconscious entertainments that thrilled audiences the world over in more innocent times.

I learned a lot about Murphy from this book, and as a result I've been inspired to hunt down a few of the movies I somehow never saw and to re-visit some of the ones I did. I'm sure this reaction will be shared by anyone who reads these pages. I'm saddened by the fact this book is being published posthumously on Bob's part, but, at the same time, I would like to acknowledge the tenacity of Bob's partner, Deidre Lassau, who, after his death, fought to have his work published and found in Boyd Magers a willing and knowledgeable co-author. Bob would have been delighted by the end result, an important career profile of an unjustly neglected actor who brought pleasure to eager kids like me, and to their parents, back in the days before multiplexes.

Foreword
by Michael Pate

It is gratifying to have been even a small part of a literary venture such as this enthralling book, especially when it has been written by two dear and much admired friends of mine, Bob Larkins and Boyd Magers, and is about one of the truly unique western film actors of the Twentieth century—Audie Murphy. Due to his courage and deadly skills as an infantryman on the battlefields of France after D-Day, this young farmhand from Hunt County, Texas, became a highly decorated war hero before he was old enough to vote. Then, after the war ended, Murphy went on to become one of the young guns of the silver screen, an icon to millions of movie fans, along with the likes of Montgomery Clift, James Dean, Marlon Brando and Steve McQueen.

Although I lived and worked in Hollywood for twenty years between 1950 and 1970, regrettably I never worked on an Audie Murphy film. Of course, because I appeared in a handful of films and television shows that were made at Universal, I remember Audie, and I nodded hullo in passing a few times on the lot. In those distant days it was a friendly lot where everyone seemed to know each other, but more important than that is the fact Audie Murphy was someone I had heard about long before I came to Hollywood. I had read all about his wartime exploits in either the U.S. Armed Forces publication *Stars and Stripes* or *New Guinea Gold*, which was the Army newspaper in the South West Pacific Area where I served with the Australian Imperial Forces during World War II. Here was a guy who had risen from private to lieutenant in the field, who had been wounded three times while he killed 240 of the enemy in just under a year of fighting, and who received every combat medal the U.S. Army could hand out, including the Distinguished Service Cross, the Silver Star and the Congressional Medal of Honor. Later the French government even bestowed upon him their Legion of Honour. What a guy! No wonder I wanted to do a film with him.

It was many years later, in 1985, that I first met up with Bob Larkins in Sydney, Australia. He got in touch with me and asked if I'd talk to him about an old mate of mine, Chips Rafferty, the iconic Australian actor who had sadly died at the young age of 62 in 1971, and about whom Bob was compiling a book. In the next few weeks we met a few times at Bob's home in the inner city and spent many hours yarning about Rafferty, who I had known and worked with in several Australian films, and met up with at sundry spots around the world over some 35 years. Bob subsequently spoke with many other film people, and in 1986 published a warmly personal and very readable biography of Rafferty. Bob was a very likeable fellow, a first-class journalist and broadcaster, a person whose encyclopedic knowledge of films of all kinds was put to good use by various talking-heads who fronted film shows as presenters on Australian TV channels.

Another ten years passed before I had the great good fortune to meet Boyd Magers (and his wife, Donna) at the Western Movie Stars Festival of 1996 in Memphis, Tennessee, to which I had been invited as one of the guests that year. The three of us have been good buddies ever since. When Boyd asked me if I had heard of Bob Larkins and the manuscript he had compiled on the films of Audie Murphy, I went straight into my best Pinkerton Man mode and was pleased as any modern-day Hercule Poirot might be when, very shortly afterwards, I was able to locate Bob's widow, Diedre (Dee) Lassau. She, after our first meeting over lunch at her home in the Blue Mountains to the west of Sydney, gave me a copy of Bob's original manuscript. A few weeks later, just after we received an expression of interest from the eventual U.S. publisher of this book, Dee was delighted when I told her that, if he was willing to (co-) write an extended version of the original compilation, there was no one else in the whole wide world but Boyd Magers into whose scholarly hands we should place Bob's initial work, thus ensuring it would be lovingly shaped into the form it now takes. Only someone with Boyd Magers' gargantuan knowledge of western movies and television shows, and his incredible network of contacts with other western movie and TV writers, researchers, curators, historians, actors and actresses, stuntmen, and film and TV directors, could have produced such a wonderful compendium of information and transformed it into such a seamless extension of Bob Larkins' original manuscript.

Enjoy this book about the films of Audie Murphy and the actor himself by two writers who have combined their talents to give us a biography that embodies all that is worthwhile in the long history of western movie biographies, a book we will not easily forget, but rather, from time to time, will want to read again — and again — and again.

PREFACE

The genesis of this book occurred some 25 years ago when Bob Larkins of Australia wrote the introductory sections and the actual film-by-film analyses of Audie Murphy's movies. It went unpublished, even after Bob's death, until an Audie Murphy devotee, Rolla Mires of Ohio, who had somehow heard about the unfinished manuscript, mentioned it to me. My interest and curiosity aroused, I contacted a friend in Australia, actor Michael Pate, hoping to somehow locate the manuscript. This proved far easier than expected, as Michael had been a friend of Bob's for years prior to his death and had worked with him on various projects, in particular a book about Australian actor Chips Rafferty. Michael quickly contacted Bob's widow, Deidre Lassau, and arranged for us to communicate regarding the completion and publication of Bob's work.

I then spent over a year of additional work and research then constructing the most complete and accurate list ever compiled of credits, casts, locations and costs on every Audie Murphy film and television show. It's worth mentioning that the hardest credits to research were those of the fabulous stuntmen who worked on Audie's films. Various assistant directors' notes were often incomplete in this area. Often a particular stuntman would only work one day on a film to do a horse fall or some other "gag." Assuredly, we have done all we could to make those credits as complete as possible — but to those uncredited "action-actors": if your name is missing, chastise the assistant director who failed to write your name down in his notes 40 years ago … then let us know who you are for future reference. I also interviewed nearly 100 of Audie's co-workers for their remembrances, perspectives and insights into Audie — the actor and the man. A "Notes and Comments" section was then added to each film to offer an idea of what was happening to Audie personally during the time each film was being lensed, and to add other interesting sidelights about the films and some of the people involved.

What Bob started a quarter of a century ago, I am gratified to finish, so those who love and respect Audie Murphy around the world may have a complete and honest perspective on Audie's films and on Audie himself.

INTRODUCTION

When Audie Murphy died in a plane crash on a Virginia mountainside on May 28, 1971, the film world remained largely unmoved. There was none of the hysteria that followed the deaths of Rudolph Valentino and James Dean, none of the wailing about lost genius that washed around in the wakes of the deaths of Marilyn Monroe and Judy Garland. To Hollywood, Audie Murphy was a forgotten man, a name and face from the past, one of a multitude of discarded relics of earlier times. Those who had known him remembered him privately with affection and regret, but the Hollywood of the superstar seventies, and, sadly, most of its public hardly noticed his passing. There were a few magazine tributes, notable for surprising sincerity and dignity, and a handful of bland newspaper features to back up the bald reporting of his death and cursory biographical details. Much was made of his wartime exploits, but little of his acting career. Anyone not familiar with his film work could be pardoned for thinking Audie Murphy was no more than a soldier who'd won a lot of medals, cashed in on them by going into movies instead of knuckling down to find a worthwhile job, made three or four good films and a batch of little westerns few people remember, and made a miserable hash of a number of shaky business ventures. Not a very honorable character — a self-exploiter who had made blatant use of his country's honors for personal gain, and even had the egotistical bad taste to star in a film glorifying his own war experiences. Such was the impression many must surely have gleaned. Nothing could be further from the truth. In this book we hope to correct these impressions through a film-by-film appreciation of Audie Murphy, film actor, as opposed to Audie Murphy, war hero. It is not intended as a definitive biography of Audie Murphy the man; that has been done quite well by Colonel Harold B. Simpson in 1982, Don Graham in 1989 and Audie himself in his autobiography *To Hell and Back* in 1949. Audie Murphy was a complex personality, and the essence of his character is hard to capture.

With grayish-green eyes, reddish-brown hair and a liberal sprinkling of freckles, Audie, in physical appearance, was as Irish as his name. By nature Audie was an idealist whom circumstances forced into becoming a realist. Forthright and sensitive, he loathed both back-scratchers and back-stabbers, hence his aversion to playing the Hollywood game and to the "suits" who run it. Loath to waste words, he often expressed himself with shocking candor. Also, because he steered clear of people and situations that annoyed him, he gained a reputation as being anti-social. In actuality, to his close-knit circle of friends he was warm-hearted and friendly, admiring sincerity and loyalty in his companions. He would never let himself or others be pushed around or belittled. Totally unimpressed by "names," he chose his friends on the basis of character. He detested snobbery and artificiality in any form, often standing up for the less important workers on a movie set. Temperamentally Irish, his moods could swing from high to low for no apparent reason — except to him. In contrast to his melancholic moods, his sense of humor tended toward outrageous practical jokes, perhaps making up in his adult life what he'd missed as a child. Possessing an inward dignity, Audie was completely self-confident and unafraid of any situation. Though sensitive over not completing a high school education, Audie was handicapped little by that fact. He possessed a penetrating mind and instinctive good taste. His one downfall was his habitual gambling — whether it be poker, craps or horses— and his inability to win at any of these. During his life he made and lost several fortunes. Perhaps because of his sharecropper background, money meant nothing to him. Also, after having lived on the edge during the war, perhaps high stakes gambling was the only thing that could once again get his adrenaline pumping.

In Hollywood he was able to transfer his war experiences into his screen persona. The audience knew what he'd done and what he was capable of. Though not a big man, he brought that sense of quiet danger and menace to the screen. When Audie spoke, you knew damn well he meant what he said. All of these personal complexities manifest themselves in his movies, with Audie Murphy the man emerging from this evaluation of his films.

This book is primarily concerned with Audie's years in the film world; his war record surfaces only as background to the subsequent developments in his life and career.

According to many public records, Audie Leon Murphy was born June 20, 1924. However, the wallet Audie was carrying when he was killed contained a driver's license issued in 1970 with his date of birth listed as June 20, 1925. As far back as the mid–1950s, Audie began explaining the discrepancy. At age 17, in 1942, Audie's oldest sister, Corinne, lied about his age so he could enlist in the Army one year before he should have been eligible for service. Therefore, many public records, even his Arlington National Cemetery tombstone, still reflect the 1924 date; but the correct year of birth is 1925. Murphy was born in Hunt County, Texas, one of eleven children of a poor sharecropping family. His father deserted the family when Murphy was 15, leaving Audie as the main provider for the family, shooting rabbits and squirrels with a borrowed rifle, at times even with a slingshot. The accuracy he developed through necessity was to serve him well as a soldier. When America entered World War II, he tried to join the paratroopers and the Marines, but was turned down because he was underweight, and was finally accepted by the army. He fought in the European campaign for three years, winning battlefield promotions from private to lieutenant, and gaining every combat medal awarded by the army, including the highest award for bravery, the Congressional Medal of Honor. He was wounded three times, twice in the legs and once in the hip, and was discharged from the army as fifty percent disabled in September 1945. Officially credited with killing 240 enemy soldiers, he returned home a national hero. It is perhaps evidence of the strength of Murphy's character that though his war experiences scarred him, both physically and psychologically, he was not defeated by them, as many others had been, but managed instead to carve himself a career in an alien industry and win world-wide respect and adulation. Inevitably, the wartime scars took their toll — he never escaped the "hero" tag, and his war-fashioned temperament often led him into serious trouble — but he kept battling until the end.

This book, then, is a purely personal tribute intended to honor a man who received a pretty raw deal from life most of the time, and who deserves a little glory and dignity, late as it may seem.

THE BEGINNING

1945. The war was over, the hero had returned. To nationwide adulation, parades, speeches, brass bands, reporters— and an uncertain future. Audie Murphy had gone off to war as a raw farm boy, and returned, still not yet 21 years old, as a battle-scarred combat veteran, old beyond his years, trained only in the efficient destruction of his fellow man, mentally and physically racked by the horrors of war. The career he wanted, he could not have. His war wounds kept him from continuing in the army full time, although he remained in the reserves. He was restless, unsettled. His closest friends had been the men who fought, and mostly died, beside him; the exploitation offers which poured in, frantically trying to cash in on his fame, held no interest.

"A lot of jobs were offered me," he said. "Selling clothes, insurance, working for oil companies ... but none of them would have given me a chance to learn the business." Audie was even offered a career by Ted Dealy of the *Dallas News*. Dealy offered to send Audie through journalism school to get him started. Then came a different kind of offer — from Hollywood. Actor James Cagney, who operated his own production company in partnership with his brother Bill, saw Murphy's photograph on the front cover of *Life* magazine for July 16, 1945. The Cagneys said they saw "poise and assurance, with spiritual overtones" in his face — the more cynical observer might say they saw a golden opportunity to cash in on the value of the Murphy medals by exploiting the somewhat unnerving contrast between Murphy's angelic appearance and his proven expertise as a killer. Murphy was invited to Hollywood to discuss a contract with the Cagneys, but took his own time about accepting their offer. Eventually,

In uniform, Audie Murphy holds a display of his World War II service medals.

after travelling back and forth from Texas to Hollywood a few times, he decided to give movies a try. He was nearly broke. "I had no qualifications and no ambitions for the job," he said. "But after a while I couldn't afford to ignore it, and then I didn't care."

In August 1946 he signed a contract with the Cagneys, and took up residence at James Cagney's Hollywood ranch. He was sent to the Hollywood Actors Laboratory to learn something about acting, but felt so out of place that he quit after two weeks.

He saw a photograph of starlet Wanda Hendrix on the cover of *Coronet* magazine. Impressed, he managed to arrange a meeting — a dinner party at the Cagney ranch — and romance blossomed. By April 1947 the "young love" angle was rapidly adopted by fan magazines, and Murphy's name was kept in the public eye, even though his film career had yet to start. Eventually, in 1948, he won a small role in Alan Ladd's movie *Beyond Glory* at Paramount, and his screen prospects seemed so promising that, on his return from an army-sponsored trip to France to receive the French Legion of Honor, he proposed to Wanda Hendrix. She accepted.

The fan magazines, gushing about the young couple on the verge of stardom, gave the impression all was well with Murphy — the poor boy who had now won himself a beautiful girl and a place in the Hollywood sun. But, in fact, all was far from well. Murphy's nascent film career had ground to a halt — the Cagneys dropped his option, leaving Audie broke and out of work. Sleeping rough and accepting handouts from friends, he withstood over a year of inactivity, keeping himself occupied by writing his own wartime autobiography, *To Hell and Back*. Its publication brought him a measure of success, some money in the bank, and the revived interest of the film world. In January 1949, with his movie career on the upswing again, he finally married Wanda Hendrix, but the match was doomed.

"She had no more right around me than a lamb around a grizzly," said Murphy later. Hendrix filed for divorce in early 1950, and the break became final in April 1951. Murphy, still suffering from his war experiences, had not been ready for marriage — he was plagued by recurring nightmares and could not sleep without a loaded pistol under his pillow. On one occasion he woke up suddenly and blasted a luminous light switch apart with three shots. Moody and wary, wanting only peace and quiet, Murphy was not interested in the Hollywood party-go-round, nor in meeting the right people, while Hendrix was ambitious and enjoyed the glamorous life. But their parting, when it came, was without bitterness, each accepting the marriage had been a mistake. For Murphy, the blow was softened by his booming film career, which had suddenly taken off after his first starring role in the low-budget independent production *Bad Boy*. His personal life also improved when he was introduced to fellow Texan Pamela Archer, an airline stewardess. They met in 1950, after Murphy had separated from Hendrix, and were constant companions until they married in April 1951, four days after his divorce became final. Their first son, Terrence Michael, was born in 1952.

If there was a unifying factor to Murphy's early film roles, it was his total lack of dramatic ability. Flat-voiced, frozen-faced, and blank-eyed, he intoned his lines with an awkwardness that should have seen him laughed off the screen; but something about him touched a chord with audiences, and his first five films for Universal-International netted the studio a tidy profit of two million dollars. Even Murphy himself could not understand his appeal to the paying customers. "It must be my damned curl," he once said. Whatever it was, the lightness of his movements, the deceptive ease with which he handled all sorts of firearms, or his damned curl, it was cunningly channeled into the right vehicles by Universal after they had purchased his contract from independent producer Paul Short, who made *Bad Boy*. If he had continued playing the sort of contemporary mixed-up roles he assayed in *Bad Boy*, his career might well have ground to a second halt, but it blossomed to promising proportions in the series of crisp little color westerns he made for U-I between 1950 and 1952. He was still no actor, and proved it several times, but he looked good, the camera loved him, and Audie seemed convincing in the pure action scenes of films like *The Kid from Texas, Sierra* and *Kansas Raiders*. However, his first real acceptance as a possible stayer in the movie stakes came with his role in John Huston's *The Red Badge of Courage* in 1951, for which he was loaned to MGM. Huston wanted Murphy for the film from the outset. Criticized for choosing a small-time cowboy actor for the starring role in what was envisioned as a major MGM production, Huston stuck to his guns and won out over the opposition. In the *Red Badge of Courage* pressbook, Huston is quoted as having chosen Murphy because "He was in the necessary age bracket, he is a good actor and can be a better one, and he has had the combat experience which helps give his role as a soldier complete credulity." Huston's comment to writer Lillian Ross, quoted in her celebrated book *Picture*, dealing with the making of the film, is somewhat more earthy, and less suggestive of publicity-department invention. "They'd rather have a star," he said. "They just don't see Audie the way I do. This little, gentle-eyed creature. Why, in the war he'd literally go out of his way to find Germans to kill. He's a gentle little killer." Huston also saw qualities in Murphy as a screen actor which few others have acknowledged. "The screen magnifies and exaggerates whatever it is that a great actor has," he said. "It's almost as though greatness is a matter of quality rather than ability.... You see it in Audie Murphy's eyes. It's like a great horse. You go past his stall, and you can feel the vibration."

Huston's working methods were totally unlike the assembly-line system Murphy experienced on the Universal westerns, and the different approach paid off on the screen. Huston rehearsed his company for two solid weeks at his ranch in California before moving to the locations in another part of the state. He coaxed and cajoled Murphy, went fishing with him, allowed him to bring his own horse on location, and treated him with respect and gentleness. After viewing the first rough cut of the movie, Huston said, "Audie is superb. He's just marvelous. Sensitive. Alive. This boy is something."

Murphy was occasionally troubled with malaria during the shooting, and kept mainly to himself. In *Picture*, Lillian Ross paints a moving word-picture of Murphy as a sad, troubled man, often lost in his own thoughts, treated by Huston like "a frightened child," and totally uninterested in anything but the actual filming. Murphy's own words, quoted in the book in conversation with Huston, partly explain his mental state at the time. "Seems as though nothing can get me excited anymore — you know, enthused?" he said. "Before the war, I'd get excited and enthused about a lot of things, but not anymore." But Huston was able to penetrate the barrier, and although the finished film was not as the director had envisioned it, Murphy emerged as a credible actor and began to earn the respect of the film world. He already had the public on his side, but his stock wasn't high in Hollywood, either as an actor or as part of the social scene, which he resolutely shunned. His habit of saying exactly what was on his mind didn't help him either. It could be argued that had *The Red Badge of Courage* been allowed to continue as Huston had conceived it, Murphy might have gone on to a more illustrious career as a serious actor; but this is only conjecture. In any case, one can see a parallel between Murphy's situation and the fine work of Tim Holt in Huston's earlier *Treasure of Sierra Madre,* after which Holt returned to low-budget westerns at RKO. But it's doubtful Murphy would have been able to continue his career in any other direction anyway, since he was under contract to Universal, and was regarded as a valuable property in the area of westerns. The studio had already refused a TV series offer by western star Gene Autry, and, upon completion of his MGM stint, immediately put him back in the saddle in *The Cimarron Kid.*

After working with Huston, Murphy was less awkward, although still carefully photographed so the more experienced players received the bulk of the dramatic footage, leaving Murphy to handle the action chores. *The Cimarron Kid* was no particular improvement on his other westerns, but, like the others, it again drew the crowds, and his next role was in *The Duel at Silver Creek* in 1952. This time costar Stephen McNally took care of the heavy dramatics, but Murphy was not disgraced. He showed the first hint of the gently cynical humor that would distinguish his best roles in the coming years, and began to display a pleasantly sardonic way of handling semi-comedic lines. The film was little more than a potboiler, with very little period feeling and a lot of talk, but Murphy, in the inevitable black hat that identified his early roles, was more relaxed than he'd ever been, and seemed ready for more dramatically adventurous roles.

THE VINTAGE YEARS

"Audie Murphy looks mild as baby food, but try to outdraw him brother, and you're dead." This comment by an anonymous fan magazine reviewer writing about *Ride Clear of Diablo* in 1954 perfectly sums up Murphy's particular appeal as a western star in his peak period, 1953–1955. His contemporaries of the time, Randolph Scott, Gary Cooper, John Wayne, Joel McCrea, Rod Cameron, Dale Robertson and Rory Calhoun, were all cast in the big, rugged, no-nonsense mold of the larger-than-life hero, the man of obvious strength and skill. Murphy, slim and slight, soft-spoken and boyish, was their complete opposite, often a seemingly soft-centered tenderfoot who posed no obvious threat to the opponents of law and order. But when the chips were down and the lead began to fly, bad guys found they had a tiger by the tail, and audiences delighted in the spectacle of the bantam-weight youth confounding his enemies with devastating expertise and exactness, while retaining his youthful charm.

With one exception, all Murphy's westerns of this period were finely crafted little gems of action and humor, carefully written and directed to make the most of his offbeat appeal. Increasing his stature, these entertaining films led up to the high point of his career, an adaptation of his own biography, *To Hell and Back.*

For Audie Murphy the vintage years were all too short, and included only seven pictures, from *Gunsmoke* to *To Hell and Back.* The superior standard attained during this brief period was to be regained only spasmodically in the ensuing years of his career. The Audie Murphy western of this period has become as much a part of the pop culture of the '50s as Elvis Presley or James Dean; and it was from 1953 onwards that Murphy began to develop a screen identity and attract a loyal following, so that a new Murphy western, though often relegated to second-feature status, became an event. Prior to that time, Murphy served his apprenticeship as the smooth-faced, pretty-boy "kid" of the early years, winning fans more through his looks than through personality, since he had remained very much a negative, cardboard hero around whom more animated performers circled. With 1953's *Gunsmoke*, however, his range seemed to suddenly broaden; he became an active rather than a passive participant in the action, and the developing ease and wry humor that had begun to show in *Duel at Silver Creek* came to full prominence. The well-scrubbed, neatly dressed look was replaced by a more believable scruffiness, the slightly bewildered blankness giving way to a combination of cynicism, caustic humor and natural charm. His gunslinger in *Gunsmoke* was a man who knew all the dirty tricks, trusted nobody but himself and had no time for those who didn't play it straight — very much like Murphy himself, in fact. Yet he was not an unpleasant character — he remained likeable in spite of himself.

In his private life, too, Murphy was enjoying a peak period. He was financially secure, after a long period of struggle following an early incident in which a business manager had made a number of poor investments and left him with massive debts. With the help of Universal's legal department, Murphy pulled himself out of the hole, and was now able to indulge in such leisure activities as horse breeding, skin-diving and adding to his collection of guns. His marriage to Pam Archer, though not without its rocky patches, solidified with the birth of his second son, James Shannon, in 1954, and picture-spreads of Murphy and his family were regular fea-

Audie Murphy is ready for action in this scene from *Tumbleweed* (1953).

tures in the fan magazines. He still maintained a polite distance from the Hollywood social scene — neither smoking nor drinking, and avoiding premieres and parties. Murphy preferred the company of his family to that of his fellow stars, and was happier consorting with studio workmen and production staff than with directors or producers. His modest little movies were proven dollar-earners, and he became a favorite son at Universal, one of the studio's "Big Four" box-office draws (along with Rock Hudson, Tony Curtis and Jeff Chandler). *Gunsmoke* was followed by *Column South*, which fell below standard due to indifferent scripting and direction, with Murphy restricted by having to play a cavalry officer. But his next four films more than made up for it. In quick succession he appeared in *Tumbleweed*, as a wagon-train guide accused of selling out to the Indians; *Ride Clear of Diablo*, as a railroad surveyor (an unusual occupation for someone so proficient as a gunfighter, but nobody really cared) seeking revenge for the murder of his family; *Drums Across the River,* an intelligent action film about Indian wars; and *Destry,* George Marshall's remake of his own *Destry Rides Again,* with Murphy in the James Stewart title role. The film and Murphy were critically acclaimed, and it became clear as a performer ("actor" was perhaps still too strong a word) Murphy had matured enough to take on his toughest role — playing himself in *To Hell and Back,* a project that had been planned as far back as 1950.

"It was like pulling teeth for the first three months when we were planning the picture — just getting Audie to talk," recalled director Jesse Hibbs. Murphy was opposed to any suggestion the film glorify his own exploits. "This isn't just my story," he said. "It's the story of all our company and of the infantry." This conviction that the film should be made as a tribute to all fighting men, and his approach to the part as merely another role (rather than a reliving of his own past), helped him through many rough patches. "I had to think throughout the picture, this isn't me. I'm somebody else," he said. But, of course, it didn't always work, and the genuine emotion which continually surfaced lifted his performance, and the film, to a level of truth above the majority of war films, many of them admittedly better-written, better-directed and better-acted, but few with so compelling a performance in the starring role. The emotional strain on Murphy was considerable, and following the completion of filming, he wrote about it in a national magazine. He wrote of his uneasiness—"...the kind you feel when your mind plays back something you don't want to hear or see or feel again"—and of the impossibility of remaining continually detached: "The charges going off in the make-believe battle are blanks, but the shrapnel goes off in your mind. You are back walking a razor's edge between fear and your control of it, your stomach contracts into a tight, hard ball, and in the hot sun you feel a cold that comes from nowhere. Suddenly I knew that 12 years isn't long enough, maybe 1,200 years isn't long enough." He described his feelings during filming as "this strange jerking back and forth between make-believe and reality, between fighting for your life and the discovery that it's only a game and you have to do a retake because a tourist's dog ran across the field in the middle of the battle." And when the shooting ended, he concluded: "I could walk away from it, and when I came back again there would be no scars, nothing to show that the battle *of* Anzio had been re-fought here. But what you can't walk away from is what you remember."

The success of *To Hell and Back* is now part of Hollywood history; but, ironically, the film that became Audie Murphy's greatest triumph also became his ticket to obscurity. Murphy was now a "star"—but the price was to be high.

THE STAR YEARS

The international success of *To Hell and Back* elevated Audie Murphy to "star" status, as opposed to the more modest heights of purely a "western star." Universal had fired all its big publicity guns for the movie, with one and two-page color spreads in the biggest national magazines, and scores of magazine articles, interviews, and personal appearances—the full works—and it paid off in unprecedented box-office returns. In countries where Murphy was known only as a western star whose films usually occupied the bottom half of a double-bill, he was suddenly "discovered." In Britain, the popular and influential weekly film magazine *Picture-*

goer listed him among the ten best actors of the year, placing him among such illustrious company as Yul Brynner in *The King and I*, Frank Sinatra in *Man with the Golden Arm,* James Dean in *Rebel Without a Cause,* Laurence Olivier in *Richard III* and Marlon Brando in *Guys and Dolls.* Even in Australia, a country notoriously skeptical about the wartime exploits of American servicemen (where the general opinion is, "the Yanks give you a medal if you cut yourself shaving"), the film was a resounding success. Critics who had been previously lukewarm about Murphy as an actor, or had simply ignored his films, were suddenly falling over themselves to find new superlatives to describe his work in *To Hell and Back.*

Murphy was the number one boy at Universal. A new, richer contract was negotiated, allowing him to make one picture a year away from the studio, and Universal cast him in a series of films which reflected, in budget and casting, his new importance in the movie world. Unfortunately, Murphy was not really ready for the diversity of roles the studio felt was his due as one of the hottest actors in Hollywood. *To Hell and Back* was followed by *World in My Corner*, a routine boxing drama, with Murphy as a young boxer caught up in corruption. The film did not fare well, and neither did Murphy.

Next came *Walk the Proud Land*, a serious-minded western biography of Indian Agent John Clum, and although Murphy gave a particularly strong performance, the film failed to impress those fans who expected more action and less thought in a Murphy western. Though popular with critics, the movie was another step backwards for Murphy's film career.

His first independent production, released through Columbia, with Murphy himself as producer (in partnership with western veteran Harry Joe Brown), was *Guns of Fort Petticoat*, again directed by his *Destry* mentor, George Marshall. It proved to be a very routine effort, with Murphy in a role which did nothing to exploit his particular charm.

Next came *Joe Butterfly*, his only outright comedy role, a total disaster with Murphy embarrassingly unfunny as a magazine photographer in post-war Japan.

With *Night Passage,* in partnership with James Stewart, he returned to his roots in an epic-scale western that failed to realize its potential. Among the strangely lackluster cast, only Murphy emerged with any real credit (as Stewart's cynical young outlaw brother); but it was a victory by default rather than merit — Murphy had the best role.

Next came his big try at serious dramatic acting — in Joseph L. Mankiewicz' *The Quiet American*, based on the controversial anti–American novel by Graham Greene set in Vietnam. Co-star Michael Redgrave was superb, while Murphy's sincere efforts paled by comparison. The film, though literate and intelligent, and generally a critical success, flopped at the box office. So did Murphy's chance of remaining a major screen personality, and *Ride a Crooked Trail* found him back in the saddle. Admittedly, it was a more expensive production than his earlier westerns; but despite the surface gloss, it was really a return to the days of *Gunsmoke* and *Diablo* (though without their clean-lined appeal).

Another modern-day drama, *The Gun Runners* (*Guns for the Rebels* in some countries), came next, with Murphy miscast as a Hemingway hero. It played mostly on action-house double bills.

Ironically, Murphy's next film, as his star began to fade rapidly, was one of his best — certainly his best and most intelligent western, and arguably his best performance outside of *To Hell and Back*. This was *No Name on the Bullet,* with Murphy cast against type as a cool, arrogant, contemptuous professional killer whose main

Introduction

Audie Murphy at the height of his popularity, in *Ride a Crooked Trail* (1958).

weapon is psychology rather than a gun. With a clever, biting screenplay, fine direction by Jack Arnold and solid support from a cast of western veterans (including Murphy's long-time friend Charles Drake), plus Murphy's own splendidly mature characterization, it came close to classic stature. Like *Walk the Proud Land*, it is often singled out for retrospective praise. Unfortunately, *No Name on the Bullet* did nothing to revive Murphy's flagging career at the time, and was followed by yet another poorly-judged effort, the backwoods comedy *The Wild and the Innocent*, which saw Murphy rather oddly teamed with Sandra Dee in a fluffy little saga about a mountain lad and his love for a wild young girl. Murphy again gave a mature, restrained performance, but the film missed out on the folksy atmosphere it aimed for, and did very little business. It was the last movie, with one exception, Murphy was to make that held any pretensions of importance. With such a string of flops and near-misses behind him (ten films and performances so variable in quality as to resemble a celluloid patchwork quilt), the "stardom" he had won with the guts and sweat of reliving his own private hell in *To Hell and Back* had dissipated.

But he was still a working actor, employable if not exactly a box-office guarantee, and still enjoyed the security of his family, who accompanied him on location jaunts to Colorado for *Night Passage,* Japan for *Joe Butterfly* and Rome for interiors of *The Quiet American.* During his five months in Saigon and Rome, Murphy was plagued by illness, including an emergency appendectomy, and later featured in a much-headlined row with his studio and with production partner Harry Joe Brown, who poured public scorn on Murphy's announced plans to film *Peer Gynt*— a project which never materialized. Murphy and Brown did not make any more films together. There was a feeling in some areas of the film business that Audie Murphy was getting too big for his cowboy boots, aspiring to artistic achievements that were beyond his capabilities. Perhaps it was true, perhaps not — Murphy was never given the chance to try. For Audie Murphy, the good life was again turning sour — despite the rewards of a happy family life. As always, Murphy was fighting — fighting Hollywood, speaking his mind, refusing to compromise and upsetting those whose influence could make or break an actor. At home, things were fine, but in the Hollywood jungle the bosses were finding that the pussycat who'd brought them such fat rewards was really a tiger who wouldn't play the star game by rules he regarded as "phony." Murphy preferred to go his own way, and it wasn't Hollywood's way — he wanted better roles and better films than he was given, and said so; but instead the films got worse, the budgets lower. Audie Murphy was no longer a viable product, and the remainder of his career would be downhill all the way — with one brief pause, which will be noted later.

THE DECLINE

The decline of Murphy's film career began in 1959, although he would appear sporadically on the screen until his death in 1971. The film that sealed his fate as a major star was *Cast a Long Shadow*, made for United Artists in black and white, laced with stock footage, and populated by many familiar B-western faces. Murphy was half-good, but was out-acted by John Dehner, and the end result was very obviously a second-rate double-bill horse opera. His next western was for Universal, *Hell Bent for Leather*, a sparse chase story directed by George Sherman. Murphy, at that time prosperous enough to own his own plane, assisted Sherman by flying him around to seek out locations; and the spectacular scenery in the Lone Pine area of California (frequently used by Randolph Scott) proved to be the film's main virtue.

Seven Ways from Sundown, Audie's next Universal western, was a resurgence of the old Murphy style — a brisk, well-written tale of a green, young Texas Ranger and his growing respect for his captive, a

Audie Murphy on horseback on the Universal backlot in 1960.

flamboyant killer played in fine style by Barry Sullivan. Murphy was excellent, but the film generally played the lower half of double bills. *Sundown* was to be his last really high-standard starring western. He followed it with *The Unforgiven,* John Huston's big-scale drama of white-Indian conflict in early Texas, with Murphy heading the supporting cast under star-billed Burt Lancaster and Audrey Hepburn. Location work in Durango, Mexico, was held up in the early stages after Hepburn was injured in a fall from a horse, and the film went well over its planned budget, but Murphy emerged with his most favorable critical comments since *To Hell and Back.* The film itself was also well received by critics, but not by the public, and was not the success that might have been expected from the powerful combination of Lancaster, Hepburn, Murphy and Huston.

Next Murphy tried television. In May 1961 he joined the already overcrowded roster of TV cowboys with *Whispering Smith,* a half-hour series co-starring singer Guy Mitchell. Loosely based on a 1949 Alan Ladd western of the same title, with Murphy as a railroad detective using scientific methods in the 1870s, it must have seemed like a good idea at the time. Murphy's contemporary westerners from the Universal stable—Jock Maloney, Rory Calhoun and Joel McCrea—had all joined the TV gold rush with considerable success. Likewise, virtual unknowns, like Hugh O'Brian, James Garner, Jack Kelly and Chuck Connors, had become worldwide hero-figures, and Murphy, as an experienced movie westerner with a loyal following, seemed assured of success. But like so many other ventures in his later years, the series flopped and was cancelled after only 18 episodes. The TV western was dying — the established favorites held their ratings, but the new entries made no impression. The rich field of the TV horse opera had been mined out in a few short years, killing not only itself, but also the low-budget theatrical western it had replaced. Tired of westerns on the small screen, audiences no longer wanted them in cinemas, unless they were big-budget, star-studded epics, and rising production costs made their low returns a luxury few studios could afford. Murphy was fortunate he still had a firm contract with Universal, but the quality of his westerns in the '60s was generally inferior to that of ten years earlier.

After *The Unforgiven*, Murphy's films received what was virtually "throw-away" treatment—released without publicity on the bottom half of double bills in unimportant theaters. Ignored by critics and most fan magazines, these pictures gave the impression Audie Murphy was now just a low-grade cowboy actor clinging somewhat desperately to stardom in a pathetic attempt to revive past glories. His efforts away from Universal-International were even cheaper, and did nothing but further diminish his status.

Posse from Hell, Audie's first film after *The Unforgiven,* was a chase-and-revenge effort with Murphy grittily believable as a single-minded gunman tracking down a gang of killers. Then came *Battle at Bloody Beach,* a mediocre World War II melodrama, and a gradual wind-down to total obscurity (with one or two bright flashes) in a series of B-westerns, beginning with *6 Black Horses,* a Dan Duryea co-starrer which benefited from a Burt Kennedy script but still looked like a reject from Randolph Scott's excellent Budd Boetticher series at Columbia. Then came *Showdown,* a black-and-white potboiler; *Gunfight at Comanche Creek* and *The Quick Gun,* a couple of poverty-row remakes of mid-'50s cheapies; *Bullet for a Badman,* almost a return to form; *Apache Rifles* and *Arizona Raiders,* two more low-grade programmers from the producers of *The Quick Gun*; *Gunpoint,* Murphy's final Universal western; a plodding spy drama called *Trunk to Cairo*, filmed in Israel; the pathetic Spanish-made *The Texican*; and, in 1967, another cheap Columbia action piece, *40 Guns to Apache Pass,* his last starring role. By now Audie was only going through the motions, and when he faded quietly from sight after *40 Guns*, his absence was hardly noted (other than by diehard Audie Murphy fans). The movie world was finished with Audie Murphy — but Murphy was not quite finished with movies. He was down, but far from out.

If Audie Murphy, Movie Star, was poor copy during the '60s and '70s (apart from a brief flurry when *Whispering Smith* began), Audie Murphy, War Hero, still managed to make the news, one way or the other. In a feature article on TV westerns in March 1959, *Time* magazine noted how Murphy had upset Hugh O'Brian, one of the reigning kings of the TV western with his *Wyatt Earp* series. O'Brian reportedly offered to bet $500 he could beat any other western hero to the draw. Murphy countered with an offer to raise the stakes to $2,500, but stipulated only live ammunition be used. O'Brian did not pursue the matter! Also in 1959, Murphy made news when he almost drowned during filming of *The Unforgiven*; and 1960 newspapers carried stories of his separation from Pamela, one of a number of estrangements that would plague the marriage. In June 1962 Murphy was charged with assault after allegedly punching a teenager and pulling a gun, but was acquitted. A further blow came in 1967 when he lost an investment of some $250,000 in an Algerian oil venture which failed after the Arab-Israeli Six-Day war. In 1968 Murphy declared bankruptcy when he was unable to pay a promissory note. Residuals from the sale of his old films to television were taken by the Internal Revenue Service for outstanding back taxes, but he remained heavily in debt, and was forced to sell one of his horse-breeding ranches to Bob Hope. In 1970 came the biggest blow of all — a trial for attempted murder after an incident in which he allegedly assaulted a greyhound trainer and his wife, firing a gun at the man and slapping the woman. The charge was later dismissed, but the worldwide publicity was a humiliating experience for a man who once commanded profound respect for his exploits as a war hero and immense popularity as a movie star. After the court hearing that saw him committed for trial, Murphy told reporters: "This charge against me has affected my career. I'm a producer of movies, and financial backers wonder what kind of man they are doing business with. I expect to be completely exonerated."

As a movie producer, he had joined forces with writer-director Budd Boetticher (described by Murphy as "a genius who just needs a chance") to make a series of low-budget westerns, with financial backing from a tax attorney and an oilman. But only one film, *A Time for Dying,* was made. Completed in 1969, the movie was still unreleased at the time of Murphy's death. It eventually screened in Europe in 1971 and saw a limited videotape release.

Following his trial, Murphy again tried to stave off financial disaster in a number of business ventures; and it was on a trip involved with one of them that he died when the plane in which he was travelling with five other men crashed into a mountainside near Roanoke, Virginia, during a rainstorm. The bodies, strewn about the burnt-out wreckage of the plane, were discovered on June 1, 1971, and on June 7 Murphy was buried, with military rites, at Arlington National Cemetery in Washington, D.C.

THE FILMS

Beyond Glory
(PARAMOUNT, SEPTEMBER 1948)

CREDITS: *Producer:* Robert Fellows; *Director:* John Farrow; *Assistant Directors:* (William) Herbert Coleman, Harry Caplan; *Screenplay:* Jonathan Latimer, Charles Marquis Warren, William Wister Haines; *Editor:* Eda Warren; *Director of Photography:* John F. Seitz; *Art Directors:* Hans Dreier, Franz Bachelin, Robert Clatworthy; *Costumes:* Edith Head; *Makeup:* Wally Westmore; *Sound Recording:* Hugo Grenzbach, Walter Oberst; *Music:* Victor Young; *Technical Advisor:* Brig. General Gerald J. Higgins.

CAST: Alan Ladd (Rockwell Gilman); Donna Reed (Ann Daniels); George Macready (Major General Bond); George Coulouris (Lew Proctor); Harold Vermilyea (Raymond Denmore Sr.); Henry Travers (Pop Dewing); Tom Neal (Captain Harry Daniels); Conrad Janis (Raymond Denmore Jr.); Dick Hogan (Eddie Loughlin); Paul Lees (Miller); Audie Murphy (Thomas); Geraldine Wall (Mrs. Daniels); Luis Van Rooten (Dr. White); Charles Evans (Mr. Julian); Margaret Field (Cora); Sean McClory (Barney); Steve Pendleton (General Prescott); Vincent Donahue (John Craig); Harland Tucker (Colonel Stoddard); Russell Wade (Jensen); Johnny Michaels (Michaels); Robert Coleman (Carson); James Burke (Bartender); Martin Lowell (Beast detail); David Ragan, Robert Winkler, Frank Mullen (West Point candidates); Jack Searl (Lt. Brown); William Challee, Lester Dorr (Sergeants); John Benson (M. P. Sergeant); Bob Simpson (Capt. in combat clothes); Marcia Yousen (young woman in church); Jerry James, John Sheehan (4Fs); Francis Pierlot (Mr. Charles); Noel Neill, Ann Sterling (Girls in hotel room); Tim Ryan (Man in hotel room); Dorothy Abbott (Girl); Rusty Marlowe (Girl in bar); Joe Whitehead (Man in bar); Julia Faye (Woman in church); Virginia Vinson (Young woman in church); Jerry James (Corporal McMullen); Billy Burt (Lt. Col. Hall); Don Shelton (Chaplain); Geraldine Jordan, Elaine Riley (Nurses); William Neff (Lt. Peters); Bob Tidwell (Cadet); Russell Arms (Milliken); William Meader, Hal Rand (Officers); Lloyd Hagerty (Congressman); Henry Crittman (Reporter Johnson); Harold Miller (Reporter); Joey Ray (Photographer); Len Hendry, James Davies (M.P.s); Tommy Summers (Plebe); Richard Gaunt (First Classman); Jack Marvin, Jack Parker (Second Classmen); James Fallet (Yearling); Glen Vernon (Yearling in mess hall); Ward Ellis (Second Classman in mess hall); Noel Reyburn, Hal Melone (Plebes in ballroom); Bob Templeton (Lt. Col.); Delia Bogart (Lt. Colonel's wife); Frank Marlowe (Boxing instructor); Robert Watson, Paul Picerni (Detectives), Mickey Phillips (Capt. at range).

RUNNING TIME: 82 minutes

FILMING DATES: August 28, 1947–September 13, 1947; October 13, 1947–November 25, 1947; retakes December 3, 1947

LOCATIONS: Paramount lot; United States Military Academy at West Point, New York.

While his courtship of Wanda Hendrix was being reported in gushing tones in the fan magazines, Murphy made his film debut in a small role in this routine Alan Ladd drama set at West Point Military Academy, with Ladd as a rebellious cadet who finally sees the error of his ways. It was ironic that Murphy, whose war wounds had kept him from a West Point career, made his first appearance on screen as a cadet officer. He was required to give another cadet a hard time, but was not over-impressed with his own performance. "I had eight words to say," he said later, "seven more than I could handle."

The film, originally titled *The Long Gray Line* (a title later used by John Ford), was the only work he obtained through his Cagney brothers contract.

In later years Murphy would be frequently compared to Alan Ladd because of his equally inflexible acting style, and in 1961 he starred in a short-lived TV series based on the title character of Ladd's first starring western, *Whispering Smith*.

Murphy's connection with the Cagneys was terminated shortly after his film debut. According to one report, the break was precipitated by an incident at a Cagney party in which Murphy floored Bill Cagney in a judo scuffle after the much bigger man had aroused the explosive Murphy temper. He did not work in films again for more than a year.

REMEMBRANCES: *Audie Murphy:* "Alan Ladd gave me the best advice I ever got in Hollywood. Just relax, do my work and get away from the studio." Ladd also advised Audie not to get upset over pressures and temperaments in the motion picture business. "I was still under contract to Cagney then. I only went to acting school [Actors Studio] for two weeks, then decided I didn't want to attend their Thursday night meetings to talk politics. Even though the school was subsidized by the government — there were a lot of leftists and Commie lovers in it. Dore Schary called and invited me to his home and asked if I would run for Congress. He said they would see to it I was elected. I

Publicity photograph of Audie Murphy in his first screen role for *Beyond Glory* (1948).

Donna Reed (*left*, in chair), Henry Travers (hands folded), and Alan Ladd (sitting behind table) in a tense moment from *Beyond Glory* (1948).

looked around the room at the bunch there and said, 'Hell, I can't even make a living. Why would I want to run for Congress?' When I said no—that ended the discussion—I didn't stay more than five minutes."

Director John Farrow: "Audie has as much natural acting talent as any newcomer I've ever worked with."

Elaine Riley: "I remember I was taller than Alan Ladd. They built a board of some kind for him to stand on when we had a scene together, that may be on the cutting room floor! [Laughs]. But I don't recall Audie."

Sean McClory: "I don't remember Audie in *Beyond Glory*. But Alan Ladd and I had a fight. Alan was a very small man. He was up on planks walking around and I was tripping over them all the time. [Laughs]"

NOTES AND COMMENTS: Still under contract to the Cagneys, for his first film Audie was paid $3,000 on a ten-week guarantee. Contractually, the Cagneys were entitled to one-half that sum; however, the corporation refused to claim any of the money. The Cagney Corporation dropped Audie's contract after this film. Cagney and Audie remained on the best of terms. Cagney, however, said of him many years later, "It turned out we had no use for him. He couldn't act." Murphy stated, "He simply had nothing for me to do, and you can't take money for nothing."

Joan Caulfield was initially cast as Ann Daniels—no explanation as to why the change was made.

Portions of General Dwight D. Eisenhower's address to the 1947 graduating class at the U.S. Military Academy are included in the film. Because there was no existing newsreel footage of the actual speech, Paramount arranged to shoot a brief close-up of Eisenhower speaking lines from the address in late 1947 at the Department of Agriculture in Washington, D.C.

On September 6, 1947, the *Hollywood Citizen News* reported Robert Montgomery was trying to get Audie for the role of a blind war veteran on TV's *Lights Out*. Nothing ever came of it.

Actress Margaret Field is also known as Maggie Mahoney, wife of actor and stuntman Jock Mahoney, and mother of actress Sally Field.

At the time this film was made, Audie was bunking on an Army cot in the back room of a Hollywood health salon.

Texas, Brooklyn and Heaven
(UNITED ARTISTS, JULY 1948)

CREDITS: *Producer:* Robert S. Golden; *Associate Producer:* Louis J. Rachmil; *Director:* William Castle; *Assistant Director:* Harold Godsoe; *Screenplay:* Lewis Meltzer (based on the story *Eddie and the Archangel Mike* by Barry Benefield); *Editor:* James Newcom; *Director of Photography:* William Mellor; *Art Director:* Jerome Pycha Jr.; *Set Direction:* George Sawley; *Gowns:* Mary Grant; *Wardrobe:* Earl Moser; *Sound:* John Carter; *Hairdresser:* Helen Lierley; *Makeup:* Mel Burns; *Musical Director:* Emil Newman; *Musical Score:* Arthur Lange; *Song:* "Texas, Brooklyn and Heaven" music and lyrics by Ervin Drake, Jimmy Shirl.

CAST: Guy Madison (Eddie Tayloe); Diana Lynn (Perry Dunklin); James Dunn (Mike); Lionel Stander (the Bellhop); Florence Bates (Mandy); Michael Chekhov (Gaboolian); Margaret Hamilton (Ruby Cheever); Moyna MacGill (Pearl Cheever); Irene Ryan (Opal Cheever); Colin Campbell (MacWirther); Clem Bevans (Capt. Bjorn); William Frawley (Agent); Alvin Hammer (Bernie); Roscoe Karns (Carmody); Erskine Sanford (Dr. Dunson); John Gallaudet (McGonical); James Burke (Policeman); Guy Wilkerson (Thibault); Audie Murphy (Copyboy); Tom Dugan (Bartender); Jesse White (Customer); Frank Scannel (Barker); Dewey Robinson (Sergeant); Ralph Peters (Cop on phone); Herb Vigran (Man in subway); Jody Gilbert (Lady); Mary Treen (wife); Charles Williams (Reporter).

RUNNING TIME: 76 minutes

FILMING DATES: Mid–January 1948– February 19, 1948

LOCATION: General Services Studio in Hollywood.

The money Murphy earned for *Beyond Glory* did not keep him properly fed and sheltered during his subsequent out-of-work period, and he frequently slept rough (and free) in a Hollywood gymnasium owned by a friend, Terry Hunt. He would later name his first son Terry as a token of his gratitude. During this period, his name was bandied about Hollywood in connection with various film roles. He was approached with offers of work aimed at exploiting his war record, but he refused to cash in on his medals by taking such exploitation roles, and nobody was prepared to give him a chance as merely *an* actor, rather than as Audie Murphy, war hero. There was publicity value in his war record, but he was an unknown quantity as an actor, and even the release of *Beyond Glory* did nothing to help a career that looked like it would die before it had even started.

Murphy began to write his wartime

Director William Castle points to Audie Murphy's small part as a copy boy in *Texas, Brooklyn and Heaven* (1948). Producer Robert S. Golden smiles approvingly.

autobiography, *To Hell and Back*. He wrote it in longhand, in the present tense, because to him there was no past or future to a soldier at the front. He showed it to journalist Spec McClure, who worked for columnist Hedda Hopper, one of Murphy's early Hollywood champions, and McClure offered to help him turn the material into a book (in exchange for 40 percent of the income). In July of 1948, Audie signed a contract with Henry Holt and Company to publish his bio. Audie received a $1,500 advance at the time of signing. Published early in 1949, the book proved a literary and financial success.

Audie's second screen appearance was a bit part, filmed in one day, as a newspaper copy boy in *Texas, Brooklyn and Heaven* (called *The Girl from Texas* in Britain), a lightweight romance starring Guy Madison and Diana Lynn, a popular juvenile leading lady of the '40s and early '50s. Madison was an untrained youngster who'd made his film debut in a small role in *Since You Went Away* while on leave from the U.S. Navy, after his good looks had been noticed during a studio visit. Like Murphy, Madison was a fairly wooden actor, and quickly faded into film obscurity, only to emerge in 1951 as TV's *Wild Bill Hickok*, and re-emerge in the mid–1950s as a rival to Murphy in the medium-budget western field. Murphy's second film made as little impression as his first, but the breakthrough to stardom was on the way.

REMEMBRANCES: *Jack Elam:* "Over the years I got to know Audie quite well. I'm proud to call him a personal friend. He was a very private person and I will say nothing to impose on that privacy. Audie and I had a relationship that extended several months before either of us were actors. He was under contract to James Cagney's company for actor training and preparing. At that time I was comptroller for Hopalong Cassidy Productions. We were at the same studio (General Services) and both had a taste for the ponies. Since we used the same bookie about a block from the studio, we ran into each other regularly and established a very friendly racing form relationship. Little did we know that years later we would be working together before the camera."

NOTES AND COMMENTS: Audie was paid $500 for three days work. He was also given four shirts for posing in an advertisement as a promotion for the film.

Originally copyrighted with a running time of 89 minutes, the film was edited before release. One wonders if any of Audie's work ended up on the cutting room floor.

At about this time (or shortly thereafter), Audie was living at 2001 Coldwater Canyon.

In July 1948 Audie went to Paris, France, to represent American troops in celebration of Bastille Day, and to retrace his division battle route up through Southern France to Colmar in preparation for his autobiography, which was then titled *For a Young Man's Heart*. Of his planned book, Audie stated, "If I can tell the story as we all saw and lived it, it will mean more to me than anything I will do in the movie business." Audie was in uniform throughout the tour of France with the 3rd Division.

Bad Boy
(ALLIED ARTISTS, FEBRUARY 1949)

CREDITS: *Producer:* Paul Short; *Associate Producer:* George Bertholon; *Director:* Kurt Neumann; *Assistant Director:* Frank Heath; *Dialogue Director:* Clarence Marks; *Story:* Robert D. Andrews, Paul Short; *Screenplay:* Robert D. Andrews; *Additional Dialogue:* Karl Kamb; *Supervising Film Editor:* Otho Lovering; *Film Editor:* William Austin; *Director of Photography:* Karl Struss; *Art Director:* Theobold Holsopple; *Set Decorator:* Raymond Boltz Jr.; *Production Designer:* Gordon Wiles; *Production Manager:* Allen K. Wood; *Costume Supervision:* Lorraine MacLean; *Technical Advisor:* William O'Donnell; *Sound:* Earl Sitar; *Makeup:* Charles Huber; *Hairdresser:* Lela Chambers; *Men's Wardrobe:* Courtney Haslam; *Ladies' Wardrobe:* Esther Krebs; *Musical Score:* Paul Sawtell; *Song:* "Dream on Little Plowboy" words and music by Gene Austin.

CAST: Lloyd Nolan (Marshall Brown); Jane Wyatt (Maud Brown); Audie Murphy (Danny Lester); James Gleason (Chief); Stanley Clements (Bitsy Johnson); Martha Vickers (Lila Strawn); Rhys Williams (Arnold Strawn); Selena Royle (Judge Florence Prentiss); James Lydon (Ted Hendry); William Lester (Joe Shields); Dickie Moore (Charlie); Tommy Cook (Floyd); Francis Pierlot (Mr. Pardee), Stephen Chase (Sheriff Wells); Florence Auer (Mrs. Meehan); George Beban (Bill, bell captain); Walter Sande (Texas oil man); Herman Cantor, Paul Bryar, Jack Lomas, George Eldredge, Harold Goodwin (Gamblers); Bill Walker (Ollie); Andy Andrews (Police officer); Michael Gaddis (Police officer in car); Barbara Woodell (Mrs. Strawn); Charles Trowbridge (Dr. Fletcher); Milton Kibbee (Constable); Lee Phelps (Bailiff); Mike Mahoney (Officer at hospital); Gerry Pattison (Blonde with Joe); Walden Boyle (Hotel clerk); John O'Connor (Mahoney, hotel detective); Carl Saxe, Ray Teal, Robert Strong (Police

Martha Vickers tries to keep her father, played by Rhys Williams, and *Bad Boy* Audie Murphy from coming to blows.

officers); Marion Gray, Catherine Price (Matrons); Marie Blake (Miss Worth).

RUNNING TIME: 83 minutes

FILMING DATES: Mid–October to mid–November 1948

LOCATIONS: Monogram Studios; Janss Ranch, Conejo Valley, California.

Murphy's first starring role, released on February 22, 1949, shortly after his marriage to Wanda Hendrix on January 8, 1949, was not a particularly auspicious event in cinema history, and, apart from "introducing" Murphy, is perhaps notable only for the fact it anticipated the juvenile delinquent cycle of the mid–1950s, which sprang to full flower after *Blackboard Jungle*. The picture was produced by Paul Short, an agent and theater man who saw an opportunity of cashing in on Murphy's medals and signed him to an exclusive contract which offered a minimum of $5,000 a film.

Financial backing for the movie came from the world-renowned charitable organization Variety Clubs International. Murphy was considered particularly appropriate for the starring role, since he was a Texan — and a famous one — and the film would deal with events that had occurred at a Club-financed Boys' Ranch for delinquents in Copperas Cove, Texas. Set on the Ranch, it depicted the efforts of its controller (played by Lloyd Nolan) to rehabilitate an arrogant, unrepentant young thief with a long record of robbery and violence. The role of the boy, Danny Lester, was tailored to fit Murphy's limitations; when Nolan was required to lament that, "You talk to him and he isn't there," proved particularly apt, in view of Murphy's glacial, totally unemotional portrayal. It was this film which gave rise to one of the most frequently quoted examples of Murphy's modesty regarding his own ability. The story goes that director Neumann was despairing at Murphy's inability to register the proper reaction, and that Murphy told him: "You forget that I've got a hell of a handicap." "What handicap?" asked the director. "No talent," replied Murphy. Whether it was true or not, it was certainly accurate in light of Murphy's wooden non-performance. He was stiff and gauche to a degree which would have been ludicrous without his unusual baby-faced appearance and soft-spoken little-boy appeal. But the combination of his almost angelic appearance and his explosions into sudden violence was an intriguing one, and his frozen-faced posing and toneless delivery was in keeping with the character. Murphy's co-stars, old movie hands like Nolan, Jane Wyatt, James Gleason, Stanley Clements and James Lydon, were solid enough to offset his daunting dramatic deficiencies. Rhys Williams, as Audie's villainous stepfather, whose false accusation that Murphy had murdered his own mother was the psychological trigger which set him on the criminal path, tended to overplay, but on the whole the performances were soundly professional. There was, of course, the added bonus of Murphy's war record, still fairly fresh in the minds of patriotic Americans, and curiosity probably played a large part in the success of the film, with audiences anxious to identify with the young hero whose innocent appearance belied his lethal achievements on the battlefield.

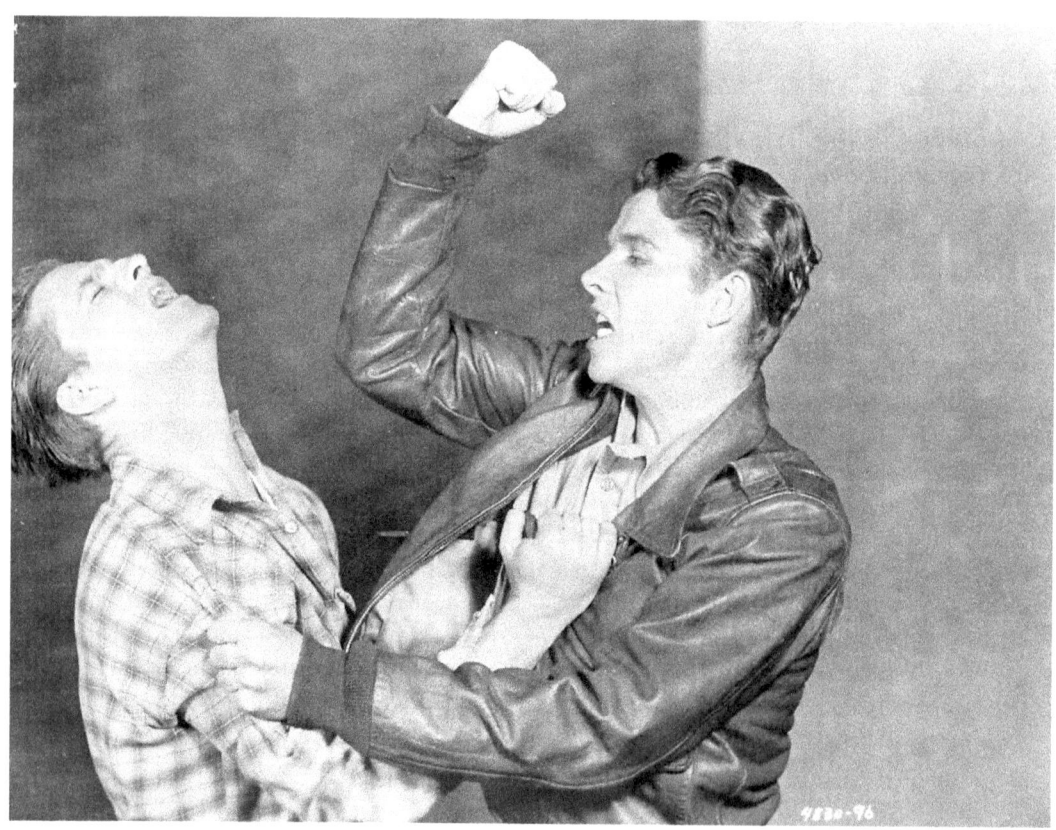

Audie *Bad Boy* Murphy just can't get along with others — in particular, Stanley Clements.

The final scene, showing the reformed Danny, now a model citizen, training at a Military Academy, was obviously inserted to get Murphy into uniform and squeeze a little more mileage from his hero status. Murphy survived the awfulness of his first performance, although it's arguable he might not have done so had he not subsequently been cast almost exclusively in western roles, where acting had always been secondary to action.

REMEMBRANCES: *Audie Murphy* (on the set of *Bad Boy*): "As a newcomer to screen acting I'm asked repeatedly about my feelings and experiences, and I'm told all the time to take it easy by my associates. They figure, I guess, that I'm plenty scared, and if I relax I might make the grade. I appreciate all this advice and concern over my acting, but I'm not easily frightened, and, after my experiences in the war where I saw some mighty big and dangerous machines, I'm not easily impressed by a mere motion picture camera. By that I mean I'm not nearly as jittery with the camera's eye upon me as my well-meaning friends think I am. I'm too interested in the progress of this picture, watching the director, the cameraman, and the technicians to give very much thought to myself. I'm getting a lot of good acting tips from Jane Wyatt, Lloyd Nolan and James Gleason, among others in the cast, and that has bolstered my confidence considerably. I like screen acting, and my fondest hope is that I'll measure up in the public's eye to the high standards established by the veterans of this business so I can make it a permanent career."

Jimmy Lydon: "Audie looked like a quiet boy, prettiest little boy you ever saw. He was only about five-eight, five-nine, couldn't weigh 130 pounds dripping wet. And he was so bashful and so shy. We were going out on location, so Audie would sit in the front seat of the car and [James] Gleason and Lloyd Nolan and I would be sitting in the back. We'd get about 15 minutes out of the city and Audie would say, 'Please sir, would you mind stopping the car?' And the driver would stop the car and Audie would get out and lose his breakfast. Then he'd get back in the car and we'd drive on to the location and start working. We'd have lunch all together and someone would say, 'Where's Audie?' And Audie was behind a bush somewhere out in the toolies losing his lunch ... this real gutsy hero. He and I dressed together on location with just a four-wall piece of canvas. And I tell you, frankly, his leg was full of holes like a Swiss cheese. And it's not very pleasant to say, but he had a hole in his butt that big (making a fist) right there. He was quite a guy — but so bashful and so shy. He always looked like he was kind of deep in thought about something else. But he apparently appreciated the cast's sympathy. After the shoot was over, he said, 'They were wonderful.' When he was angry, he never raised his voice but he had those steel gray eyes that looked right through you. When he said I'm gonna kill you he meant it! He did that one time and the guy left. Believe me."

With due respect to Lydon's observations of Audie's vomiting, following the war Audie suffered from dyspepsia, was on medication for a nervous stomach and was treated for ulcers. Referring to it as his "trick stomach," he tried to maintain a strict diet and stay away from spicy Mexican food, which he dearly loved but which upset his stomach. The scars on Audie's legs were from wounds received during action at Genevreuville, France, in 1944, and later at a battle in Riedwihr Woods, France, in January 1945. The right buttock wound came at Les Rouges Eaux, France, in October 1944.

Jane Wyatt: "I, along with others, regarded Audie as a curiosity. He was the cutest little boy and so very nice, but he was by no means a forceful figure on the set. A very nice kid — that's all."

NOTES AND COMMENTS: Audie's autobiography *To Hell and Back* was published

Lloyd Nolan and Jane Wyatt are only trying to help troubled youth Audie Murphy in *Bad Boy*.

by Henry Holt and Company in February 1949. Later that month, on February 22, *Bad Boy* premiered in the 43 cities in which the Variety Club was then operating. The world premiere was in Dallas on February 16.

Marshall Brown, the character portrayed by Lloyd Nolan, was the real-life superintendent at Copperas Cove.

When Paul Short, connected with Interstate Theatres Inc. of Dallas, Texas, cast Audie in *Bad Boy*, he put him under personal contract. Short owned the story rights (then called *The Police Story*), and made the deal with Allied Artists on the condition Audie would star.

Short also had plans to star Audie at Allied Artists in *Buckskin* (about the Indian wars, and based on War Department records), but these plans were discarded when Universal-International bought out Short's contract with Audie.

By now Audie and new wife Wanda were living at 4404 Jacaranda in Burbank.

Ralph Edwards peered into Audie's world on March 7, 1949, on his popular NBC radio show *This Is Your Life*. While the show was portrayed as a surprise, it was actually part of the publicity tour set up by the publisher of Audie's book, *To Hell and Back*. Audie was aware the broadcast was going to take place. It has been reported Audie appeared on a televised version of *This Is Your Life* in 1954, but Edwards' office has confirmed this never took place. It was his policy never to do more than one show (radio or TV) about one person.

The Kid from Texas
(UNIVERSAL-INTERNATIONAL, MARCH 1950)

CREDITS: *Producer:* Paul Short; *Associate Producer:* George Bertholon; *Director:* Kurt Neumann; *Assistant Directors:* Joe Kenny, Phil Bowles; *Story:* Robert Hardy Andrews; *Screenplay:* Robert Hardy Andrews and Karl Kamb; *Editor:* Frank Gross; *Director of Photography:* Charles Van Enger; *Technicolor Consultant:* William Fritzsche; *Art Directors:* Bernard Herzbrun, Emrich Nicholson; *Set Decorators:* Russell A. Gausman, Oliver Emert; *Gowns:* Rosemary Odell; *Music:* Milton Schwarzwald; *Sound:* Leslie I. Carey; Robert Pritchard; *Hair Stylist:* Joan St. Oegger; *Makeup:* Bud Westmore; *Unit Manager:* Dewey Starkey. Technicolor.

CAST: Audie Murphy (Billy the Kid); Gale Storm (Irene Kain); Albert Dekker (Alexander Kain); Shepperd Strudwick (Jameson); Will Geer (O'Fallon); William Talman (Minninger); Martin Garralaga (Morales); Robert H. Barrat (General Lew Wallace); Walter Sande (Crowe); Frank Wilcox (Pat Garrett); Dennis Hoey (Major Harper); Ray Teal (Sheriff Rand); Don Haggerty (Morgan); Paul Ford (Sheriff Copeland); John Phillips (Sid Curtis); Harold Goodwin (Matt Curtis); Zon Murray (Lucas); Tom Trout (Denby); Rosa Turich (Maria); Dorita Pallais (Lupita); Pilar Del Rey (Margarita); Edward Gargan (Blacksmith); Dick Wessell (Jailer Barnes); Edmund Cobb (Hale); Watson Downs (Bookkeeper); Pierce Lyden (Hagen); William Fawcett (Line Cook); Jack Ingram (Wagon Driver); Jim Hayward (Cowboy); Jack Shutta (Deputy); Bob Wilke, Johnny Carpenter (Gunmen); Beulah Parkington (Mrs. Hale); Terry Frost (Townsman); Al Ferguson, Robert O'Neil, Jack Curtis, Martin Cichy, Rory Mallinson (Men). Parley Baer (voice-over narrator). Stunts: Fred Carson, Glen McCarthy (doubled Don Haggerty), Guy Teague (doubled Zon Murray), Warren Fisk, Dale Van Sickel, Billy "Sailor" Vincent, Willard Willingham, Ralph Willingham, John Lilley, Bob Burrows, Chuck Roberson (doubled Shepperd Strudwick), LeRoy Johnson, Bud Wolfe, Bert LeBaron, George Sowards, Jeremy Brown, George McMahon, Tom McDonough, Roy Bucko, Clem Fuller, Bill McCoy.

Audie Murphy out-shot everyone in picking off ground squirrels with a rifle during the making of *Kid from Texas* (1950). Co-star Gale Storm admires Audie's shooting eye, but doesn't appreciate the noise.

The Kid from Texas

RUNNING TIME: 78 minutes
FILMING DATES: May 26, 1949–June 29, 1949
LOCATIONS: Jack Garner Ranch near Idyllwild, CA. (Pine Meadows—desert, Billy's camp; Hurkee Creek—where Minninger kills Morgan; Garner Ranch—Jameson funeral, ranch countryside); Morris Ranch (adobe ranch); Universal backlot.
BUDGET/COST: $592,924

For his first starring role at Universal-International, as the notorious young New Mexico outlaw William (Billy the Kid) Bonney, Murphy found himself working for the studio which was to mold his screen image and carefully manage his career for the next decade. To finance the film, producer Short was forced to share Murphy's contract with U-I, a merger which gave the film the advantages of Technicolor and the high-gloss professional finish which characterized the studio's westerns of the early '50s. The *Bad Boy* production team was reunited—producer Short, director Neumann, writers Robert Hardy Andrews and Karl Kamb—resulting in a tight, somewhat detached but soundly entertaining little western, told in semi-documentary style with voice-over narration by noted actor Parley Baer. Previous Billy Bonney sagas had starred Johnny Mack Brown and Robert Taylor, but this was the most factually accurate version, allowing for a contrived (but unconsummated) romance between Billy and the young wife (Gale Storm) of lawyer Alexander Kain (Albert Dekker). Billy's character was glossed over to match Murphy's romantic image, and the film's claim to authenticity received a serious setback via the immaculate two-gun, black-hat-and-leather-jacket outfit Murphy wears.

Audie's first scene was one of the most beautifully staged launching pads any western star has ever received. Bad guy William Talman, in the process of terrorizing Shepperd Strudwick and Albert Dekker, contemptuously tells one of his cohorts (veteran B-western badman Pierce Lyden) to disarm the watching Murphy. Murphy backed up his flatly-intoned "Nobody takes my guns!" with a dazzling display of two-handed shooting that shattered wrists in all directions, and set the pattern for many such scenes in which the bad guys underestimated the baby-faced youth with the deceptively mild manner. Following this initial outburst of violence, rancher Jameson (Strudwick) persuaded Billy to put away his guns. But the reformed outlaw took them up again following Jameson's murder, only to cut a swathe of revenge through the territory, refuse an offer of amnesty from Governor Lew Wallace, escape from jail, and finally meet death at the hands of Sheriff Pat Garrett (Frank Wilcox).

Murphy's wooden performance made him seem for all the world like a life-size wind-up doll, but there was no denying his deadly expertise with firearms. His total lack of emotion actually added to the image of Billy as a cold and unemotional killer. The serious acting was again left to the old hands—Dekker, Strudwick, Will Geer and Talman (who would later win fame as Perry Mason's TV opponent, Hamilton Burger).

The film gained a sharp edge from the callousness of some of its violence, with Murphy shooting men in the back without a flicker of emotion. And it offered one horrific death scene that proved quite surprising for its era, and would not have been out of place in the gore-spattered westerns of the late '60s and early '70s (highlighted by the slow-motion butchery of 1969's *The Wild Bunch*). The scene depicts the death of William Talman during Murphy's escape from jail. Having already dispatched sympathetic jailer Richard Wessell, Murphy takes a double-barreled shotgun and hides behind a door. As Talman passes, he steps out and calls to him, then fires both barrels as Talman turns. The image of Talman's bloody face, with staring, sightless

William Talman and Audie Murphy on location near Idyllwild are "held up" by three young visitors to the set of *Kid from Texas* (1950).

eyes, sliding down the shot-splattered wall is a chilling one.

The film, though disregarded by serious critics, was a solid commercial success, and Murphy became an immediate pin-up favorite. A great deal of careful thought had obviously gone into "packaging" him as a saleable commodity, and it was to pay off handsomely for the studio, if not always for Murphy.

REMEMBRANCES: Audie, in a brief "The Role I Liked Best..." article in the *Saturday Evening Post* (January 13, 1951), wrote, "As a youngster, I read everything about Billy I could get my hands on. I always figured him as a boy who might have gone straight under different circumstances. So I was glad when producer Paul Short agreed I could play him as a quiet guy, a real human being who made mistakes at times, instead of as a swaggering superman. Even so, the script had me killing off twenty-one men before the final fade-out. The biggest laugh in connection with this film never reached the screen. It came when the revolver of a fellow we called Bucko [Roy Bucko] went off unexpectedly and blew the end out of his holster. After that we called him Fast-draw Bucko, and assured him he was the only man in the country who could shoot a gun before he drew it."

Gale Storm: "Audie was never difficult to work with, but rather impersonal. You never felt like you got to know him. Normally you come in in the morning and you say 'hi' or 'good morning.' One day he'd say 'hi' right back at you, another day, he wouldn't even see you, like looking through you. I'm sure he had problems. He was not moody, but sometimes the distance would

The Kid from Texas 34

be there. But he was very professional. He always knew his lines and everything he was doing. He'd just been married to a beautiful girl, Wanda Hendrix. We were on location and she was along. It was kind of interesting. I think she was still a little confused about him too. [Laughs]"

That is not Gale Storm playing the piano in two scenes. "I didn't play piano that well, but I knew enough to make it look believable."

Don Haggerty, interviewed by Tom and Jim Goldrup for their *Feature Players Vol. 2* book, mentioned that one actor, though hired for the full run of the picture, had only one line of dialogue to say: "And Danby." "That's all he had to say, which became a big gag because all the way through the picture if anybody ever blew a line and there was a little silence, this guy would say, 'And Danby.' Well, comes the day towards the end of the picture when he has to say it. Shepperd Strudwick, Audie, and these six guys and myself were in this room, and they are trying to find out what happened; who saw anything; who was there. Audie says, 'Well there was so and so and so and so,' and I say, 'MacArthur,' and this guy's supposed to say, 'and Danby.' Well, he could never get it out. We'd all go into hysterics and start to laugh. After about nine takes, the director said, 'Damn it, it isn't funny.' Someone would say, 'The hell it isn't,' and here we'd go again. If you look at the picture, you'll see the only way we got it. I don't know how many takes, because everybody was slaphappy. [Laughs]"

Dr. William Russo, author of *A Thinker's*

Shepperd Strudwick, Martin Garralaga, Albert Dekker, Paul Ford and Audie Murphy in the Lincoln County Sheriff's office.

Damn, which concerns the making of Audie's *The Quiet American*, commented on Audie's stunt double for many years, Willard Willingham: "Willard said during *Kid from Texas*, their first movie together, they never spoke. He said Audie was an extremely strange person when he returned from the war. After the second picture with Willard, Audie sat down next to Willard between takes for 30 minutes and never said a word. But they were best friends after that. In fact, Audie [later] did *The Quiet American* based on Willard's advice that this was an important story."

NOTES AND COMMENTS: For his first major film role, and not yet a U-I contract player, Audie was paid $10,000 on a 12 week work guarantee. Gale Storm also received a flat $10,000 for the 29 days of filming. Scripter Karl Kamb earned $6,000. Production notes indicate 1,200 bullet "hits" were expended at 75¢ apiece.

Producer Paul Short originally considered Shelly Winters (who was ultimately paid $1,000), Peggy Dow, Lloyd Nolan, Herbert Marshall, Charles Bickford, Ann Blyth and Mona Freeman for various roles.

A planned Fort Sumner, New Mexico, sequence involving a dance, or ball, was eliminated, as was a scene depicting President Rutherford B. Hayes (to be played by Robert Warwick), who ended up mentioned only in the dialogue.

William Talman was injured during an onscreen "fracas" and was charged $35 for sewing up his cut arm. Later found "blameless," Talman was reimbursed and received an apology from U-I.

On location on June 9, Audie's stuntman/double hurt his shoulder in a saddle fall during a shoot-out with Minninger (William Talman) and was taken to the hospital in nearby Hemet for X-rays. Because of Willard Willingham's resemblance to Audie, it was that day he inherited the long-standing job as Audie's double.

On June 21, four buildings on Universal's backlot 'western street' burned in a brush fire which also threatened several nearby residences. On the studio lot, Audie, Albert Dekker and others joined studio firemen in fighting the blaze.

Joseph J. Breen at the MPAA (Motion Picture Association of America) objected to the number of killings, brutality, overall callousness and disrespect for human life in the film.

Universal hired expert gun coach Arvo Ojala to teach Audie the fast draw. Audie's new wife, Wanda Hendrix, has said Audie constantly practiced before a mirror to become proficient.

Art Gilmore provided the voice-over narration for the film's trailer, for which he was paid $75.

At the time *The Kid from Texas* was filmed, Audie was living at 753½ N. Croft in Hollywood.

The Kid from Texas premiered in Houston, Fort Worth, Dallas and San Antonio, where Audie made personal appearances to promote it.

In Larry McMurtry's book *The Last Picture Show*, it is *The Kid from Texas* that closes down the theater in the small Texas town. For Peter Bogdanovich's film, this was changed to John Wayne's *Red River*.

Audie appeared with Eddy Cantor, Van Johnson, Virginia Mayo, Jimmy Durante, Tex Williams, Jeanette MacDonald, Alan Young and others on *I Am an American Day*, a patriotic spectacle at the Hollywood Bowl on May 15, about two weeks before filming *The Kid from Texas*.

Color photos of Audie and Gale in costume appeared on the covers of two comic books, *Western Life Romances #2* (March 1950) and *Real West Romances #5* (December/January 1950).

Sierra
(Universal-International, May 1950)

Credits: *Producer:* Michael Kraike; *Director:* Alfred E. Green; *1st Assistant Director:* Jesse Hibbs; *2nd Assistant Directors:* Mickey Bennett, Marshall Greer; *Story:* Based on the novel *The Mountains Are My Kingdom* by Stuart Hardy (1937); *Screenplay:* Edna Anhalt, with additional dialogue from Milton Gunzburg; *Editor:* Ted Kent; *Director of Photography:* Russell Metty; *Art Directors:* Bernard Herzbrun, Robert F. Boyle; *Set Decorators:* Russell A. Gausman, John Austin; *Costume Designer:* Yvonne Wood; *Makeup:* Bud Westmore; *Sound:* Leslie I. Carey, Glenn E. Anderson, Martin Brown; *Hair Stylist:* Joan St. Oegger; *Special Effects:* Herman Townsley; *Music:* Walter Scharf; *Music Score:* Frank Skinner; *Songs:* "End of the Road," "Hideaway," "Black Angus McDougal," "Drift Along" words and music by Arnold Hughes and Frederick Herbert; "The Whale Song," "Sarah the Mule" words and music by Burl Ives. Color by Technicolor.

Cast: Audie Murphy (Ring Hassard); Wanda Hendrix (Riley Martin); Burl Ives (Lonesome); Dean Jagger (Jeff Hassard); Richard Rober (Big Matt Rangone); Elliott Reid (Duke Lefferty); Roy Roberts (Sheriff Knudsen); Houseley Stevenson (Sam Coulter); Tony Curtis (Brent Coulter); Griff Barnett (Dr. Hank Robbins); Elisabeth Risdon (Aunt Susan); Gregg Martell (Tom Hogan); Jack Ingram (Al); Sara Allgood (Mrs. Jones); Erskine Sanford (Judge Prentiss); James Arness (Little Sam Coulter); Ted Jordan (Jim Coulter); John Doucette (Jed Coulter); I. Stanford Jolley (Snake Willens); Timmy Hawkins (Johnny); Jessica Kraike, Stark Bishop, Norman Kent (Children Ives sings to); Bud Osborne, Jim Toney, Roy Butler, John Beck, Frank Austin, Irvin Berwick (Townsmen); Dodey Bottoms (Posse member). Stunts: Jimmy Van Horn, Willard Willingham.

Running Time: 83 minutes

Filming Dates: August 30, 1949–October 3, 1949; Additional filming October 14, November 1, December 5, 1949

Locations: Kanab, Utah, including Robinson's Ranch; Cedar City, Utah, including Mirror Lake, Tippet's Field Trail below waterfall, Cedar Breaks, Cascade Meadows. Background shots: Brainhead, Utah.

Budget/Cost: $627,805.

Murphy's second western co-starred him with his wife, Wanda Hendrix, in a handsomely-mounted outdoor drama in which Murphy played a young mountain man raised from boyhood in a secluded valley with his father, an escaped convict who had been unjustly accused of murder many years previously. Hendrix played a somewhat unlikely lady lawyer who accidentally invades the mountain hideout and is ultimately instrumental in helping Murphy prove his father's innocence.

By this time, Murphy was under contract to Universal, the studio having bought out Paul Short when Universal decided to take over Audie's career. The most memorable aspects of *Sierra* were the magnificent mountain locations, filmed around Kanab, Utah, and a climactic wild-horse roundup, a sequence of near-epic proportions.

Murphy was again wooden and awkward, but remained as effective as always in the action sequences. The serious acting was left to Dean Jagger as Audie's father, in his first film role since winning an Academy Award for *12 O'Clock High* in 1949.

Burl Ives, still many years away from his own Oscar win and recognition as a fine serious actor, appeared in a role that was almost a throwback to the singing cowboy era, playing a folksy, whimsical character called "Lonesome" who rode around the mountains on a mule, strumming his guitar and singing, and helped out Jagger and Murphy by selling the wild horses they tamed. Ives was billed as "America's Beloved Balladeer," and advertising copy promised prospective patrons that they would hear him sing "six wonderful songs." His only really constructive contribution to the action was to sing a jailer to sleep in order to break Murphy out of a cell.

Ives and the action scenes aside, *Sierra* was routine, but always good to look at, and the supporting cast included a rich array of professional talent and promising newcomers. Richard Rober, as the chief heavy, was a solid supporting actor who added weight to a number of crime thrillers and westerns in the early '50s. Elliott Reid, playing Rober's boss, was an accomplished light comedian who played second-fiddle to many top romantic leading men in early 20th Century–Fox CinemaScope films; and a strikingly handsome young man named Anthony Curtis played a member of an outlaw gang who helped Jagger and Murphy round up their horses. Also riding with the gang was a hulking blond actor names James Arness, destined to become a TV legend as Marshal Matt Dillon in the *Gunsmoke* series.

Murphy's war record was still being milked by studio publicists, with the film's pressbook urging exhibitors to "Play up the catch line: Audie Murphy.... Most Decorated Hero to Come Out of the War." A second promotional angle, the husband-and-wife co-starring of Murphy and Hendrix, was scotched by Murphy when, at the completion of the picture, he announced that the marriage was washed up. The *Sierra* pressbook does not even hint at the marital relationship between the two stars. Although not a resounding commercial success, the film again drew in piles of fan mail for Murphy, and the studio immedi-

Audie Murphy and his wife Wanda Hendrix co-starred in *Sierra* (1950).

ately put him into his third western, *Kansas Raiders*.

REMEMBRANCES: *James Arness*, in his autobiography, recalled, "We went up to Kanab to shoot the film. While we were making it they'd pull [Audie] out to make personal appearances, make speeches about the war, you name it. The nation wanted to honor him in every way, but he wasn't into that sort of thing. He just wanted to be left alone and get on with his life. He loved to shoot craps, and during every break, he and a bunch of the guys would be in a corner doing some serious crap shooting. He was a natural at the game and seemed to win everything. There was something unique about Murphy, a kind of mystique, which probably helped him through his harrowing war experiences. He was lucky, at that stage in his life, everything he touched turned to gold. Sadly, in later years his luck ran out."

NOTES AND COMMENTS: Universal first adapted Stuart Hardy's novel as the basis for *Forbidden Valley* (1938), starring Noah

Audie rides the hills of Kanab, Utah, in *Sierra*.

Beery Jr., and scripted and directed by Wyndham Gittens. The story was recycled again in 1965 as *Hideout,* an episode of TV's *The Virginian*, featuring Roberta Shore.

Audie and Wanda's relationship was always stormy and volatile. Although they remained the darlings of the press, at home they clashed over her clothing, money, attending Hollywood parties and Audie's interest in other women. Wanda also told a columnist, "Audie fights the war in his sleep constantly. He despised his father. He told me every time he shot one of the enemy during the war, he pretended he was killing his Dad. Audie had the most terrible nightmares. He had guns all over our home. He even slept with a loaded gun under his pillow." She also said Audie was troubled by his two ulcers. Audie's problems took their toll on her health and their marriage. On September 6, 1949, Audie told the press, "In eight months of marriage I've been fighting harder than on eight European fronts." However, they both said no divorce was planned. They hoped the romantic backdrop of Kanab, while they filmed *Sierra*, would help rekindle their marriage. It did not. Wanda was still recovering from a broken foot when she arrived on location. Audie had painful fever blisters and a severe case of cracked lips from sunburn, and literally could not smile because of the pain. This problem is quite noticeable in the film. Several scenes had to be re-shot back on the Universal lot in December because of this condition. For Wanda, the altitude caused nosebleeds and shortness of breath. Also, in one scene she was stung on her neck by yellow jackets. On September 29, a flash flood that followed a 30-minute thunderstorm sent a

Wanda Hendrix, Dean Jagger, Burl Ives and Audie Murphy receive a plaque from Heber Bennion, the Utah Secretary of State, commemorating the filming of *Sierra* as the 100th movie to photograph in Utah over the last 25 years.

four-foot-deep rush of water down the narrow draw of Kanab Creek. Audie and Wanda were almost trapped between the steep walls of the draw, but (according to press releases) Audie leaped on his horse, grabbed Wanda and rode up the canyon walls to safety. Some $10,000 worth of Technicolor photographic equipment was damaged in the flash flood. The picture wrapped on October 3, and on October 4, back in Hollywood, Wanda announced their trial separation. "It's his wish. This is what he wanted. What can I do? It isn't final. I hope it won't be. I don't want a divorce. Audie is not well. He's all mixed up and I guess I'm just about as mixed up as he is." Audie told the press he was going to Texas for a while. In November of 1949, the couple tried a reconciliation, spending time at a Texas guest ranch. However, by February 16, 1950, the headlines read, "Reconciliation fails. Hendrix to divorce Murphy." When Wanda filed for divorce she cited "extreme cruelty" and "grievous mental suffering" that had "seriously impaired my health and destroyed my happiness," explaining that from the outset Audie criticized her both privately and publicly over the way she dressed and prepared food, her expressions, the way she talked, any little thing. His unpredictable rages also kept her on edge. On April 14, 1950, the plea for divorce was granted. Due to the impending divorce, Universal scrapped plans to publicize the co-stars as a married couple.

In the mid–1950s Wanda married James Stack, actor Robert Stack's brother. When that marriage ended, she married businessman Steve LaMonte in 1969. That union ended in divorce when she became ill in 1979. After lying in a semi-conscious state for over a year, Wanda died in February 1981 of double pneumonia in Burbank, California.

For acting in *Sierra*, Audie was paid $10,000, while Wanda Hendrix received $15,000 and Burl Ives earned $17,500, which included the use of two songs he wrote for the picture. Dean Jagger also received $10,000.

Four horses were injured and two killed in the stampeding horse sequences filmed on September 29, costing Universal several injury and loss claims paid out to local owners of the horses.

Sara Allgood held up production on her second and third day because she "didn't know her lines," according to production notes, requiring as many as fifteen takes. Similarly, Erskine Sanford held up production one whole day for the same reason.

First assistant director Jesse Hibbs graduated to a full director in 1953, helming Audie's *Ride Clear of Diablo* that year, as well as five subsequent Murphy films.

One of the children Burl Ives sings to in the street is Jessica Kraike, the daughter of producer Michael Kraike.

In the Kanab area, Murphy is remembered as quite a gambler. The Black Cat, a log cabin behind Parry Lodge, was off-limits to locals but a popular drinking and gambling spot for the movie folks. Audie was a frequent patron of the Black Cat. The star also befriended Dee Crosby — one of Utah's top three WWII soldiers, and a former fellow patient with Murphy in an Italian hospital — often inviting the Panguitch resident and his German wife to Parry Lodge for dinner.

The black stallion and the wild horse herd seen in the picture consisted of stock footage from Universal-International's *Red Canyon*, filmed earlier in 1949. U-I reused this footage in several subsequent westerns.

Kansas Raiders

(UNIVERSAL-INTERNATIONAL, NOVEMBER 1950)

CREDITS: *Producer:* Ted Richmond; *Director:* Ray Enright; *1st Assistant Director:* Ronnie Rondell; *2nd Assistant Director:* George Loper; *2nd Unit Directors:* Yakima Canutt, Cliff Lyons; *Screenplay:* Robert L. Richards (Luci Ward, Jack Natteford, Russell Hughes, D. D. Beauchamp and Gene Lewis also contributed to the screenplay); *Editor:* Milton Carruth; *Director of Photography:* Irving Glassberg; *Art Directors:* Bernard Herzbrun, Emrich Nicholson; *Set Decorations:* Russell Gausman, Ruby R. Levitt; *Costume Designer:* Bill Thomas; *Makeup:* Bud Westmore; *Sound Recording:* Leslie I. Carey, Glenn E. Anderson; *Hair Stylist:* Joan St. Oegger; *Dialogue Director:* Gene Lewis; *Musical Director:* Joseph Gershenson. Color by Technicolor.

CAST: Audie Murphy (Jesse James); Brian Donlevy (William Clarke Quantrill); Marguerite Chapman (Kate Clarke); Scott Brady (Bill Anderson); Tony Curtis (Kit Dalton); Richard Arlen (Union Captain); Richard Long (Frank James); James Best (Cole Younger); John Kellogg (Red Leg leader); Dewey Martin (Jim Younger); George Chandler (Willis); Charles Delaney (Pell); David Wolfe (Rudolph Tate); Richard Egan (1st Lieutenant); Robert Anderson (Captured Farmer); Lee Fredericks (Union Corporal); Sam Flint (Bank President); Edward Piel Sr. (Bank Teller); Buddy Roosevelt (Second Red Leg); Henry Wills (Quantrill man); Mira McKinney (Crying woman); Ray Grimes (Union Sergeant); Dick Carter, David Newell, Tom Hawthorne, Ted Elliott, Frank McGrath, Richard Farmer, Warren Fisk, Helen Gibson, Jennings Miles, Bob Burrows, Roy Bucko, Leo McMahon (Soldiers/Townsmen/Quantrill men); Stunts: Ken Terrell, Paul Baxley, Henry Wills, Fred Carson, Sailor Vincent, Jerry Ambler, Warren Fisk, Carl Sepulveda, Chet Bias.

RUNNING TIME: 81 minutes

FILMING DATES: May 22, 1950–June 24, 1950

LOCATIONS: Jack Garner Ranch and Johnson Flats at Idyllwild, California; Universal backlot.

BUDGET/COST: $609,156

In his third Universal western, Murphy again played a real-life wild west badman—Jesse James. The film *purported* to be an account of Jesse's career as a member of the notorious guerrilla gang led by Colonel Quantrill in post–Civil War Kansas, tracing his recruitment, hero-worship of Quantrill, romance with a female member of the gang, and ultimate disillusionment after the infamous massacre in Lawrence, Kansas.

An action-packed, often bloody film which moved smartly from one action sequence to the next, *Kansas Raiders* was well served by Brian Donlevy's authoritative presence as Quantrill and the personable playing of its group of attractive young "heroes." Murphy, still ill at ease (especially with longer dialogue sequences, and particularly in his romantic moments with Marguerite Chapman), was carefully costumed for maximum glamour, but acquitted himself with his usual crisp confidence in the action scenes. Murphy also had the advantage over other Hollywood portrayals of Jesse in that he looked the right age, since the outlaw was only 16 when he reportedly rode with Quantrill. The obligatory line of dialogue about his youthful appearance, a sort of studio apology to those who might expect a western hero to look like John Wayne, was the prelude to a vicious knife fight in which Murphy dispatched one of Quantrill's men, thus proving himself guerrilla material. Errol Flynn, another unlikely westerner at first glance, was subject to the same "insurance cover" in his Warner Bros. westerns in the '40s, when a line was often inserted to explain his vaguely British accent as being due to his Irish ancestry. There was little or no subtlety in either the acting or screenplay of *Kansas Raiders*, but it served its purpose as gutsy western entertainment, and also as a showcase for a formidable line-up of talent. Scott Brady, already established as a leading man, switched to villainy with a convincing display of sadistic viciousness as Quantrill's lieutenant, "Bloody Bill" Anderson. Old-time western star Richard Arlen added a touch of quiet competence as a cavalry

Union Captain Richard Arlen (left) confronts Audie Murphy as Jesse James in *Kansas Raiders* (1950).

officer whose torture by Brady leads to the inevitable showdown between Jesse and Anderson. Later, Arlen repays the debt by allowing Jesse and his friends time to surrender Quantrill. But the main focus was on Murphy and four other handsome youngsters—Tony Curtis (no longer billed as Anthony), in his second consecutive Murphy western, as Kit Dalton; Richard Long, who would emerge as one of the most durable and likeable stars of a number of TV shows (including *Big Valley*) in the '60s, as Frank James; Dewey Martin, soon to attain brief stardom via Howard Hawks' vigorous pioneering epic *The Big Sky*, as one of the Younger Brothers; and James Best, another durable TV performer of the '60s, as the other Younger. Uncredited (and with only one line of dialogue) as Arlen's lieutenant, Richard Egan was to scale greater movie heights than any of the others except Curtis. He was built up as a "new Clark Gable" in a series of big-budget CinemaScope movies for 20th Century–Fox in the mid–1950s, went on to TV stardom in the *Empire* series in the '60s, and settled down to a comfortable position as a reliable leading man and guest star in TV dramas of the '70s.

Director Ray Enright, who died in 1965, was on familiar ground with the film, as he'd already directed a movie about the Younger Brothers (*Bad Men of Missouri*) in 1941, and had a reasonable list of western credits behind him, having directed such stars as Randolph Scott, Joel McCrea and Errol Flynn. Inevitably, *Kansas Raiders* proved a whitewash job regarding Jesse and his companions, but it did offer plenty of old fashioned horse opera gusto.

Dialogue director Gene Lewis, Marguerite Chapman, Audie Murphy and director Ray Enright discuss a scene for *Kansas Raiders*.

REMEMBRANCES: *James Best* thinks the most interesting scene in the film comes when Audie shoots Scott Brady. "I turned and looked into Audie's eyes, and I saw a man who went through WWII and had killed a lot of guys. He was killing Scott Brady. His looks chilled me. The hair on the back of my neck stood up because I saw a man who enjoyed killing. He enjoyed reenacting that. I don't mean *joy* joy. He was really into it. I saw death in Audie's eyes. Audie was one of the most interesting people I've ever worked with. Audie either liked you or did not. But you knew immediately ... he would let you know very quickly. Audie was very, very serious but he loved to play gags on you. [During the making of the picture] we'd shoot at each other with quarter loads and try to beat each other to the draw. Tony Curtis would draw his weapons and challenge Audie to a fast draw contest. But you didn't mess with Audie. He doesn't kid around [like that]. Tony kept challenging him and Audie kept saying I don't wanna draw. Audie was fast. Finally, Audie came over to me and said, 'Jimmy, give me your weapon.' He took my pistol and put a full load in it and held it behind his back. He left his gun in the holster, of course, which was empty. He walked up to Tony and said, 'Ok, Tony, you've been wanting to draw on me, draw!' Well, Tony reached for his weapon, but before he could even clear leather, Audie stuck his empty revolver in Tony's stomach and fired my gun behind his back. When it went off, Tony Curtis went totally white! They had one heck of a time getting Tony to ever take his gun out of the holster again."

Many westerns, such as *Kansas Raiders*, were shot at the Garner Ranch. Jack Garner, often an extra in cattle-drive scenes to protect his father's stock from the Hollywood cowboys, has fond memories of making western films. The eccentric Audie Murphy, he remembers, "didn't say much. He just sat behind a rock and fired his gun."

NOTES AND COMMENTS: Historical inaccuracies abound in *Kansas Raiders*, as they usually do in westerns dealing with real-life personalities. William Clarke Quantrill, referred to in the film as "Colonel," was most likely never commissioned a colonel by any military authority, as no records exist to confirm such a ranking. A captain ranking *is* confirmed by some sources. Also, it is not historically verifiable that Jesse James rode with Quantrill at the time shortly before or during Quantrill's historic bloody raid on Lawrence, Kansas, on August 21, 1863. Jesse *may* have tried to join Quantrill in the summer before the raid, but because he was only 15, and reportedly tending a tobacco crop that summer, he most likely did not become a guerrilla until the following summer when he joined Bill Anderson's band, who quite often operated separately from Quantrill. Decades later, after Jesse had become famous, some Lawrence survivors manufactured stories of Jesse being in the raid, but these "tales" are just that, historically inaccurate visualizations. Brother Frank James may have been with Quantrill since May 1863. Coleman Younger was definitely with Quantrill during his raid on Lawrence. Cole's brother James had ridden with Quantrill, but it is unconfirmed as to whether or not he took part in the Lawrence raid. Following Lawrence, Quantrill moved on to Baxter Springs, Kansas, then Texas, where he was deposed as the guerrillas' leader. He ended up in Kentucky in early 1865 with vague plans to assassinate Abraham Lincoln. He was eventually ambushed by federal authorities at a farmhouse near Taylorsville, Kentucky, where he died of bullet wounds June 6, 1865, at 27 (obviously much younger than Brian Donlevy in *Kansas Raiders*). Certainly neither Jesse or Frank James, nor the Younger brothers, were with him at this time, nor was he blinded as portrayed in the film. The "Kit Dalton" character in *Kansas Raiders* is manufactured out of whole cloth. None of the Daltons—all of whom weren't even born at the time of the Lawrence raid—had the name Kit. Bill Anderson's participation in the Lawrence raid is also unconfirmed, but it's certain he was not gunned down there by Jesse James, as his own atrocity against Centralia, Illinois, in 1864 is well documented. Anderson was ambushed and killed by Union troops on October 27, 1864, near Orrick, Missouri.

A grasshopper plague on June 5 forced the film company to remain in Los Angeles rather than travel to Idyllwild as planned. The grasshoppers cut a five-mile swath across the filming locale. The company eventually arrived in Idyllwild on June 12.

On June 17 it became necessary for assistant director Ronnie Rondell to call Carl Sepulveda out of a riding scene at Idyllwild because he was making excessive noise and disrupting the morale of the other riders. Sepulveda, asked to return to "base," was accompanied by Chet Bias. Later that evening, in the lobby of the hotel, Sepulveda spoke in a "belligerent and profane manner" to Rondell and second assistant director George Loper. Sepulveda publicly admitted he had been drinking that day, then struck Rondell in the chest. Rondell did not return the blow. Both Sepulveda and Bias were restrained at this time by Roy Bucko and other members of the crew, and were sent back to the studio the next day.

For this film, Audie earned $12,500, while Brian Donlevy, a star name for years, was paid $37,500. Scott Brady gained

Audie Murphy stops to sign autographs for youngsters between scenes of *Kansas Raiders*.

$10,000, Marguerite Chapman $7,500, Richard Arlen $4,000 and Richard Long $7,000.

Civil War stock footage from *Tap Roots* (Universal-International, 1948) was utilized in the montage battle scenes for this film.

Before Audie's next film, *The Red Badge of Courage*, began filming in August, Audie joined the Texas National Guard on July 5, 1950, to train between films.

Now between marriages, Audie and East Indian Princess Sita Singh became a gossip column "item" for a while in July 1950, before she transferred her affections to actor Louis Hayward. By August 20, 1950, Audie was being seen "around town" with actress Peggie Castle. In September 1950 Audie personally took her to Universal and wrangled Peggie her first film role, in *Air Cadet* (1951).

The Red Badge of Courage
(MGM, SEPTEMBER 1951)

CREDITS: *Producer:* Gottfried Reinhardt; *Director:* John Huston; *Assistant Director:* Reggie Callow; *Second Assistant Director:* Bill Beaudine; *Story:* Based on the novel *The Red Badge of Courage* by Stephen Crane; *Screenplay:* John Huston; *Adaptation:* Albert Band; *Editor:* Ben Lewis; *Director of Photography:* Harold Rosson; *Art*

The Red Badge of Courage

Directors: Cedric Gibbons, Hans Peters; *Set Decorations:* Edwin B. Willis, Fred MacLean; *Sound Recording:* Howard Voss; *Special Effects:* Warren Newcombe; *Makeup:* William Tuttle; *Music:* Bronislau Kaper.

CAST: Audie Murphy (Henry Fleming); Bill Mauldin (Tom Wilson, the Loud Soldier); Douglas Dick (Lieutenant); Royal Dano (Tattered Man); John Dierkes (Jim Conklin, the Tall Soldier); Arthur Hunnicutt (Bill Porter); Andy Devine (the Cheery Soldier); Robert Easton Burke (Thompson); Smith Ballew (Captain); Glenn Strange (Colonel); Dan White (Sergeant); Frank McGraw (Captain); Tim Durant (General); Emmett Lynn, I. Stanford Jolley, William "Bill" Phillips, House Peters Jr., Frank Sully (Winterside Veterans); George Offerman Jr., Joel Marston, Robert Nichols (Union Soldiers); Lou Nova, Fred Kohler Jr., Dick Curtis, Guy Wilkerson, Buddy Roosevelt (Veterans); Jim Hayward (Soldier); Gloria Eaton (Southern Girl); Robert Cherry (Soldier Who Sings); Whit Bissel (Wounded Officer); William Phipps (Officer); Ed Hinton (Corporal); Lynn Farr (Confederate); Lee Roberts, John Crawford, James Dobson, Todd Karns, William Greenburg, Norman Leavitt, William Schallert, Gregg Barton, Ivan Perry, Billy Dix, Cliff Lyons, Terry Wilson, John Cliff, Larry Harmon, King Moody (Soldiers); James Whitmore (Voice-over narrator).

RUNNING TIME: 69 minutes (edited from approximately 78–90 minutes)

FILMING DATES: Rehearsal from August 25, 1950 to September 1, 1950; actual shooting from September 2, 1950 to October 11, 1950

LOCATIONS: Sacramento River area near Chico, California, and the John Huston Ranch in the San Fernando Valley, California.

BUDGET/COST: $1,642,017

Murphy was loaned to MGM to star in John Huston's adaptation of Stephen Crane's Civil War novel *The Red Badge of Courage*. A classic of American literature, the novel dealt with the exploits of a youth in the Union Army who faces his first battle, runs from it, then redeems himself in a later skirmish, emerging as a hero.

Huston envisioned the film as a full-length, artistic, prestige product, a plan initially endorsed by the studio but later vetoed due to changes in administrative personnel and top-level power struggles. The end result was a "condensed" version running little more than an hour, and Huston's struggles to maintain his original concept formed the basis of a book by Lillian Ross called *Picture*, now generally regarded as the definitive statement on the problems facing the serious artist in conflict with the studio system. In this wider area of discussion, Murphy's contribution is often ignored, but what remains of Huston's film shows the first evidence of a potential talent awaiting release under the right guiding hand. Murphy was completely convincing as the young soldier, and displayed depths of emotive acting he would rarely achieve in future roles. It is significant, and evidence of Huston's skill, that (with the exception of *To Hell and Back*) Murphy did not achieve similar heights until *The Unforgiven*, which Huston directed in 1960. Both films showed Murphy was capable of more depth than the pleasant blandness that characterized most of his work, but he obviously needed an exceptional director to guide him.

A complete assessment of *The Red Badge of Courage* is impossible in its existing butchered condition, but what remains is impressive, offering a superb sense of the chaos and stupidity of the conflict, a rewarding roundness of characterization, and remarkable affinity with the tone and atmosphere of the book. Huston deliberately cast "non-star" actors, including World War II cartoonist Bill Mauldin, thus generating a feeling of almost total realism and period identification. In later years, Mauldin remembered incidents that were indicative of Murphy's still tense and unpredictable emotional state, even five years after the end of the war. In one scene Murphy was required to admit to his cowardice, but (reported Mauldin) found it impossible to do until Mauldin also admitted to being "skeered." Mauldin also related how Murphy had arrived on location one morning with skinned knuckles after a brawl with a couple of toughs who had tried to force a young cyclist off the highway. Murphy had stopped their car, dragged them out and beat them up so badly that they both wound up in the hospital, claiming they had been attacked by a "maniac." It was not the last time Murphy would be involved in this sort of incident, and not always with right on his side.

The possibility of Murphy gaining recognition as a serious actor was nullified by MGM's handling of *The Red Badge of Courage*. The studio released it in supporting spots, half-heartedly promoting it as a Civil War action drama. A prominently-displayed still showed Murphy gazing fondly into the eyes of starlet Gloria Eaton, who actually appeared only briefly in one background shot as a farm girl teased by the soldiers. But *The Red Badge of Courage* was neither the action movie promised by its poster art of Murphy with rifle and bayonet at the ready, nor the cozy romance suggested by the Gloria Eaton still. Consequently, it proved a failure on all counts.

Serious moviegoers largely ignored it because of its lowly B-feature status, and Murphy fans stayed away because it was such a radical departure from his previous western hero roles. Now regarded as a cult movie, and always mentioned as one of Murphy's few worthwhile films (it was one of his own favorites), it did nothing for his career at the time.

REMEMBRANCES: *Harry Carey Jr.:* "I did a screen test with Audie for *Red Badge of Courage*. I was back in Oklahoma with Ben Johnson publicizing *Wagon Master* and got a call to come back to California, that John Huston wanted to see me. He tested a whole buncha young guys. We all did the same scene with Audie, who was a real nice guy, very mild mannered, very quiet. The scene was for the loud soldier [the part which eventually went to Bill Mauldin]."

House Peters Jr.: "I spent a week on that set, and about all I did was sit under a tree watching John Huston direct Audie. Huston spent *hours* with him! I kinda envied him because I had nothing but a coupla of lines. I worked at my regular salary and got a week's work out of it." As to Audie's performance in *Red Badge*: "Rehearsal. Rehearsal. Rehearsal. Rehearsal builds business and rehearsal builds characters. It makes such a difference. Huston only said hello to *me* once. Audie I never talked to. Huston worked quietly with Murphy, he was trying to build a character out of him. Huston spent *hours* with Audie. I noticed they even sat cross-legged under a tree. I was leaning against a nearby tree smoking my pipe thinking, 'what a lucky guy to have all that attention.'"

Robert Easton: "Working with Audie on *Red Badge of Courage* was a wonderful experience for me. I enjoyed it immensely and I learned a great deal. In fact, as an actor, I've done 80 features, and I can say this is one of the ones I'm most proud of having worked on.

"I was particularly pleased to work with Audie because I knew about his incredible record in World War II. I didn't know what kind of a person he might be because I knew he had won the Congressional Medal of Honor and the Distinguished Service Cross, and the Silver Star, and the Legion of Merit, and all of it. He was the most decorated soldier of World War II. When I met Audie he was very shy and very down to earth. There was no arrogance or no bullshit about him. He was just a very nice, very down to earth kind of guy. As I learned a little bit more about him, I learned he had been raised in Texas, as in fact I was, but he was six years older. He had a tough childhood, I know he'd been a sharecropper. Sometimes war brings out amazing qualities in people that would

Audie Murphy holds the American flag as a group of soldiers prepare for another confrontation in *The Red Badge of Courage* (1951).

in 1945, and again, very down to earth, very natural. Years later I met General Doolittle, who had led the raid on Tokyo, and again, same thing, quiet, unassuming. I thought how different from the way Hollywood usually thinks of war heroes, that they've gotta be loud and braggadocio. The typical Hollywood thing of the war hero is the kind of stereotypical guy with 'three balls.' Meeting Audie, I was very, very impressed with him, and we all had a great working rapport with him. He was very professional. Everything John Huston suggested to him, he did; there was no arguing or fighting. Audie had great confidence in John Houston.

"One of the things that struck me as being very interesting from the original book, the regiment was clearly identified as being from Ohio. In fact, what happened, Huston cast a whole lot of people who were really from the south, like Audie and I had both been raised in Texas, Bill Mauldin I believe came from Oklahoma, and then you had people like Arthur Hunnicutt. You remember that wonderful line he had: 'A woman, a dog, and a walnut tree. The more you beat 'em the better they be.' Glenn Strange was from the south, an enormous number of the roles were. Now, I know at the time some people questioned that. They said, well, you know, this is supposed to be a union regiment. Why do they all sound southern? But John Huston has always done his homework. He had all the [noted Civil War photographer Mathew] Brady photographs and quite often if you look at the film, there are little tableau scenes that are really structured the same

not otherwise have surfaced. When I met him and I saw how unassuming and down to earth and nice he was, immediately it brought back memories of Sergeant York, who had been a similar type person in World War I; I liked him immediately.

"I've always been kind of personally over-awed by war heroes more than any other type of person in my work [as a dialect and speech coach]. I've met all the top actors and actresses in the world and a lot of political figures, but I've always had the most admiration for war heroes, and I felt the same way when I met Audie that I had when I met Captain Eddie Rickenbacher. I had done a radio show with him

Audie Murphy learns the intricacies of the sound department from mixer Jimmy Brock (left) and sound recorder Howard Voss (right).

way as Brady's photographs, groups of three and four and five people right out of Brady. He used the same photographic style Brady did to give the feel. When we were working on *The Red Badge of Courage*, in fact, Huston wanted the kind of speech ... it's not deep south, but it's technically called midland speech, which goes all the way from the Appalachians up across the Ohio River into southern Ohio, southern Indiana, and southern Illinois. [Watching the film] you can see Huston went against the prevailing thing. He didn't over-dramatize anything. He did it with a very kind of underplayed, almost semi-documentary style.

"You notice in the film I get credited as Robert Easton Burke. That was my birth name. Easton was my mother's family name. I thought rather than the triple barrel ... and because I did a lot of rural stuff, people were saying, well, Bob Burke, that's too close to Bob Burns. He did a lot of rural humor from Arkansas. But it just seemed better to shorten my name to Robert Easton. I had established the name Robert Easton Burke years before when I'd been on a radio show called *Quiz Kids*. I was one of the original Quiz Kids on radio. When I met Huston, he was very interested in that. He asked me a lot about it, so, that was really my entrée into show business.

"On the set what was very interesting … Audie and most of the rest of us didn't get into actor talk—about 'Stanislavsky would have said this,' and all that stuff. Everybody just kind of created that kind of a feeling of a bunch of people who were in an outfit and were friends. That became our reality, and quite often—this was amazing to me 'cause I don't gamble—John Huston and Audie and a whole bunch of extras would be down on their knees in the dirt right in the middle of a big crap game. That really amazed me, 'cause I had worked for other directors who were kind of aloof. So here Huston and Audie and the extras are all in this crap game. The first assistant director was a very elegant man from the Isle of Man, they called him Manx. His name was Reggie Callow. He was very elegant and soft spoken, but he would have to go in and break up the crap game and tell them the cameras were ready and everybody was waiting. Quite often, Huston and Audie would be so involved in the crap game they really didn't want to stop and go to work. I thought that was hilariously funny.

"Now, let me tell you about Lillian Ross. I did not know who she was. I didn't know she wrote for the *New Yorker*. I noticed there was this very frumpy, colorless, pleasant, but looked-like-somebody's-maiden-aunt who was hanging around. She wore very frumpy, dowdy clothes, and didn't seem to know anything about picture making, and so she'd go up to people in a very nice way and ask a lot of questions. Everybody tried to explain everything to her. She hung around talking to everybody. Later, this savage book comes out where she has betrayed everybody's confidences and has made a lot of people—who I knew to be very nice people—out to be idiots. I thought, gee, I hope *I* didn't say anything to her. Looking back on it, I'm sure that I was always very tactful and diplomatic and didn't say anything she could have used. But it was interesting because I felt the way she operated … instead of being openly a very sophisticated witty woman that was out to write a satiric book and destroy reputations, she didn't … she didn't come across that way. She came across like a little maiden aunt you felt sorry for that didn't really seem to know anything about movies or anything. That taught me a lesson. I thought, my God, the woman missed her calling, she should have been an international spy. The book was just absolutely savage. A lot of those people she savaged were really good people, like Gottfried Reinhardt, who was the producer. He was the son of the great Max Reinhardt. Then Huston had an assistant named Albert Band, and she just savaged Albert Band. Ever since that book came out, I've been exceptionally careful when I'm working on something and there's anybody from the press that asks questions. I don't say anything I don't want to have be in print.

"Then, of course, just being an actor on *Red Badge*, I didn't realize all the power politics involved. I knew John Huston had this dream of wanting to bring Stephen Crane's book to life as realistically and accurately as possible, but I didn't know at the time there was all that power struggle between Louis Mayer and Dore Schary. Schary wanted to make it. Mayer didn't want to make it, and I didn't know any of that stuff. Allegedly, it ran probably somewhat over two hours, and I believe at Louie Mayer's orders it was chopped down to 69 minutes. Huston apparently did not keep an original director's cut at all. He just turned it over to MGM and Mayer and therefore....

"Huston himself had a role in the film. A lot of people don't know that. I've seen a still of Huston himself. He played a guy who wasn't in the Army. He was kind of a hermit type character in regular civilian clothes that Audie runs across in the woods. It's gone.

"John Dierkes had a wonderful death scene, then Royal Dano had one, and they were quite different, but the people who cut the film said it's too downbeat. We can't have two big death scenes. So they cut out Royal Dano's, and I remember scenes I was in that were cut. There was a wonderful long tracking shot of us all marching into battle. It was a long shot, the camera would be on one platoon and do all the faces and then the next platoon would come up behind, then the next one, and the next one, and the next one. I do remember, in fact, that particular scene; Lillian Ross was there that day, and she said, oh, that's a wonderful scene. I remember her personally complementing me. She said, 'I liked the way you marched.' And there was the scene where I got wounded and that was cut."

As to Easton receiving billing when so many others did not, "Huston wouldn't have done that unless he liked what I did. One particular sequence was kind of interesting, that long monologue ... he tested a lot of actors for that, and the testing went on for days and days. Originally, he had me read for the Bill Mauldin part, which of course I wasn't right for, then he called me back and said, 'I've got another part I'd like to have you test for.' So I tested for it, and a whole lot of people ... lot of well known young actors came in and tested and tested, and he didn't use them in the film. After I tested for that scene, one of the things he liked was where I'm quoting. In the script it's marked 'ahem.' Instead of going [cough] like that, I just said 'a-hem.' And Huston loved that. So, when I'm rehearsing ... a lot of the actors are saying you're not really supposed to say 'a-hem,' that's just kind of a clearing the throat designation. I said, well, Mr. Huston likes me saying 'a-hem,' but they were all trying to help me. They thought it sounded a little amateur that I was saying 'a-hem.'

"We did a scene where I'm breathless, and I give 'em this key news that Audie was a hero and so forth and so on, and after several days Huston said to me, 'You know, I'd like to do that scene again.' So I thought, 'Oh God, he didn't like it.' But he gave me a little different direction on it so that the final result is that you see a guy who's really what we would call ... in World War I you'd call them shell shocked or World War II you'd call it battle fatigue. He wanted me to just be in really bad shape psychologically, so he had me running up and down hills until I was just absolutely totally out of breath. Then he shot it, and it gave it that kind of semi-hysterical kind of thing. It happens to a lot of guys in the war. It gave it that hysterical urgency. When I first saw the film, I gotta tell ya, as many actors, I was a little disappointed in my performance, but in ensuing years since I've seen it, I realize what Mr. Huston wanted, and I

Audie Murphy, Royal Dano (as the Tattered Man) and John Dierkes (as the Tall Soldier).

see that it works in the context and it's interesting.

"John Dierkes was very interesting. He'd never done any acting. He was a friend of John Huston and he worked for the treasury department. He had that wonderful craggy face. He had one of the world's great, great faces. That was always the hallmark of Huston films. He liked people that had an unusual look or an unusual quality.

"Douglas Dick plays the young lieutenant. Everybody was popular with one another and everybody liked one another except Douglas Dick, and it may be to some extent the characterization he chose, but he was rather pompous. He didn't quite fit in with the rest of the bunch, and that may have been intentional. He may have chosen, you know, [the attitude] 'I come from an upper class family and here I am commanding all these louts, trying to whip them into being soldiers.' He was not very popular. One day he was doing a thing of derring-do with his saber and he ran his saber right down into his foot. So you'll see scenes where he's limping, and that's because he actually jammed his own saber into his foot. Now you know when you get a bunch of guys that are playing a bunch of guys that know each other, the humor gets quite raunchy. So when he stabbed his saber in his foot, Audie Murphy said, 'Oh, Dickless Doug has done it again.'

"The thing about it … nobody came across as being 'actor-y,' and that's what Huston wanted. He wanted the feel of real sweating, bleeding guys who felt fear and anxiety. Huston was a great psychologist, and I remember when I tested for the part, I was kind of overanxious. I said to him, 'Now, Mr. Huston, this line here, I can do it like this, or I can do it like this, or I can do it like this, which do you like,' and he didn't wax directorial like some of the old German directors I'd worked for. He just said, 'Which one do you like?' He always let the actors make a lot of their own choices. Then if it wasn't quite right, he'd give them a little guidance, as, in fact, when he had me redo that one scene with a little more hysterical urgency."

As to whether Huston personally coached Audie, "I did notice that he did it very surreptitiously. When he'd talk to me, he'd take me aside, and that's very good because actors are nervous, and if a director gives them too much stuff in front of other actors, they get nervous. So he had a very confidential way of … he'd put his arm on your shoulder and ask you questions and stuff. But he was a very fatherly figure. The fact Audie played his role so kind of quiet and self-effacing and down to earth, I think made it work all the better when he then did become a hero. Huston had that ability to get performances out of people. He knew which buttons to push or he knew how to create. Huston created an aura where he led you to believe you were gonna do really wonderful stuff, and that he was counting on you and he was proud of you.

"For locations I know they went up to Chino and did a lot of stuff in Chino, which I was not involved in. My stuff was all at Huston's ranch. I do remember we'd be between battle scenes, and a knobby-kneed little girl used to come wandering down the hill and stand there and look at everything wide-eyed. Of course, that was [Huston's daughter] Angelica."

Royal Dano: "We had a good group. Compatible fellows. Most of 'em had been in the Army and come out a few years before. So we were all full of Army stories. Since it was a Civil War picture, just about everything we'd do would remind somebody of something. Audie used to take an awful lot of static that he was a war hero who was exploiting his medals. Audie was hurt by that. He tried very hard to deliver on this picture. He talked with me one time, 'Boy they gave me a bad time in so and so's column!'

"Now, I had seen Audie working on the backlot at Universal on what we called the old 'Phantom Stage,' used in *The Phantom of the Opera*, but it was a real stage. It had a place for the audience and a place for the actors. Universal used to have their contract players do plays there. I watched Audie do a Sayroan one-act play called *Hello Out There*—and it was a hell of a piece of acting. He did a fine job on it. Then I watched him in *Red Badge* and he did a good job on that. Then in the other pictures he did—f'instance *Posse from Hell*—he was very good. Murph was a lot better actor than people gave him credit for being.

"While rehearsing *Red Badge* we were running up and down hills. Murphy would run all doubled up. I couldn't even roll in that position. He could run so close to the ground he'd make a damn difficult target.

"I think Bill Mauldin brought this into the group: we played a game taking the rings off of Civil War rifles, throwing them up in the air and trying to spear it with a ramrod. I was never able to do that! Kept stabbing the air to get the damn thing and I couldn't do it. Mauldin managed to at least hit it a couple of times, and Murphy actually caught it once! He had that kind of natural coordination between eye and physical movement, which made him a very difficult guy for the Germans to deal with.

"[Audie] was a kind man. When we finished *Red Badge* they wrote a lot of newspaper articles and there was a book written. A lot of people said Royal Dano the first year in the movies is gonna win the Academy Award for this one, saying what a great performance it was. But I didn't know what was happening at Metro Goldwyn Mayer. There was a lot of arguments about the movie. And they began to cut it. Unbeknownst to me they had cut out my big [death] scene, all the meat of it. Well, Audie had heard about it. He knew my wife Peg and I would be hurt when we went to see it. He drove about 20 to 25 miles from the studio and sat down and chatted with us and gradually led up to telling us what had happened. That was a hell of a nice thing to do. Audie went out of his way to break it gently for us. That shows a side of Murph you don't usually get from the newspapers and things."

(Note: In checking the facts of the following story, it became clear either Dano's memory or Audie's retelling of the story is slightly askew, but the basics of the incident are true.) "Murph looked like a baby for a guy who had been decorated so many times. He was driving his car down to Texas and he picked up a hitchhiker. The hitchhiker, as they went along in the car, reached under his jacket, leaned over to Murph and said, 'I've got a .45 here—now pull the car over and get out.' Well, Murphy, instead of doing that, jammed this ostensible .45 caliber with his hand, thinking about the safety that's on the muzzle of the .45 automatic. He hit that with his hand, hooked the wheel to the left, jammed his foot down on the brake, and this guy went sailing down into the corner of the car, Murph helping to push him. When the guy was down in the bottom of the car, Murph took his foot off and stomped him in the face, opened the door and rolled him out. Now it turned out the .45 was a piece of pipe, but underneath his coat you couldn't have told. I said to Murph, 'What if it had been a revolver?' He said, 'I didn't think about it, when I think about '45s I think about the Army automatic.' That's why he jammed the safety on it. Well, he took this guy into the police station and they took a picture of him. And, by golly, the blood was pouring out of his scalp, and he had a shiner and he was just a bloody mess. Newspapers came out and said, 'War Hero Beats Up on Transient.' Well, Audie got clobbered in everybody's column. Hedda took a shot at him, and so did some of the others. So while we were shooting *Posse from Hell* he came in one morning and said, 'I had a hell of a time last night!' I said, 'What happened?' He said, 'There were two guys in a car and they were hurrahing these kids on bicycles over on Ventura Boulevard.' Murph was driving home and these guys were hurrahing the kids, honking their horns, chasing the kids along the edge of the road. So Murph pulled over to stop them,

he sorta cut them off. He then tried to drive away and they followed him, calling him all sorts of dirty names. Murph stopped. Guy came up and threw a punch at Murphy, so Murphy belted him. The other guy got a hand-hatchet and came after Murphy. Well, Audie had a riding crop, which was pretty heavy on one end. So he fought this guy with the hatchet, grabbing the hatchet arm and started to belt him with the crop. A man that was living in an apartment on Ventura saw this two-to-one fight going on and came down to help out. Between them they dumped these two guys all over the sidewalk. So anyway, Murph came to work and said 'I had a hell of a time last night.' I said, 'What happened after that?' He said, 'Well the fella that was helpful, I took his name and I'll be in touch with him. He wanted to take 'em in to the police and I said no, the hell with it, 'cause if we ever get to the police they'll turn the story around again.' So the guys left. About a day or so later there was a little item in the Valley newspaper: 'Two Pacoima men were admitted to Valley Hospital after being assaulted by unknown assailants.' Poor Murphy couldn't win for losing on a lot of those things."

NOTES AND COMMENTS: This film was one of several that brought about the head-to-head confrontation between MGM studio boss Louis B. Mayer and his chief of production, Dore Schary. Mayer did not like the script for *Red Badge*—although Schary did. Mayer had no faith in the picture making any money. Mayer tried to talk Huston and producer Reinhardt out of doing the film when Schary was away from the studio for a few weeks with a bad back. Soon Mayer was on his way out—to be succeeded by Schary, whose productions had brought in more capital than those Mayer had spearheaded (although this was not the case with *Red Badge*). Huston left the production immediately after completion to make *The African Queen*, leaving Schary and others to edit *Red Badge* as they saw fit. The studio reduced it to barely over an hour. It didn't play well with premiere audiences, and MGM dumped it, unheralded, as a second feature. Huston himself never knew how long his final print was, although it was reported to be 78 minutes. Huston did not hold on to a copy, so the truncated version is all that remains.

The Breen office of the MPAA was concerned about many words and lines in the film. "Dum [dumb] animals" they were afraid sounded like "damn," which was unacceptable. Also unacceptable was "Lord knows...," "Gawd," "Good Lord," "Oh Lord," "Hell to pay," "T'hell with yeh," "You can go straight to hell," and "Th' hell you say."

Huston was approached and contacted by hundreds of actors and their agents as this film was in pre-production. It is noteworthy that Huston filled his supporting cast with over a dozen primarily B-western character players, chosen, obviously, for their gritty or soldierly look — Glenn Strange, House Peters Jr., Lee Roberts, John Crawford, Smith Ballew, Dan White, Emmett Lynn, I. Stanford Jolley, Frank Sully, Billy Dix, Gregg Barton, Dick Curtis, Fred Kohler Jr., Lou Nova, Buddy Roosevelt, Guy Wilkerson, Jim Hayward. Also strongly considered but not cast were such people as Jack Larson, Dick Erdman, Bill Hudson, Robert Wagner and Harry Carey Jr.

Audie said the psychology in all wars was the same—he believed the psychology of a raw recruit in the Civil War was the same as that of a young man in the World Wars.

For *Red Badge* Audie earned $2,500 a week over 47 working days (about $20,000). Bill Mauldin was paid $2,000 per week ($15,667) for the same 47 days. John Dierkes earned $600 a week ($3,000 for 30 days), Douglas Dick made $800 per week over 46 days ($6,133), Royal Dano made $750 per week ($3,000) over 24 days, and Huston was paid $4,000 per week, earning $156,010 for his work.

The Cimarron Kid
(UNIVERSAL-INTERNATIONAL, JANUARY 1952)

CREDITS: *Producer:* Ted Richmond; *Associate Producer:* Muriel Whitson; *Director:* Budd Boetticher; *1st Assistant Director:* Joe Kenney; *2nd Assistant Directors:* George Lollier, Gordon McLean; *Story:* Louis Stevens, Kay Lenard; *Screenplay:* Louis Stevens; *Editor:* Frank Gross; *Director of Photography:* Charles P. Boyle; *Art Directors:* Bernard Herzbrun, Emrich Nicholson; *Set Decorations:* Russell A. Gausman, Joe Kish; *Costume Designer:* Bill Thomas; *Makeup:* Bud Westmore; *Sound Recording:* Leslie I. Carey, Corson Jowett; *Hair Stylist:* Joan St. Oegger; *Dialogue Director:* Gene Lewis; *Music Director:* Joseph Gershenson. Color by Technicolor.

CAST: Audie Murphy (Bill Doolin); Beverly Tyler (Carrie Roberts); James Best (Bitter Creek); Yvette Dugay (Cimarron Rose); Hugh O'Brian (Red Buck); John Hudson (Dynamite Dick); William Reynolds (Will Dalton); Leif Erickson (Marshal John Sutton); Roy Roberts (Pat Roberts); David Wolfe (Sam Swanson); John Hubbard (George Weber); Noah Beery Jr. (Bob Dalton); Palmer Lee (Grat Dalton); Frank Silvera (Stacy); Richard Garland (Big Jim Moore); Rand Brooks (Emmett Dalton); John Bromfield (Tulsa Jack); Wheaton Chambers (Thompson); Eddie Dew (Railroad Detective); Garnett Marks (Second Railroad Detective); Tris Coffin (Silk Conrad); Ann Robinson (Stella); Frank Ferguson (Warden); Tim Graham (Mr. Gans); Charles Delaney (Swanson's Deputy); Elizabeth Root (Lola Plummer); Dave Sharpe (Charlie); Rory Mallinson (Deputy); Forbes Murray (Postal Union Telegrapher); Harry Harvey (Storekeeper); Suzette Harvin (Stacy's wife); Jack Ingram (Train Passenger); Joe Bailey (Jed); Blaine Turner (Eddie); Dusty Walker (Singer in Dallas bar); Eugene Baxter (Tilden); Jack Shannon (Joe, wagon driver); Stanley Blystone, Charles Sherlock, Richard Farmer (Men on train); Tom Hubbard (Man in Swanson's office); Clem Fuller, Ethan Laidlaw, Paul Webber, Eddie Parker, Philo McCullough, William Marks, Jack Davidson, Martin Cichy, Brick Sullivan, Harold Lockwood, George Barton, Frank Roderick (Men). Stunts: Jimmy Van Horn, Wayne Burson, Dave Sharpe, Willard Willingham, George Sowards, Bob Burrows, LeRoy Johnson, Dick Farnsworth, Clyde Hudkins, Ellinor Lannon, Fay Johnson, Larry Randall.

RUNNING TIME: 84 minutes

FILMING DATES: May 17, 1951–June 15, 1951

LOCATIONS: Sonora area, including nearby historic town of Columbia and Jamestown Roundhouse; Juaregui Ranch; Universal backlot. All California.

BUDGET/COST: $491,202

For his next film, Murphy was back in the saddle as another real-life western badman, Bill Doolin, a member of the Dalton gang who took over its leadership when the Daltons were killed in a bank raid in Coffeyville, Kansas. With the expected gallons of whitewash slung over the hero, Doolin emerged as a misunderstood youth hounded by a vindictive railroad detective after his release from prison. Forced to take up a life of crime, Doolin is eventually captured after all his gang have been killed in an abortive train robbery.

Well handled by director Budd Boetticher, the film takes advantage of two rousing action sequences—the Coffeyville raid and an escape through a railway yard after yet another failed bank robbery. The acting ability suggested by Audie's work in *The Red Badge of Courage* was conspicuous by its absence here; but, in any case, a close examination of the film will reveal Murphy really had very little to do, and tended to

The Cimarron Kid

Title lobby card depicting (clockwise from top) Audie Murphy, Yvette Dugay, Noah Beery Jr., James Best, Hugh O'Brian. Bottom left shows Audie and Beverly Tyler.

get lost in the somewhat over-populated shuffle of supporting characters, many of them played by members of Universal's talent school. One of the main reasons why Murphy survived so many bad performances in his early roles is because of the high standard of supporting players assigned to his films, and this was to continue right up until the end of the 1950s. In *The Cimarron Kid* he was flanked by young character actor Hugh O'Brian, impressive in a fiery beard as outlaw "Red Buck," who challenged Doolin for leadership and lost; handsome youngsters William Reynolds (later to star on TV in *The F.B.I.*) and Palmer Lee; veteran westerner Noah Beery Jr.; the darkly intense James Best as "Bitter Creek," whose romance with Yvette Dugay received more attention than Murphy's dallying with Beverly Tyler; Rand Brooks, a one-time Hopalong Cassidy sidekick; solidly dependable Leif Erickson, who would eventually gain recognition as a serious actor in *Tea and Sympathy*, and fame as the star of TV's *High Chaparral*; black actor Frank Silvera, who also starred in *High Chaparral*; as well as Richard Garland, John Bromfield and John Hudson, who all achieved a small degree of popularity in low-budget movies of the 1950s.

Factually, the film was more accurate than the earlier Randolph Scott version, *The Doolins of Oklahoma*, in which Scott died a self-sacrificial hero's death at the end. Murphy's Doolin surrendered quietly to lawman Erickson and trotted off to jail, as had the real-life badman, although the real Doolin later escaped and was gunned down.

The sparse, bleak style which was to earn director Budd Boetticher an enduring cult reputation for his Randolph Scott westerns of the late '50s was not yet in evidence in his conventional handling of this rather routine effort.

REMEMBRANCES: *James Best:* "*Cimarron Kid* is one of my favorite films. I got a leading lady [Yvette Dugay], and I didn't get killed so soon. One time I asked Audie, 'You're very hard to get close to.' He said, 'There's a reason for that. In the war I lost so many friends and acquaintances, it's very hard for me to get close to someone. I'm still afraid I will lose them.' Audie was a dangerous man. You didn't mess with Audie. We'd done *Cimarron Kid* and we were down in Texas on a personal appearance [in January 1952]. He'd just married a young lady, an airline hostess [Pamela Archer]. Four or five guys that looked like football players were driving the other way past our car and they yelled something obscene at Audie. Audie slammed on the brakes and shoved his young wife out the door. He said, 'Get out, this second!' slammed the door and took off. I said, 'What are you doing?' He said, 'We're gonna catch 'em.' I said [making an astonished face], 'We?' I said, 'Audie, I'm 155 pounds wringing wet and these guys look like football players.' He said, 'I have an equalizer' and he pulled a .45 out of the glove compartment. Thank God we didn't find those guys! Audie was a very, very sweet, honest, sincere man, but he didn't take any guff off anyone."

How it's done: filming a close-up with Beverly Tyler facing the camera and delivering dialogue to Audie Murphy, who stands on a ladder beside the camera lens. Director Budd Boetticher has his foot on a film box.

Gregg Palmer: "Audie was a different cut. He admitted, 'I'm not an actor.' What makes a star? There has to be something that sets you off— whether it's the speech, the hesitation of a Jimmy Stewart or the walk of a Walter Brennan — there has to be something. Audie had this sweetness. You could look in his eyes and try to figure out what the hell was going on. He had that quality of a cat moving. And if you ever crossed him, he had those narrow eyes, you could see them narrowing. But Audie was natural, he didn't try to put on, he didn't try to over-exaggerate. Audie was not one to yell. If he got mad he would do it with his eyes. He never tolerated anyone being yelled at or belittled. I just remember his eyes, the deepness of them. He wouldn't scream at anyone, he'd just take 'em aside and that would be it. You don't have to be a big man or scream at someone to threaten them. Also, people knew who he was, knew his background. What I admired about him, Audie looked out for the crew, for the wrangler, and made sure they were happy. I found him to be very congenial.

"He was a very fast draw. His hands weren't big, but he was quick."

Rand Brooks: "I liked Audie tremendously. I only had the two [screen] relationships; one where I was his first commanding officer, and I died real quickly in *To Hell and Back*. But on *Cimarron Kid* I saw a lot of him. Two things impressed me very much. An assistant director, nice young fella, came up to him and said, 'Mr. Murphy, we're ready for you.' Audie asked, 'When is my wife coming out?' I guess he'd been expecting her. 'Right after lunch we'll be bringing her out,' the fella said. 'I'll do the scene when she's here.' Everything was so quiet. No outbursts. No hysterics. But you knew damn well that's what he meant! The other thing—[director] Budd Boetticher made us load our bags robbing the bank. Audie didn't have a bag, but the rest of us did. Budd wanted 'em heavy so they'd look real. And damn! To mount horses quickly with a heavy bag is not too much fun. And Audie at that time was not the horseman he became later. We went out of there ... Audie got a hold of the [saddle] horn as a group of horses went out, and he followed with him hanging on to the horn. He hit the light scaffolding going out, not many people saw it; I did. The scaffolding is a platform they put all the lights on when they want 'em up higher. They're iron pipe. Anyway, if he'd been a more expert rider he could have done a pony express and gotten on [the horse], but he just kept hanging on. As he went by this light scaffolding, he hit, just slightly, but at a running speed a horse hitting some iron with Audie's knee being in-between is not fun. When he came back he never made one complaint whatsoever. He wouldn't acknowledge he was hurt. I don't know how badly but he just wouldn't mention it. I could see he had a little limp. In that film, Noah Beery Jr. was a very fine actor, as everyone knows. James Best never found the success he should have had. He was a very, very good actor. Eddie Dew later directed a picture I did up around Eugene, Oregon, called *Stump Run*. Eddie and I drove up together."

John Bromfield: "Audie was a very quiet guy. I think he did a good job, but the director there was much needed. Audie never said, 'Look at me, I'm the greatest,' I don't think he needed that. I remember him as a kind person ... you wouldn't think that with his war record. He was an amazing guy. And he did pretty good box office."

NOTES AND COMMENTS: Audie's paycheck was $15,000, while other players earned far less— Beverly Tyler, $2,500; James Best, $1,200; Hugh O'Brian, $1,800; Leif Erickson, $3,333. Director Budd Boetticher earned $7,500.

An accident that should never have happened occurred at 9:25 A.M. on May 22. Hugh O'Brian began to play around with his pistol. He apparently accidentally discharged the gun, firing a shot into the nose

Left to right: Beverly Tyler (seated), Frank Silvera, Audie Murphy, Hugh O'Brian, William Reynolds (seated), Roy Roberts, John Hudson (seated), Yvette Dugay, James Best, and John Bromfield (seated) in *The Cimarron Kid*.

of Yvette Dugay's horse as she was mounted alongside Murphy and Best. The horse reared, throwing Dugay to the ground. Murphy and Best dismounted, grabbed the girl and pulled her away before the startled horse could tromp on her. Dugay required one stitch to the side of her face and returned to work by 11 A.M. The stitch was removed four days later. The cast and crew were so upset by O'Brian's action that they gave him the silent treatment for several days.

On May 24, stuntman Dave Sharpe (doubling John Hudson) performed a spectacular fall down an embankment by a waterfall during a chase sequence. Displeased with his first effort, Sharpe insisted on taking the fall a second time, this time injuring his ankle.

The original script called for Audie (as outlaw Bill Doolin) to be shot in the back by Swanson, but director Boetticher felt Audie's fans would reject this ending, so he rewrote the script to have Audie captured.

Cameraman Irving Glassberg replaced an ailing Charles Boyle on the final day of lensing. Glassberg had been filming *Battle at Apache Pass*.

In written memos, censors at the Breen office objected to the film's "excessive slaughter" and wanted the script changed to "indications of surrender on the part of the outlaws," or to simply "show men being wounded." The censors also felt a "religious medallion on a criminal like Bitter Creek might prove offensive to certain people."

The Cimarron Kid, like most Hollywood westerns, mixes fact and fiction. Bill Doolin was indeed a member of the Dalton gang as of late 1891; however, he did not participate in the infamous Coffeyville bank hold-ups of October 5, 1892, as the movie depicts. He was busy robbing a bank in Spearville, Kansas, with Bitter Creek Newcomb (who is shown in the movie to participate in the Coffeyville raid and escape). Grat and Bob Dalton were killed in Coffeyville, and Emmett was wounded, whereas the film shows all three being gunned down. John Moore (referred to as Jim Moore in the movie) was also killed, as he is in the film. Bill Dalton (referred to as Will in the picture) was not in the real raid; he joined Doolin's gang later in 1892, as did Tulsa Jack, "Dynamite" Dick Clifton and "Red Buck" Waightman. Bill Dalton was killed on June 8, 1894, by a deputy. Bitter Creek and others were slain on May 1, 1895. Red Buck was killed by marshals on March 4, 1896. "Dynamite" Dick (who was never a traitor to the gang, as the film depicts) was arrested in June 1896. Bill Doolin, actually married as of March 14, 1893, was arrested by Marshal Bill Tilghman on January 15, 1896. He, "Dynamite" Dick and twelve others escaped a Guthrie, Oklahoma, jail on July 5, 1896. Doolin was ambushed and killed by deputies on August 24, 1896, and "Dynamite" Dick was killed by deputies on November 7, 1897.

Audie's personal life went through some dramatic changes just prior to filming *The Cimarron Kid*. The final divorce decree from Wanda Hendrix came through on April 20, 1951, and he promptly married Pamela Archer, age 28, on April 23, 1951, in Dallas, Texas. Pam, a former airline hostess, then holding an office position with Braniff Airlines in Dallas, met Audie when she came to California on a summer vacation in 1950. The pair honeymooned in Dallas, but even then, trouble followed Audie. On his wedding night Audie almost shot a prowler; only his bride's screams stopped him. Audie told the *Los Angeles Herald and Express,* "I was trying to have a honeymoon and didn't want the publicity. We had a ground floor apartment. Very late in the night, I heard a scratching noise at the bathroom window. Pam was sleeping. I got my automatic and waited. The guy unhooked the screen and lifted it off. Then he forced the window up. This made a squeaking noise. Pam bolted up in bed. I told her to be quiet. There were venetian blinds inside the window. Suddenly they rattled and Pamela screamed. The guy took off in a hurry. I didn't have my clothes on and couldn't chase him."

Audie's new bride accompanied him to Sonora, California, for the filming of *The Cimarron Kid*. Following the shoot, the couple purchased a small bungalow just off the Sunset Strip in Los Angeles. Pam was described by a Hollywood columnist as "dark eyed, soft-spoken, petite, with raven hair, olive skin and a quiet wisdom that bespeaks her Cherokee [one-eighth] heritage."

In early 1952 Audie appeared as a guest on CBS' *The Ken Murray Show*, an hour-long Saturday night variety show hosted by the one-time vaudevillian. Murphy didn't appear again on TV for three years.

The Duel at Silver Creek
(UNIVERSAL-INTERNATIONAL, AUGUST 1952)

CREDITS: *Producer:* Leonard Goldstein; *Director:* Don Siegel; *1st Assistant Director:* Ronnie Rondell; *2nd Assistant Director:* H. Greene; *Story:* Gerald Drayson Adams; *Screenplay:* Gerald Drayson Adams, Joseph Hoffman; *Editor:* Russell Schoengarth; *Director of Photography:* Irving Glassberg; *Art Directors:* Bernard Herzbrun, Alexander Golitzen; *Set Decorators:* Russell A. Gausman, Joe Kish; *Costume Designer:* Bill Thomas; *Makeup:* Bud Westmore; *Sound Recording:* Leslie I. Carey, Corson Jowett; *Hair Stylist:* Joan St. Oegger; *Musical Director:* Joseph Gershenson. Color by Technicolor.

CAST: Audie Murphy (Luke Cromwell, the Silver Kid); Stephen McNally (Marshal "Lightning" Tyrone); Faith Domergue (Opal Lacey); Susan Cabot (Jane "Dusty" Fargo); Gerald Mohr (Rod Lacey); Eugene Iglesias (Johnny Sombrero); Kyle James [aka James Anderson] ("Rat Face" Blake); Walter Sande (Pete Fargo); Lee Marvin (Tinhorn Burgess); George Eldredge (Tim Ryan); Griff Barnett (Dan Musick); Frank Willcox (Dr. Clayton); Steve Darrell (Sheriff Barton); Wheaton Chambers (Dr. Hargrove); Harry Harvey (Dad Cromwell); Lee Morgan (Card Player); Stanley Blystone (Sam — at Ft. Lowell); David Newell (Man at Ft. Lowell); Jennings Miles (Stagecoach driver); Taylor McPeters [aka Cactus Mack] (Posse member); Jeff York, Johnny Carpenter, Carl Andre, Forrest Burns (Outlaws); Frank Hagney, Billy [Sailor] Vincent, Scoop Martin, Cap F. Summers, Bill Bailey, Monte Montague, George Brand, Tex Terry (Townsmen); Alma Maison (Lady). Stunts: John Epper, Jimmy Van Horn, Henry Wills, Clem Fuller, Carl Pitti, Willard Willingham, Emile Avery.

RUNNING TIME: 76 minutes

Daring the outlaw guns on this title lobby card are Audie Murphy and Stephen McNally. On the left (top to bottom) are Faith Domergue, Susan Cabot, Eugene Iglesias, Gerald Mohr, Lee Marvin and Walter Sande.

The Duel at Silver Creek

FILMING DATES: November 26, 1951–December 29, 1951; February 9, 11–16, 1952

LOCATIONS: Iverson's Ranch; Corriganville (Ft. Lowell); Vasquez Rocks, Universal backlot (all California).

BUDGET/COST: $604,894

Although it boasted Don Siegel as director, Murphy's next Universal western was again strictly routine, and rarely receives a mention in any retrospective analysis of Siegel's early work. Murphy, still cast in the glamour mold in fancy black-leather-and-silver-decorations outfit, played a character called "the Silver Kid"—the son of a murdered miner who teams up with lawman Lightning Tyrone (Stephen McNally) to track down claim jumpers who are making life miserable for the local mining community. Matters are complicated by the fact McNally has a non-operative trigger finger and a blind passion for bad girl Faith Domergue. Events are resolved after Murphy kills a hired gunman to save McNally, and the two of them rout the claim jumpers.

The Duel at Silver Creek offers little of interest to the cinema historian, other than the presence of the young Lee Marvin (in his first western role) as a gambler of rather indeterminate character, and possibly the presence of Domergue, a Howard Hughes protégée who never really made the big time. Filmed in Universal's crisp, high-gloss Technicolor, the film ran its short course at a brisk pace that didn't allow for character development and didn't get it, with McNally supplying enough strength and authority to compensate for Murphy's limitations. However, though he displayed no spectacular improvement, Murphy appeared more relaxed and at ease here than in his previous western roles, and the screenplay provided him with some wry comedy lines, which he handled with the gentle irony that was to become one of his most attractive features in his best westerns.

Even so, Siegel was taking no chances, and it's indicative of his skill as a director that although Murphy was ostensibly the star, he actually played a supporting role to McNally, who received all the close-ups *and* the final shoot-out with chief villain Gerald Mohr. Apart from one or two romantic interludes with Susan Cabot, Murphy mainly lurked around looking glamorous and handling the fancy action chores. But audiences, conditioned by the studio publicity machine, accepted Murphy as the star, and his popularity continued to grow.

REMEMBRANCES: *Faith Domergue:* "I loved to ride. I was fu-

Audie Murphy gives Faith Domergue a lesson in the proper use of a six-gun on the set of *Duel at Silver Creek*.

rious if they put in a stand-in for me. Riding was my great sport, but there was one scene where the posse is chasing us. We came around the corner at the end of Vasquez Rocks, across the sand and rocks at full speed. My horse slipped — almost went down, with the posse right behind us — but luckily it got back up, or else I would have been trampled by all those people following us! The others wouldn't have been able to stop and help me. As a result, the studio said I could no longer do my own stunts. They complained about all the costs, time, trouble there would be if they had to re-shoot — they didn't seem to care about me at all. Audie was terrific. One day he asked my advice about a kitchen appliance he was going to purchase for his new wife. Although I am not domestic, I gave him my opinion, and he was very pleased. Susan Cabot was his girlfriend in the picture, but when we were making it, she was on the 'outside,' as Audie and I became great chums."

Susan Cabot gets a lift from Stephen McNally and Audie Murphy on Universal's backlot between scenes of *Duel at Silver Creek.*

NOTES AND COMMENTS: The first nine minutes of *Duel* were added to the film by director Don Siegel after principal photography wrapped, because the picture clocked in at only 67 minutes, too short by U-I standards. You'll notice that although Audie's father is killed in the opening scenes, nothing further is ever made of that fact — Audie later simply appears as the Silver Kid. That's due to the fact those early scenes were written later and added to the extra seven days filming in February 1952, over a month after the picture officially 'wrapped.'

The working titles for *Duel* were *Claim Jumpers* and *Hair Trigger Kid*.

Some of the music cues used in *Duel* are riffs on standard Universal chase music often heard in their Johnny Mack Brown B-westerns of the 1940s.

The censors at the Breen office complained of "excessive brutality and gruesomeness," as well as a "muttered curse" and a "lustful and sex suggestive" scene.

Gunsmoke
(UNIVERSAL-INTERNATIONAL, MARCH 1953)

CREDITS: *Producer:* Aaron Rosenberg; *Director:* Nathan Juran; *1st Assistant Director:* William Holland; *2nd Assistant Directors:* George Lollier, J. Welch; *Source novel:* Roughshod by Norman A. Fox; *Screenplay:* D. D. Beauchamp (and Louis Stevens, uncredited); *Editor:* Ted J. Kent; *Director of Photography:* Charles P. Boyle; *Art Directors:* Alexander Golitzen, Robert F. Boyle; *Set Decorators:* Russell A. Gausman, Ray Jeffers; *Costume Designer:* Rosemary Odell; *Makeup:* Bud Westmore; *Sound Recording:* Leslie I. Carey, Robert Pritchard; *Hair Stylist:* Joan St. Oegger; *Music:* Joseph Gershenson. Color by Technicolor.

CAST: Audie Murphy (Reb Kittredge); Susan Cabot (Rita Saxon); Paul Kelly (Dan Saxon); Charles Drake (Johnny Lake); Mary Castle (Cora Dufrayne); Jack Kelly (Curley Mather); Donald Randolph (Matt Telford); Jesse White (the Professor); William Reynolds (Brazos); Chubby Johnson (Doc Farrell); Mike Ragan (Buck Jimson); Henry Wills (Clint Jimson); Frank Cordell (Ed Jimson); James F. Stone (O'Shay); Gregg Barton (Sig Bratton); Denver Pyle (Greasy); Bill Lester (Irish); Bill Radovich (Bartender); Carl Andre (Train engineer); Monte Montague (Railhead tallyman); George Taylor (Railhead

Jesse White, Paul Kelly and Audie Murphy tend to a wounded William Reynolds during a trail drive scene in *Gunsmoke* (1953).

doctor); Ed Cobb (Stage driver); Forrest Taylor (Station Master); George Eldredge (Stage passenger); William Fawcett (Hotel clerk); Leroy Johnson (Cavalryman #1); Carl Pitti (Cavalryman #2); Bill Williams (Cavalryman #3); Don Happy (Cavalryman #4); Jimmy Van Horn (Clay Larkin); Clem Fuller (Two Dot); Al Haskell, Frank Cordell (Men). Stunts: Henry Wills, Willard Willingham, B. Miles, Don Happy, Emile Avery, Bill Williams, Leroy Johnson, Polly Burson, Ann Duncan, Carl Pitti. Stand-in for Audie Murphy: Arvo Ojala. Stand-in for Susan Cabot: Ann Duncan.

RUNNING TIME: 79 minutes

FILMING DATES: June 12, 1952–July 11; July 23, 1952 (for pickup shots)

LOCATIONS: Big Bear, California; Juaregui Ranch, California; Universal backlot.

BUDGET/COST: $514,604

Gunsmoke remains one of the most satisfying of Murphy's conventional westerns, and marked the beginning of his most rewarding period as a western star. Tightly constructed, photographed in Technicolor against some magnificent mountain locations, and blessed with a witty and interesting screenplay, it possessed a wide-open, buoyant aura of freewheeling gusto totally removed from the studio-bound strictures of *The Duel at Silver Creek*.

In the sort of role that would in later years be tagged "anti-hero," Murphy played Reb Kittredge, a professional gunslinger hired to harass rancher Paul Kelly for villain Donald Randolph. Inveigled into a card-game with Kelly, Audie emerges as the reluctant owner of Kelly's ranch, and is forced to undertake a hazardous trail drive to protect what is now his own property. Charles Drake played Johnny Lake, a former friend of Murphy who hires his gun to Randolph; but after his numerous attempts to stop Murphy fail, Lake switches sides and wipes out the bad guy, leaving Murphy free to live happily ever after with Kelly's daughter, Susan Cabot.

For the first time in a western, Murphy discarded the glamour image and appeared in stained and scruffy trail clothes, sporting a stubble beard and often behaving in a decidedly unheroic and ungentlemanly manner towards Cabot, who had more to do here than in *Silver Creek*, and provided a spirited heroine. Murphy handled the well-written, often quite funny dialogue with sardonic ease, and displayed an authority never before evident, even in scenes with such a seasoned professional as Paul Kelly. Kelly, as the wily old rancher, was equally entertaining but did not overshadow Murphy; and Charles Drake, after playing weak-kneed heavies in earlier Universal westerns like *Winchester 73*, was solid and dependable as Murphy's cheerfully amoral former partner. Murphy and Drake were to team up again, to excellent effect, in four more films. Future *Maverick* TV star Jack Kelly gave a good showing as the jealous former boyfriend of Cabot.

Director Nathan Juran, an underrated talent who was responsible for some outstanding minor westerns of the 1950s, extracted maximum tension from a number of confrontation scenes, particularly an early shoot-out between Murphy and Paul Kelly; the poker game in which Murphy wins the ranch (by virtue of Paul Kelly's cardsharp skills); and a taut little sequence in which Murphy, his gun-hand out of action, bluffs Jack Kelly out of a gunfight. Action sequences are handled with speed and vigor, and there is a brutal maiming scene in which Murphy's gun hand is shattered by a pick-handle — almost as effective as the more frequently mentioned sequence in the later James Stewart western *The Man from Laramie*, in which Alex Nicol put a bullet through Stewart's palm. Another James Stewart western, *Bend of the River* (1952), was put to unfortunate use in *Gunsmoke* when its canyon ambush sequence was used nearly intact, even to showing the death of *Bend* villain Howard Petrie in a fall from a white horse. This

tended to confuse the issue, but was a minor flaw in a choice little action melodrama that heralded a bright start to a new look in Audie Murphy westerns.

NOTES AND COMMENTS: For *Gunsmoke* Audie earned $12,000; while Paul Kelly received $10,000; Susan Cabot $1,750; Charles Drake $7,000; Jack Kelly $1,200; Mary Castle $800; Donald Randolph $875; and Chubby Johnson $1,000.

Working titles for the film were *Roughshod* and *A Man's Country*.

On June 25 Susan Cabot turned her ankle, but nothing was broken.

Production was held up one day on Universal's backlot when actor Joe Mell,

Left: Between scenes on the set of *Gunsmoke*, Susan Cabot treats Audie Murphy to a bite of food. *Below:* Audie Murphy has been wounded, and Susan Cabot affectionately cares for him as trail drive cook Jesse White watches.

assigned to play the stagecoach passenger, failed to show up at 7:45 A.M. for his scene. After a few hurried calls, he was replaced by old pro George Eldredge, who arrived on the backlot at 9:30 A.M.

John Dehner was originally considered for the part of Matt Telford.

Mary Castle's saloon song, "See What the Boys in the Backroom Will Have," was previously sung in *Destry Rides Again* (1939) by Marlene Dietrich. Castle sings the song a la Dietrich.

Versions of Mary Castle's other song, *True Love*, were heard again in four other Universal-International westerns—*Law and Order* (1953), *Dawn at Socorro* (1954), *War Arrow* (1954) and *Quantez* (1957).

Considering Audie's war record and his penchant for always carrying a gun (even to sleeping with one under his pillow), his response in the film to Susan Cabot when she confronts him in his room, saying, "You don't need that gun," becomes very prophetic: "I sorta feel undressed without it."

Audie and the crew put in an extra hour's time after work on June 25 to shoot a black and white promotional trailer for Los Angeles County Sheriff Gene Biscailuz's annual rodeo.

Just three months prior to the start of filming on *Gunsmoke*, Audie became a father. Terence (Terry) Michael, named after Audie's friend and health instructor, Terry Hunt, was born on March 14, 1952, at Santa Monica Hospital.

Column South

(UNIVERSAL-INTERNATIONAL, JUNE 1953)

CREDITS: *Producer:* Ted Richmond; *Director:* Frederick de Cordova; *1st Assistant Director:* Fred Frank; *2nd Assistant Director:* George Lollier; *Story/Screenplay:* William Sackheim; *Editor:* Milton Carruth; *Director of Photography:* Charles P. Boyle; *Art Directors:* Alexander Golitzen, Hilyard Brown; *Set Decorators:* Russell A. Gausman, Ruby Levitt; *Costume Designer:* Rosemary Odell; *Makeup:* Bud Westmore; *Sound Recording:* Leslie I. Carey, Glenn E. Anderson; *Hair Stylist:* Joan St. Oegger; *Musical Director:* Joseph Gershenson; *Technical Director:* Col. Paul R. Davison, U.S.A. Ret. Technicolor.

CAST: Audie Murphy (Lt. Jed Sayre); Joan Evans (Marcy Whitlock); Robert Sterling (Capt. Lee Whitlock); Ray Collins (Brig. General B. N. Stone); Palmer Lee (Lt. Ben Chalmers); Dennis Weaver (Menguito); Russell Johnson (Corp. Biddle); Jack Kelly (Trooper Vaness); Bob Steele (First Sgt. Macafee); Johnny Downs (Lt. Posick); James Best (Trooper Primrose); Richard Garland (Lt. Frye); Ralph Moody (Joe Copper Face); Rico Alaniz (Trooper Chavez); Ray Montgomery (Trooper Keit); Ed Rand (Trooper Sabbath); Alan Dexter (Tom Kehler); Monty Montague (Wagon driver); Steve Darrell (Dan, rancher); Britt Wood (Wint Miller); Frank Ellis (Bartender); Denver Pyle (Confederate supply wagon officer); Jimmy Gray, Ed Colebrook, Jack George (Card players in saloon); Sidney Mason (Garcey, businessman in Gen. Stone's office); Tyler McVey (Miller, businessman in Gen. Stone's office); Jack Ingram (Sgt. in stable); Kermit Maynard, Boyd Morgan, Joe Bailey (bit roles); Dave Sharpe (saloon double); Maxine Garrett (Joan Evans' double); Stunts: Fred Carson, Billy Williams, Carl Pitti, Emile Avery, John Epper, Clem Fuller, Don Happy, Willard Willingham, Boyd Stockman, Clint Sharp, Ray Shaman, LeRoy Johnson, Jack Williams, Jerry Brown, Bobby

Herron, Saul Goross, Al Wyatt, Chick Hannon. Wagon drivers: Frosty Royce, Joe Hooker, Phil Schumacher.

RUNNING TIME: 84 minutes

FILMING DATES: July 29, 1952–August 27, 1952

LOCATIONS: Apple Valley, California, near Victorville; Universal backlot.

BUDGET/COST: $623, 358

After the sprightly humor of *Gunsmoke*, *Column South* proved a reversal to the straight-action format of *Kansas Raiders* and *The Cimarron Kid*, with Murphy again wooden, seeming uncomfortable in the uniform of a cavalry lieutenant, and ill at ease in his romantic scenes with leading lady Joan Evans. Set in Fort Union, New Mexico Territory, 1861, just prior to the Civil War, the plot had Murphy averting an Indian uprising arranged by Southern spies, and winning the hand of Joan Evans, as the sister of fort commander Robert Sterling. The treatment was plodding, performances routine, and even the action sequences lacked any particular excitement. Director Fred de Cordova was much better suited to comedies like *Bonzo Goes to College* and *Here Come the Nelsons*.

Sheer professionalism came to the rescue of screen veterans Ray Collins and Robert Sterling, but the rest of the supporting cast, including a number of Universal's star hopefuls, hardly registered as anything more than background figures. Dennis Weaver, who played an Indian chief, proved to be the most successful in the long run, going on to join James Arness in *Gunsmoke*, then on to TV super-stardom in the 90 minute *McCloud* series. Palmer Lee, who received special "Introducing" billing in *Column South*, and was built up as a romantic leading man (with his name changed to Gregg Palmer) through important roles in such prestige films as *Magnificent Obsession*, failed to measure up to the studio's plans for him. His last significant role for Universal was in Murphy's *To Hell and Back* two years later. Jack Kelly, James Best and Russell Johnson were all to appear in later Murphy films, as was old-time western star Bob Steele, who played a cavalry sergeant in *Column South*. Joan Evans possessed the pert teenage appearance that seemed obligatory for Murphy's leading ladies.

REMEMBRANCES: *Joan Evans:* "My first opinion was, I had no idea what Audie was all about. And it never changed! I was interested to meet him because I knew who he was and what his background was, so I found that intriguing. I had never met anybody who had the kind of war

Audie Murphy and *Column South* (1953) co-star Joan Evans.

background he had. I didn't know what kind of person are you who can do that ... and I still don't know what kind of person he was. I came from a show business family. I knew a lot of actors and he wasn't *like* actors. He was not outgoing ... he was not unpleasant, he just wasn't anything to me, except odd. But I was not sure until later how much that oddness was what I brought to it. I mean, before I met him, I thought this must be an odd character, so I found him an odd character. He was an enigma."

Joan said she felt Audie was uncomfortable as an actor, and would "never run lines" with her. "The rehearsal was only whatever the director needed to do to set up. Never privately."

Joan feels Audie was uncomfortable in the romantic scenes with her. "I always loved to be on the set. I was not a girl who couldn't wait to get away. I liked the set action. I liked what was going on. I was interested in what everybody else was doing; and in watching Audie, he always seemed much more comfortable with the men. He hung out with the wranglers, that's who his cronies were, he played cards with them, that's where you could find him when somebody needed him."

Joan's second film with Audie, *No Name on the Bullet*, came six years later. "He never changed! [Laughs] There was acknowledgement that he knew me, but his attitude was the same. He did two things over the period of those two pictures that was personal to me. In *No Name on the Bullet* I had to have a gun in my hand. When I was 14 years old and was working on *Roseanna McCoy* (1949) I had accidentally been shot. There was a blank, but I was hurt and it was very traumatic. After all, I was a city girl, I didn't know anything about guns. So, in this picture with Audie, I found myself uncomfortable about *the gun*. Granted, the girl in the picture would not have been particularly comfortable with a gun, but probably more comfortable than I. So Audie did show me how to hold it right, he did show me how not to be uncomfortable with it. And I was grateful to him for that. But that was the only personal kind of contact we had. I didn't want to look awkward and I was glad to be shown how not to."

"Then the only other personal move was at the end of *Column South*. I had just gotten married ... just days before the picture started. And we had gone to Apple Valley, to the God-awful dry lake bed in August—just horrible. Then we came back and did the rest of it at the studio. [The] picture is over, toward the last day. And he said to me — much to my amazement, we had barely passed any words as co-actors—he said to me he was having a little close-down-the-picture party in his suite of rooms at the studio and would I like to come? I said, 'Of course.' Well, when I got there I was the only person there. It wasn't a party. It was me. Now I was very young and I had never had anybody do that. So when I realized I was the only one there I said, 'Gee, it's been lovely working with you. Thanks for inviting me, but I've really gotta get home.' And I left. The intention was comparatively clear. As [producer] Gordon Kay said to me once, 'Don't flatter yourself, Joan. You weren't the only one!' I said, 'A, I didn't flatter myself. B, of course I wasn't the only one.' I handled it, there was no problem. What surprised me was, I made another picture with him. I would have thought once he discovered I really wasn't *available*...."

"On *Column South* I was loaned from Goldwyn. I was still under contract to Goldwyn. On the second picture [Samuel] Goldwyn had virtually closed down operations. I had been the last person under contract to him. By then I was freelancing.

"Fascinating story: During one of these pictures, we were all in the commissary together for lunch. Audie didn't usually go into the commissary, but he did this day. And whomever the actors were that were working, we were all sitting at the same table. It was the time of the Miss Universe contest. And several of the girls were brought to tour Universal. At lunchtime they brought several of these girls into the commissary. They were walked around and introduced. One of them was quite taken aback. We discovered she was Miss Germany, and Audie said, 'She probably knows how many of her brothers I killed!' But he was rarely that forthcoming.

"I think the camera loved Audie. I was astounded, when, after working with him, and then seeing the pictures, I was just amazed what happened on screen! But it sure didn't happen in person ... during a scene. Whatever that weird magic is that sometimes happens, certainly happened with him.

"I don't know that Freddy De Cordova was much of a director, but he was such a darling man. The idea of Freddy doing a western has always been funny to me. He was a very sophisticated fellow. Freddy looked the part of a New York sophisticate out there in the middle of the desert. My husband and I were both just crazy about Freddy. But in a picture like *Column South*, the people handle the camera and you just sorta do it.

"Of course, Audie's gambling habit was just ... when I learned what he was doing every day, what he was betting every day, I just couldn't believe it. Besides playing poker, he was betting on the horses every day. Lots of money! Every day! He didn't know how to handle money—or anything. That was the problem. There was no background, and I don't mean that in a snobbish way, there just wasn't. I always found him fascinating because here this boy, with no real talent, and yet what happened on the screen was this strange magic. Even in the early—really, really awkward days—there was a credibility because you knew what he'd done [in the war]. He really could do that—that little baby-looking kid.

"On *Column South*, in the middle of the dry lake bed in [snoring sound] Apple Valley, we were working and it was really hotter than hell. It always seemed to me that we made whatever movie we made out of season. We were either dressed for winter in the summer or dressed for summer in the winter. In the film, I was coming from the East to see my brother at the outpost, and I was wearing green velvet trimmed in fur—[in] August. So, the first day of wearing the outfit—the hat, the whole routine, somebody said at lunch, 'Oh Joan! Get out of those clothes,' because we were way in the middle of nowhere ... they'd brought the truck out for lunch. So the wardrobe lady helped me out of these clothes, unhooked 4,000 hooks, got me out of all this stuff and gave me a smock to put on. I wasn't hungry, I was dying of the heat. Somebody gave me a couple of glasses of ice tea. Do you know what happens to you when the weather is 190º and you drink ice tea? You swell up, and I couldn't get back in my clothes! [Laughs] So I learned, don't take your clothes off! [Laughs]"

Gregg Palmer: "One day we were having lunch at the Universal commissary. We got up to leave and went to the cashier. Audie reached in his pocket to get his money and pulled out an envelope. 'What have you got there?' I asked him. He said, 'I went down to Arizona to make a film and I picked up some rattlesnake eggs.' I said, 'What? Rattlesnake eggs?' I stepped back about four paces and he said, 'You can have these if you want, but I can use them to make a bracelet for your girlfriend. I can string them together and make a necklace. Here, take a look.' And he starts reaching for his wallet, but I can see he's watching me out of the corner of his eyes, and I figured, 'What the hell, there's no rattlesnake in there,' and I went to open the damn envelope, released the pressure and there was this rattling sound—I jumped about six feet! He had rigged a hairpin with a rubber band wound up taut—a button was attached to spin and hit the inside of the envelope, and the sound made you think there was a rattlesnake in there. That was Audie.

Joan Evans, Audie Murphy and Gregg Palmer between scenes of *Column South*.

"I remember when we were filming *Column South*, Bob Steele came on the set; he was going to play my sergeant. I used to pay ten cents to go see him jump on and off horses. When visitors came on the location to visit one day, all the parents went to visit Bob Steele, and all the youngsters went to see Audie Murphy.

"Willard [Willingham] saved my ass. He was doubling Audie. We were going through this pass with about 27 troopers. As I'm riding through, the cinch on my horse breaks. I yelled, 'Willard —' and he says, 'Lean in!' I just leaned in towards him and we made it on through; otherwise I could have gone off and the other horses would have run over me."

Russell Johnson: "You can see why Audie was the most decorated hero of the Second World War. There was something dangerous about Audie. That sweet face of his. He was a madman; he'd half kill you. He was a very, very tough little bastard. He was an interesting star of the period. There was that spark behind that sweet little look of his. Once you saw it, you knew that, man, there's a guy that could go berserk in a moment. He was absolutely an amazing fellow. Having come out of the Second World War myself, I had a great admiration for his exploits during the war. If he'd decide he was going to do something, he was going to do it."

In his memoir *Johnny Come Lately*, the late Frederick de Cordova, who became executive producer of Johnny Carson's *Tonight Show*, remembers Audie had such "frightening eyes" that camera angles had

Audie Murphy treats Joan Evans to a "lunch break" on *Column South*. Note the tissue paper around Audie's collar, placed there to keep the makeup off his cavalry costume.

to be changed in a scene involving anger in order to avoid a close-up—for fear of frightening the audience. De Cordova also relates an off-camera incident that occurred when Audie learned General Mark Clark was going to visit the set. Audie told de Cordova to watch what happened when the general approached. Military protocol required all soldiers, including officers, to salute a Medal of Honor winner, and when Clark came into view with his entourage, Audie said nothing, waiting until Clark realized the gaffe and saluted Audie first. Later Audie told de Cordova why he had one-upped the commander of American forces in Italy in World War II: "Too many soldiers, who didn't have to, died at Anzio."

NOTES AND COMMENTS: Audie earned $12,000 for his role, while co-star Joan Evans received $11,000. Salaries diminished greatly from there, as many of the cast were U-I contract players who were paid anywhere from $900 to $2,000. Of the non-contract players, second lead Sterling made $4,333, while old veteran Ray Collins was paid $6,000. Former B-cowboy star Bob Steele received $1,267.

On the second day of filming, Joan Evans received a bump on the head when she fell and hit her head against a door during the bedroom scene.

Considered by Universal for the role of Marcy, which Joan Evans played, were Terry Moore, Mona Freeman, Geraldine Brooks, Eleanor Todd and Barbara Britton. Jay Silverheels was considered for Menguito, Arthur Kennedy for Capt. Whitlock, Guy Williams for Lt. Frye and Dennis Weaver for Corp. Biddle.

According to studio files, Audie was accepted for insurance — except for disability due to gastric ulcers.

Technical advisor Colonel Paul R. Davison offered many military comments on rank, language and facts about Confederates leaving the Union Army to fight for the South.

Although Ray Collins is credited as General Storey, an onscreen identifier lists his name as General Stone.

While filming around Apple Valley, the cast and crew stayed at the Apple Valley Inn, later owned by Roy Rogers.

At one point, assistant director Fred Frank called upon three wagon drivers to drive their wagons in a scene. Frosty Royce, Phil Schumacher and Joe Hooker refused any more wagon runs unless their pay was adjusted up to $75 a day from $35 a day. Frank refused, and director de Cordova shot the scene without wagons.

Just prior to the start of *Column South*, Audie's wife Pam entered the hospital for 10 days on July 24, feeling run-down since the birth of their son Terry Michael Murphy on March 14, 1952.

Tumbleweed
(UNIVERSAL-INTERNATIONAL, DECEMBER 1953)

CREDITS: *Producer:* Ross Hunter; *Director:* Nathan Juran; *Assistant Director:* John Sherwood; *Story Source:* Based on the novel *Three Were Renegades* by Kenneth Perkins; *Screenplay:* John Merdyth Lucas; *Editor:* Virgil Vogel; *Director of Photography:* Russell Metty; *Art Directors:* Bernard Herzbrun, Richard H. Riedel; *Set Decorators:* Russell A. Guasman, John Austin; *Costume Designer:* Bill Thomas; *Makeup:* Bud Westmore; *Sound Recording:* Leslie I. Carey; Glenn E. Anderson; *Hair Stylist:* Joan St. Oegger; *Musical Direction:* Joseph Gershenson. Color by Technicolor.

CAST: Audie Murphy (Jim Harvey); Lori Nelson (Laura Saunders); Chill Wills (Sheriff Murchoree); Roy Roberts (Nick Buckley); Russell Johnson (Lam); K. T. Stevens (Louella Buckley); Madge Meredith (Sarah Blandon); Lee Van Cleef (Marv); I. Stanford Jolley (Ted); Ross Elliott (Seth Blandon); Ralph Moody (Aguila); Eugene Iglesias (Tigre); Phil Chambers (Ross); Lyle Talbot (Max Weber); Ezelle Ponte (Mrs. Clark); Harry Harvey (Prospector); King Donovan (Mac, Buckley wrangler); Ed Cobb (Fred); Lee Roberts, Tom Hart, Gregg Barton, Roy Butler, Eddie Dew, Don Nagel (Townsmen); Felipe Turich (Mexican in jail); Belle Mitchell (Lady); Emile Avery, Jennings Miles, Ken Terrell, Clem Fuller (Possemen). Stunts: Clem Fuller, Jack Williams, Jack Carey, Don Happy, Jimmy Van Horn, Billy Williams, Allen Pinson, Dave Sharpe, Willard Willingham.

RUNNING TIME: 79 minutes

FILMING DATES: March 11, 1953–April 2, 1953

LOCATIONS: Red Rock Canyon and Vasquez Rocks, California; Universal backlot.

BUDGET/COST: $523,975

Audie Murphy's next western more than compensated for the weakness of *Column South*, offering another entertaining package of attractive locations, tightly-developed plot and crisp production values under the sure hand of director Nathan Juran.

Tumbleweed featured less humor than

Audie Murphy urges his horse Tumbleweed up a steep Red Rock Canyon trail.

did *Gunsmoke*, but Murphy was again relaxed and in command as a rugged young wagon-train boss accused of betraying his charges to the Indians. Arrested and jailed, he is broken out by a young Indian he had earlier befriended, then sets off across mountain and desert country to prove his innocence. Managing to stay one jump ahead of pursuing sheriff Chill Wills, with the help of the title character, Tumbleweed, is a mangy white horse that made up in sagacity and stamina what it lacked in looks.

Specifically tailored to Murphy's emerging image as the laconic, self-sufficient young westerner, the film was a fast-moving mystery-western, enlivened by spirited action sequences and gaining a degree of gentle humor from Murphy's relationship with his ungainly mount. Chill Wills, more often found providing folksy comic relief (and the voice of Francis the Talking Mule), presented a nicely rounded performance as the humane lawman; and Russell Johnson, in a more substantial role than in *Column South*, was an ingratiating heavy. Lori Nelson, however, made for a dull heroine. Lee Van Cleef, who would emerge some 20 years later as the King of the Italian "Spaghetti" westerns, played a more-or-less sympathetic member of the pursuing posse, shot down by Johnson in the closing stages of the film. At that time one of the screen's busiest villains, Van Cleef menaced just about every western star of the 1950s, but usually didn't survive as long as he did in *Tumbleweed*.

The climactic fight between Murphy and Johnson, with the latter falling to his death from a Vasquez Rocks cliff top, was

How it's done: Director Nathan Juran (in dark coat) watches as Chill Wills and Audie Murphy film a scene for *Tumbleweed* (1953).

a concession to standard western cliches and didn't match the originality shown in the rest of the film; but, overall, *Tumbleweed* proved to be an excellent piece of entertainment, its strongest elements being Murphy's attractive, assured presence, and the expansive outdoor feel of the narrative.

REMEMBRANCES: *Lori Nelson (as told to writer Robert Nott):* "Audie was mischievous in terms of his sense of humor. He just kind of had that twinkle in his eye, like he was just about ready to pull a stunt on somebody or say something that would be shocking. Surprisingly, he was very good [as an actor]. I guess it was because he was so natural. He didn't try to act. He didn't try to mug. He just played himself. And it was so natural that it was good. Universal thought he was a very, very hot commodity. The films he made obviously made money—they put him in quite a few. *Tumbleweed* was a fun movie. That horse was amazing. He could do just about anything—except talk. But that film was light-hearted and not real complicated.

"[Our later film together] *Destry* was a remake. I didn't think it was as good as the first one, but it was a nice little movie. I was the good girl and Mari Blanchard was the bad girl. I got to be the bad girl in other movies later in my career, so that made up for it. George Marshall [the director of *Destry*] was very good, very instructive. Nathan Juran was more of an action director, but Marshall would take more time with characterization and such, whereas

Pardoned after serving two years in Tehachapi prison as a conspirator in a kidnapping case, Madge Meredith makes her return to movies in *Tumbleweed*. Lori Nelson and Audie Murphy welcome Madge to the set after Governor Earl Warren, then U.S. Chief Justice Warren, commuted her sentence "in the interest of justice."

Juran was more of 'Stand there, say your lines, then move here...' type. Sometimes when you're working on a really good script, and the character is interesting, that kind of direction can be disappointing, but on a picture like *Tumbleweed*, where it was this light-hearted, easy-to-take film, you figured, 'What the heck, it's gonna come off okay anyway!' [Laughs]"

NOTES AND COMMENTS: For *Tumbleweed* Audie received $15,000, and Chill Wills made $10,000. Lori Nelson and Russell Johnson earned $3,000 and $3,250, respectively, under contract to U-I. Up-and-coming heavy Lee Van Cleef took home $750 a week.

Tommy Hart, a friend of Audie's, was a former longshoreman and fight referee whom Audie found parts for in several of his films.

Hugh O'Brian and Faith Domergue were originally considered for the roles played by Russell Johnson and Lori Nelson. Suzan Ball was also tested. Maureen O'Sullivan, Jane in many Tarzan films, was considered for the role K. T. Stevens essayed.

Ride Clear of Diablo
(UNIVERSAL-INTERNATIONAL, MARCH 1954)

CREDITS: *Producer:* John W. Rogers; *Director:* Jesse Hibbs; *1st Assistant Director:* Fred Frank; *2nd Assistant Director:* W. Cody; *Story:* Ellis Marcus, Inez Cocke, George Zuckerman; *Screenplay:* George Zuckerman (Additional Dialogue: D. D. Beauchamp); *Editor:* Edward Curtiss; *Director of Photography:* Irving Glassberg; *Art Directors:* Bernard Herzbrun, Robert Boyle; *Set Decorators:* Russell A. Gausman, Julia Heron; *Costume Designer:* Rosemary Odell; *Makeup:* Bud Westmore; *Sound Recording:* Leslie I. Carey, Richard De Weese; *Hair Stylist:* Joan St. Oegger; *Dialogue Director:* Harold Goodwin; *Dance Director:* Kenny Williams; *Musical Director:* Joseph Gershenson. Color by Technicolor.

Ride Clear of Diablo

CAST: Audie Murphy (Clay O'Mara); Susan Cabot (Laurie Kenyon); Dan Duryea (Whitey Kinkade); Abbe Lane (Kate); Russell Johnson (Jed Ringer); Paul Birch (Sheriff Fred Kenyon); William Pullen (Tom Meredith); Jack Elam (Tim Lowerie); Denver Pyle (Reverend Moorhead); Lane Bradford (Harry Lowerie); Mike Ragan (Jim Lowerie); Eddie Dew (Matt Grove); Ray Bennett (Frank, stableman); Tim Graham (Pat O'Mara); Bob Camp (Andy O'Mara); Harold Goodwin (Bartender); Lee Aaker, Bob Mims (Boys); Leo Curley (Dr. Hyatt); James Griffith (Henry, train conductor); Hank Patterson (outlaw); Carol Henry (Gunman); Ray Boyle [aka Dirk London] (Pete, saloon patron); Robert Bray (Saloon patron); Paul McGuire, Ewing Brown (Men in El Paraiso saloon); George Lynn, Frank McGrath, Larry Williams, Frank Hagney, John Goddard, John Savage, Joe Morrisey, Bob Lawson, Volney Peavyhouse (Cantina patrons/townsmen). Stunts: Wayne Van Horn, Alan Pinson, Billy Williams, Bob Miles, Eddie Parker, Fred McDougal, Jimmy Van Horn.

RUNNING TIME: 81 minutes

FILMING DATES: July 15, 1953–August 11, 1953. Pickup shots: September 16, 1953

LOCATIONS: Burro Flats; Apple Valley (Victorville) desert, California. Universal backlot.

BUDGET/COST: $495,409

A brisk and tightly constructed western, *Ride Clear of Diablo* marked the first teaming of Murphy and Dan Duryea, later to make two more westerns together. Their

This title lobby card for *Ride Clear of Diablo* (1954) depicts (left to right) Susan Cabot, Audie Murphy, Dan Duryea and Abbe Lane.

contrasting screen personalities made the most of the economical and witty script. Duryea's manic gunfighter, with semi-deranged laugh, sloppy appearance and totally amoral outlook, was the perfect counterpoint to Murphy's relaxed, wryly comic understatement.

Murphy played a young railroad surveyor, Clay O'Mara, on the trail of cattle rustlers who have murdered his father and brother. A crooked sheriff deputizes him to arrest notorious gunman Whitey Kincaid (Duryea), in the hope Clay will be killed. Clay not only captures the gunman but wins him over as an ally. They eventually expose the sheriff as the leader of the rustlers, Whitey dies a hero's death, and Clay settles down with the sheriff's niece (Susan Cabot).

In her third co-starring role with Murphy, Cabot was again an effective heroine, although singer-dancer Abbe Lane, at that time being built up as a Latin sex-bomb, added decoration but little else as Russell Johnson's saloon-singer girlfriend. The film's highlights include the initial meeting between Murphy and Duryea—a neat, explosive saloon duel; a sequence in which Murphy and Duryea recover a stolen horse, climaxing with Murphy hotly pursued by the villains while Duryea rides behind at his leisure, enjoying the spectacle; and the final shoot-out, with the wounded Duryea bursting from a saloon to go down in a hail of bullets, followed by Murphy, who disposes of the heavies in a spirited burst of gunfire and fisticuffs.

Director Jesse Hibbs was one of Universal's regular western directors of the 1950s, and would later work with Murphy on two more westerns, as well as his biggest success, *To Hell and Back*.

REMEMBRANCES: *Jack Elam:* "The basis of my relationship with Audie Murphy was gambling. The very first place I met him was in a bookie's office. This guy worked out of a gas station in Hollywood. So we had the same bookie. This was before Audie ever did anything in Hollywood, when Jimmy Cagney had him under contract. He was out playing the horses, and so was I. And that's when we began our relationship. So when we worked in pictures, our relationship was very well established. I saw him many times at the [General Services] studio where he was taking dancing lessons and fencing lessons and all kinds of shit, and he had never done a picture and neither had I. I was Hopalong Cassidy's controller. I was making big money then for an auditor, about 300 per week. Anyway, I'd run down and make my bets, and there'd be Audie. So we got to trading handicaps. He handicapped horses, and he liked to gamble. One day I made the biggest bet I'd ever made in my life. I bet $50 on a horse and parlayed it on the seventh race, and parlayed it to the eighth race. I walked away with $1,600. And I bought a new Cadillac.

"Audie was a very fast draw. I'd done the thing where I was supposed to be the fastest draw in the world. In the movies, that is. We were always drawing all the time. And I was, really; in the line of actors, I don't think there was an actor in town who could outdraw me—except Audie Murphy. The big difference between him and me was that if I drew I couldn't hit anything. I just got the gun out. That was my glory. But he could get the gun out and get it aimed before he pulled the trigger. But we never did it with real bullets. We don't play that game. We did do it with blanks sometimes, just to see, you know. I'd get it out and he'd say, 'Jack what are you doing? You're shooting at the goddamned ground.' But it was a game we played, not too often. I gave up in a hurry. I knew when I was beat.

"He had a shorter fuse than anybody I've known. And he didn't like bullies. I saw him jerk a guy off a horse one time when the guy got smart with a lady—he didn't like that at all. Maybe the lady was Susan Cabot. He liked Susan Cabot. I knew Susan. I did pictures with her before I worked with

Tourists wave goodbye — or is it hello? — to Audie Murphy on the Universal backlot during the filming of *Ride Clear of Diablo*.

Audie. She was pretty cute and she was tiny, and so she worked great with him. She was only about five feet tall, and they had a great look together. Audie liked girls. I mean Audie *really* liked the girls.

"He wasn't afraid of anybody. One time, on some show, it'd have to be *Ride Clear of Diablo*, I guess, Audie was the star of the picture so he had his own car, and he said, 'Jack, ride in with me tonight.' Because I had to ride in a station wagon with three other guys. So he said, 'Come on with me, Jack.' We came down off the hill and we hit a little town at the foot of the hills. Because it was a western, I had a week's growth of beard and the long hair, which today would be short. We stopped at a bar for a drink. Audie didn't drink. But I said, 'Gimme a straight shot of Cutty Sark.' And Audie ordered a straight shot of Cutty Sark and a Coke chaser. We were sitting at the bar, and that way he could just slip me his drink. It would look like he was drinking, so he didn't have to explain to the bartender, 'I only want a Coke.' Anyway, some guy came down from a table at the end and walked behind me. And I had this hair, you know. And the guy got ahold of the back of my hair and squeezed it and said, 'You need a haircut, buddy.' And he touched the back of my head. Audie spun around and hit him and never said a friggin' word. Just hit him. And he went flat. The guy was with two other guys at a table down at the other end of the room. The guys got up and looked at Audie — and you know Audie was short — and these were big guys. Audie just looked at 'em. Not a word. They picked their friend up — he was kind of coming together — and they left the bar. We figured we might be meeting them after we finished my drinks, on the way to the car. But there was no sign of 'em. They were gone. I mean, they knew they don't mess with Audie at that point. They could tell. He had that attitude about him of 'Don't tread on me.'"

Denver Pyle told writer Robert Nott, "Audie was a pretty good actor. People didn't look on him as an actor, but I think he was very underrated and I think that's a matter of management. I think Audie needed better handling than he got. He was a tough little bugger. I just think he could have used ... they kept letting him slide back into scripts that weren't all that good. I attribute it to poor management. That could be his agent's fault for not getting in there and taking advantage of Universal's PR department. To promote him. I always thought he took his whole career with a grain of salt. I don't think he thought it was any kind of achievement. I had a feeling he didn't think it was a very manly thing for somebody to be doing. [Laughs]"

NOTES AND COMMENTS: Audie was paid $22,000 for *Ride Clear of Diablo*, while Dan Duryea, an outside talent, earned $20,000. Susan Cabot earned $1,000; Russell Johnson $2,600; and Abbe Lane $4,000.

Audie rode his three-year-old quarter horse Flying John in both this film and *Drums Across the River*. Audie rented Flying John to the studio for $125 a week.

The company lost considerable time during the first day of filming due to dialogue fluffs by Paul Birch. William Pullen had problems with his lines in the early evening of July 18.

Dan Duryea cut his hand during a fall in front of the saloon on July 31 while filming the movie's final shootout. He was treated at the studio hospital.

Audie received a gunshot powder burn on his chest August 10; and on the next — and final — day of filming, skin was torn from his right hand when he held a rope on a stallion in an Apple Valley action sequence.

Anthony Caruso was tested for a role in the film but not hired.

The working title for the film was *The Breckenridge Story*. What that possibly related to is anybody's guess, as there is no one named Breckenridge in the completed film.

On the set of *Ride Clear of Diablo*, Dan Duryea and Audie Murphy attempt to "run" their lines, but are interrupted by Audie's dog, Long John, a gift from (and named for) director John Huston (*The Red Badge of Courage*).

Drums Across the River
(UNIVERSAL-INTERNATIONAL, JUNE 1954)

CREDITS: *Producer:* Melville Tucker; *Director:* Nathan Juran; *Assistant Director:* Tom Shaw; *Story:* John K. Butler; *Screenplay:* John K. Butler, Lawrence Roman; *Editor:* Virgil Vogel; *Director of Photography:* Harold Lipstein; *Art Directors:* Bernard Herzbrun, Richard H. Riedel; *Set Decorators:* Russell A. Gausman, Julia Heron; *Costume Designer:* Jay Morley Jr.; *Makeup:* Bud Westmore; *Sound Recording:* Leslie I. Carey, Richard De Weese; *Hair Stylist:* Joan St. Oegger; *Musical Director:* Joseph Gershenson. Color by Technicolor.

CAST: Audie Murphy (Gary Brannon); Walter Brennan (Sam Brannon); Lyle Bettger (Frank Walker); Lisa Gaye (Jennie); Hugh O'Brian (Morgan); Mara Corday (Sue); Jay Silverheels (Taos); Emile Meyer (Nathan Marlowe); Regis Toomey (Sheriff Jim Beal); Morris Ankrum (Chief Ouray); Bob Steele (Billy Costa); James Anderson (Jed Walker); George Wallace (Les Walker); Lane Bradford (Ralph Costa); Howard McNear (Stilwell); Gregg Barton (Fallon); Ken Terrell (Captured Indian); Chief Yowlachie (Medicine Man);

Director Nathan Juran, Morris Ankrum (in costume) and Audie Murphy discuss a scene from *Drums Across the River.*

Audie and Lisa Gaye on the set of *Drums Across the River* (1954).

Robert Bray (Sheriff Ed Crockett); Ed Cobb (Deputy Beal); John Alvin (Doctor); Willard Willingham (Crockett deputy); Steve Darrell, Rusty Westcoatt, Lee Morgan (Townsmen). Stunts: Ken Terrell, Cliff Lyons, Jack Williams, Willard Willingham.

RUNNING TIME: 78 minutes

FILMING DATES: October 8, 1953–October 31, 1953

LOCATIONS: Kernville; Red Rock Canyon; Burro Flats (all California); Universal backlot.

Rated by many film writers as the best of Murphy's early-fifties westerns, *Drums Across the River* again had the advantage of Nathan Juran's clean-lined direction, and boasted one of the most impressive supporting casts of any medium-budget western of the decade. More outdoor than *Ride Clear of Diablo*, but lacking the witty dialogue, it was nevertheless a thoroughly satisfying little film.

Murphy played Gary Brannon, a young freight-line operator who teams with businessman Frank Walker (Lyle Bettger) to invade Ute Indian land for gold exploration. Realizing Walker is rally intent on starting an Indian war for his own profit, Gary joins his father, Sam Brannon (Walter Brennan), in an attempt to thwart the conflict. Framed for a Wells Fargo gold robbery, Gary is sentenced to hang, but is rescued by Walker when he learns only Gary knows where the gold is hidden. Gary leads Walker and his men into an Indian ambush and clears his name. The switch-about ending—with the Indians, rather than the U.S. Cavalry, riding to the rescue of the hero—was another touch of originality in a screenplay that effectively reworked many of the standard western clichés.

Murphy appeared sincere and believable, but his impact was blunted by the lack of humor in the dialogue, with villains Bettger and Hugh O'Brian more effective. Bettger, then at the peak of his career as a velvet-voiced heavy, was by far the most formidable villain Murphy had yet encountered on the screen; and O'Brian, lean and angular, clad entirely in black, made only a brief appearance as a professional gunman but stole every scene. Lisa Gaye, another young actress in the big-eyed, cute-faced mold of Murphy heroines, was colorless and unnecessary, and her short-lived screen career proved less successful than that of her sister, Debra Paget. James Anderson, an extremely good, but virtually unknown supporting actor of the 1950s, whose physical resemblance to actor Mark Stevens may well have hindered his career, headed the solid supporting cast, which featured such B-western stalwarts as George Wallace, Lane Bradford, Gregg Barton and Robert Bray (later to win critical acclaim as the bus driver in Marilyn Monroe's *Bus Stop*). Old-time western star Bob Steele here made his second appearance in a Murphy western. He and Murphy engage in one of the best screen fights in all of Audie's westerns.

This film marked the end of the brief, but vastly entertaining, teaming of Murphy and director Nathan Juran, and Murphy's straight westerns would never quite attain the same satisfying level in the future.

REMEMBRANCES: *Mara Corday:* "Audie was psychotic—insane! After killing all those people during the war, you'd have to be a little nuts! We were shooting on the backlot—it got to be suppertime and Audie asked me out for a little dinner. We got in his car, anxious to get that prime rib! It was turning dark and we were at a stoplight. There were kids in back of us, and when the light changed, they honked because Audie didn't start right away. The teenagers gave him the finger—and took off up the street. And right behind were Audie and me. He reached in his glove compartment—while rolling down his window. He got a gun and said, 'I'm gonna get them!' We followed along Ventura Boulevard. I said, 'My God, I just signed a contract. I can't die now!' Audie then said to me, 'Oh, I scared you, didn't I?' I told Tony Curtis, 'I'm terrified of him!' Tony told me a story about Audie shooting up one of his sets one day. Audie was very quiet, soft-spoken and boyish—yet a flirt with the girls. But he had a short fuse, so you walked around on eggshells whenever he was near.

"[Walter Brennan was] a sweet, professional man. One time, Lyle Bettger asked, 'What is my motivation?' Walter said, 'Just say the goddamn line!' Hugh O'Brian was very intense—didn't kid around. He was about as serious as Jeff Morrow!"

Lisa Gaye: "Audie was a gentleman—always! Friendly. Of course, I was still a teenager when we worked together, but he was very nice, very protective of me. Audie was like a big brother to me. He took care of me, watched out for me. [At the time] I was the only girl there besides the script girl. I received some lusty looks from some of the men, but I always handled myself where they knew not to put the make on me. It's how you handle yourself. I had an attitude and I knew to 'always be aware of what goes on around you.' They knew I was a lady—they may have looked, but they didn't touch or say anything. If they had, Audie would have come to my rescue.

"[Walter Brennan] was a sweetheart, like a daddy to me."

Gregg Barton: "Audie Murphy was a small, very quiet and pleasant person, but had notoriety thrust upon him so fast I don't think he could adjust to it."

Jack Williams: "Audie has to back this wagon up and dump the gold in the Kern River. Willard [Willingham] was doubling Audie with four mules trying to back 'em up to dump this gold. [Director] Nathan Juran says, 'Why won't they back?' This wrangler, Slim Cramer, says, 'That's why they call 'em mules.' [Laughs].

"Audie had this stand-in, Arvo Ojala, who was the world's quick draw artist. Arvo lived right across the street from Universal and he had the most beautiful wife you've ever seen in your life. Absolutely gorgeous! Arvo would tell people, 'You can't believe what a great friend Audie is!' Arvo would be the first one on the set, and Audie would see to it that Arvo was there even after the drivers had left. This guy got overtime [Laughs] I mean, 'til midnight! Arvo says, 'What a buddy! Here I come home and here's Audie sitting there with the martinis already made!' [Laughs] What a buddy! [Laughs]"

Director Nathan Juran: "They were all B scripts. On a B picture, an 18-day shooting schedule was considered generous. My strength on these [Murphy] films was in planning and organizing, and having some input on the sets and camera angles. There

Sheriff Regis Toomey holds a gun on Audie Murphy as Audie is restrained by Rusty Westcoatt and another man. Lee Morgan (hand on hip) watches.

wasn't time to have any doubts about the next shot. I don't like to get arty."

NOTES AND COMMENTS: In an article in *Newslife* magazine (10/13/53), Audie was named Universal's "favorite product" by film exchange heads. Audie termed himself "a western star in search of a guitar."

During the filming of *Drums Across the River*, for realism, Audie insisted the prop guns be loaded with full charges instead of the usual quarter loads. Consequently, when Hugh O'Brian carelessly fired off his pistol near Audie's face, Murphy received powder burns on his face and neck.

Destry

(UNIVERSAL-INTERNATIONAL, NOVEMBER 1954)

CREDITS: *Producer:* Stanley Rubin; *Director:* George Marshall; *Assistant Director:* Frank Shaw; *Story:* Felix Jackson; *Source Novel: Destry Rides Again* by Max Brand; *Screenplay:* Edmund H. North, D. D. Beauchamp; *Editor:* Ted J. Kent; *Director of Photography:* George Robinson; *Art Directors:* Alexander Golitzen, Alfred Sweeney; *Set Decorators:* Russell A. Gausman, John P. Austin; *Costume Designer:* Rosemary

Odell; *Makeup:* Bud Westmore; *Sound Recording:* Leslie I. Carey, Glenn E. Anderson; *Hair Stylist:* Joan St. Oegger; *Choreographer:* Kenny Williams; *Musical Supervisor:* Joseph Gershenson; *Songs:* "Bang! Bang!"; "If You Can Can-Can"; "Empty Arms" all by Frederick Herbert and Arnold Hughes. Color by Technicolor.

CAST: Audie Murphy (Tom Destry); Mari Blanchard (Brandy); Lyle Bettger (Phil Decker); Thomas Mitchell (Reginald T. "Rags" Barnaby); Edgar Buchanan (Mayor Hiram J. Sellers); Lori Nelson (Martha Phillips); Wallace Ford (Doc Curtis); Mary Wickes (Bessie Mae Curtis); Alan Hale Jr. (Jack Larson); George Wallace (Curley); Richard Reeves (Mac); Waler Baldwin (Henry Skinner); Lee Aaker (Eli Skinner); Mitchell Lawrence (Professor); Trevor Bardette (Sheriff Joseph Bailey); Ralph Peters (Bartender); Frank Richards (Dummy); Jimmy Hawkins (Boy); John Doucette (Rowdy Cowhand); Henry Wills (Stage Guard); Rex Lease (Townsman by wagon); Wayne Burson, Charles Perry, Jack Mower, Sailor Vincent, Robert Perry, Frank Mills, Kit Guard, Dave Ledner, Jack Davidson, Frank Cordell, Arvo Ojala, Harry Hines, Stanley Blystone, Michael Forrest, Herb Golden, Philo McCullough, Billy Bletcher, Monte Montague, Sam Bagley, Fred Carson, John Conde, Tex Driscoll, Billy Engle, Franklyn Farnum, Dick Gordon, Don House, Donald Kerr, Jennings Miles, Clyde McLeod, Joe Rickson, Harry Tenbrook, Wayne Van Horn, Fred Weller, Ann Cornwall, Harry Harris, Frances Osborn, Betty Lynn, Mardorita Hellman (Townspeople). Dancers: Peggy Gordon, Jean Mahoney, Lucille Lamar, Lari Thomas, Edna Ryan, Dale Logue, Jerry Farnum. Stunts: Ken Cooper, Bobby Hoy, Bob Herron, Frank Mills, Emile Avery, Polly Burson, Lucille House, Charles Horvath, Reg Parton.

RUNNING TIME: 95 minutes

FILMING DATES: May 10, 1954–June 15, 1954

LOCATIONS: Universal backlot.

BUDGET/COST: $697,759

George Marshall's remake of his own 1939 hit *Destry Rides Again* can be seen as the definitive western of Murphy's early career, before *To Hell and Back* lifted him into more prestigious realms. It was the culmination of all the screen qualities Murphy had been gradually developing from *Gunsmoke* onwards—the quiet sincerity, the gentle humor, the taut control of action scenes. Actor and role were fused in total harmony, and a comparison with James Stewart's performance in the original reveals Murphy's Destry as a shade less forced, a shade more human—the actor is less in evidence, the technique less obvious. Perhaps this is because, unlike Stewart, Murphy was not an actor of any particular versatility, relying almost entirely on his own personality, and in the character of Tom Destry he found the most complete extension of that personality he'd yet encountered in a script.

Loosely based on Max Brand's novel, the action revolves around Destry, the son of a famous lawman, who is made deputy sheriff of the tough town of Restful. His appointment is something of a joke to the corrupt elements that control the town, as are his habits of drinking milk and not wearing a gun; but by virtue of some quiet sleuthing, amateur psychology and basic scientific principles, Destry triumphs—although in deference to western tradition he must resort to the gun for the final showdown.

For most of the time, the tone of the film was definitely tongue-in-cheek, demanding of its players a slightly larger-than-life acting style; and all of the principals responded with vigor, stopping just short of the point where it might have become self-indulgent. Lyle Bettger was never more effective as a heavy than as the insinuating, treacherous town boss Decker, his confidence gradually eroded by Destry's gentle gibes and small victories; while Thomas Mitchell added another character to his gallery of rich and enjoyable performances. Edgar Buchanan, Wallace Ford, Mary Wickes and Alan Hale Jr. were other long-time professionals who entered into the spirit of the fun with gusto, and only Mari Blanchard and Lori Nelson emerged with less than credit. Blanchard was faced with the almost impossible task of following Marlene Dietrich's performance in the original, and although the character was re-named, and the songs given a more raucous beat, her spirited performance always seemed to be showing signs of strain. Lori Nelson, on the other hand, showed no spirit whatever and seemed to be the only cast member not in on the joke. No matter, her role was quite minor anyway.

Although George Marshall's classic *The Sheepman* (1958) is more highly regarded as a comedy western (due in large measure to the big-name presence of Glenn Ford and Shirley MacLaine), *Destry* displayed the same skillful blend of semi-satire and hard action. The opening, played straight, relied strongly on the traditions of the western, with the murder of a sheriff by Lyle Bettger's gang, and the contemptuous election of the town drunk (Thomas Mitchell) as his replacement. But the slide into comedy was adroitly achieved with the first appearance of Murphy, alighting from a stagecoach in city clothes, and carrying a birdcage and parasol — to the disgust of Mitchell, who has been loudly touting the town-taming reputation of his new deputy.

Mitchell at first mistakes the obviously tough Alan Hale Jr. for Destry, a gag later pirated by Elliot Silverstein in his enjoyable but overrated *Cat Ballou* (1965) when a two-gun tough is mistaken for the legendary Kid Shelleen. *Destry's* most satisfying scene occurred when Destry was called upon to display his gun skills. A group of drunken cowboys, led by John Doucette, are shooting up the saloon. When Destry intervenes, Doucette attempts to make him "dance" by shooting holes in the floor close to his boots. Destry does not move. There is total silence; then Destry quietly commandeers a pair of six-guns and, in a dazzling display of gunmanship, begins shooting pieces off a large roulette wheel. The amusement of the onlookers turns to apprehension, leaving the cowboys thoroughly demoralized.

When, at the film's climax, after the murder of Mitchell, Bettger is informed Destry is coming, he remains unworried — until told Destry is wearing a gun. The tension builds to near breaking point as the heavies wait in ambush, only to be themselves ambushed by Destry's guerrilla tactics. This expertly choreographed final shoot-out proved explosively exciting, bringing the film full circle back to traditional western action, yet there was never any feeling of awkwardness in the transition from fun to fury.

Destry, filmed on a more lavish scale and with a bigger budget than any of Murphy's earlier works, was a perfect combination of bravado and quietness, comedy and action, and earned Audie his first serious critical acclaim. Many critics, prepared to scoff at the studio's temerity in attempting to remake a film regarded as a comedy-western classic, were totally disarmed by Murphy's charm and the film's infectious good humor. While most still regard it as inferior to the Stewart-Dietrich film, many consider it (Dietrich aside) the more entertaining version.

REMEMBRANCES: *Director George Marshall* (who also directed the original *Destry Rides Again*): "I only filched what was best of the old picture. Audie is a grass roots actor because of the many qualities which overlap between his real life and his reel life."

Lori Nelson: "Audie was very shy and quiet, and stayed to himself a lot, but very much a gentleman. He liked the working guys at the studio. Since he'd never acted before, he turned out to be quite a good actor. If you came from the generation of Jimmy Stewart and Marlene Dietrich, you probably liked [the earlier version] better.

The newer generation who were big fans of Audie Murphy ... I'm sure that colors how they feel about it."

Lee Aaker says he was unaware of Audie's background when he acted in the picture as a child of eleven. "That was done the same summer we did the pilot for *Rin Tin Tin*. I didn't realize the magnitude of what I was doing. I'd been around [movies] so long by then, and I was very busy, I worked almost steady. There was one scene I did with Lori Nelson. She did a thing where she shot her guns off in the office and the prop man dropped a bird on her head. [Laughs] [Note: Notice Lori's surprised reaction in the film.] I remember walking with Audie in a scene, imitating him with a rope. I like Audie's cowboy boots, and I either bought some or got some boots like his. He was a nice person who took time to talk to me."

Jimmy Hawkins: "My brother, Tim, is in *Sierra*. I did *Destry* with Audie. My scene was with Thomas Mitchell. We both remember Audie Murphy as being very nice. He did take time to talk with us. I remember he had a great smile. And whenever a kid would ask a question he would look at them very amused and smile down at them before he would give his answer. I found out years later from actress Joanna Moore [she acted opposite Audie in *Ride a Crooked Trail* in 1958] that he always carried a gun. She said she was driving with him in a car once, and he showed her the gun and said that having it evened things out. She would see him across the street just looking at her house. She thought that something deep was going on inside him. Knowing what he went through during WWII, I don't blame him. He deserves great respect and thanks. He was a great warrior and, when

Audie Murphy and Mari Blanchard on the sound stage of *Destry*.

called upon, served his country very well. They trained him well for war. [They] just didn't train him for life when he returned home."

Bobby Hoy: "I was doubling Audie in *Destry*, and I got a job to double Charles Buchinsky [Bronson] down in Sedona, Arizona. I said, 'Jeez, Audie, this is a couple weeks work,' as opposed to one or two days to double Audie. Willard was out of town or something, and Jimmy Sheppard wasn't yet around as a stuntman. I said, 'There's nothing to this, you jump over the bar, Audie. Just figure you're in a bar in Texas and you gotta get outta there.' [Laughs] He said, 'Ok, I'll do it.' That released me to take the better job. He was a good guy."

NOTES AND COMMENTS: For *Destry*, Audie was paid $18,000 under contract to Universal, while non-contractee Thomas

Proud Papa Audie Murphy with sons Terry Michael and James Shannon on the Universal backlot while filming *Destry*.

Mitchell signed on for $20,000. Wallace Ford received $6,500 and Edgar Buchanan $6,000, while villain Lyle Bettger earned $7,500. Lori Nelson and Mari Blanchard, both under contract to U-I, were paid $5,500 and $4,500 respectively. Child actor Lee Aaker made $1,917.

The company was all set up, ready to shoot a scene on May 26 when Audie received an emergency phone call at 5:55 P.M. regarding an illness with his son. His second son, James Shannon, had been born on March 23, 1954.

Following their screen catfight, filmed on June 2, both Mari Blanchard and Mary Wickes went to the doctor at the end of the day to check out bumps and bruises received in their fight sequence. Mari complained of an injured nose and upper lip. The following day Mari was sent in for x-rays at the end of the day. Earlier in the production, on May 13, Mari tripped on a cable on the set and cut her foot. This also delayed production when x-rays were required.

Further mishaps included Sailor Vincent cutting his face in a saloon brawl on May 27, and Betty Lynn injuring her foot on June 7 while chasing a man in the saloon. With all the wild melees that took place in the film, it's a wonder there weren't more injuries.

The working title of the film was *Son of Destry*.

Just prior to filming *Destry*, Universal announced on April 20 their intention to make *To Hell and Back*, Audie's next movie project.

To Hell and Back
(Universal-International, October 1955)

CREDITS: *Producer:* Aaron Rosenberg; *Director:* Jesse Hibbs; *Assistant Director:* Tom Shaw; *Source:* Based on Audie Murphy's autobiography *To Hell and Back*; *Screenplay:* Gil Doud; *Editor:* Edward Curtiss; *Director of Photography:* Maury Gertsman; *Art Directors:* Alexander Golitzen, Robert Clatworthy; *Set Decorations:* Russell A. Gausman, John P. Austin; *Makeup:* Bud Westmore; *Sound Recording:* Leslie I. Carey, John A. Bolger Jr.; *Hair Stylist:* Joan St. Oegger; *Song:* "Dog Face Soldier" by

Bert Gold, Ken Hart; *Musical Supervision:* Joseph Gershenson; *Technical Advisors:* Major Leonard J. Murray, Infantry, USA; Colonel Michael Paulick, Infantry, USA; Audie Murphy (uncredited). Color by Technicolor.

CAST: Audie Murphy (Audie Murphy); Charles Drake (Brandon); Marshall Thompson (Johnson); Jack Kelly (Kerrigan); Gregg Palmer (Lt. Manning); Paul Picerni (Valentino); David Janssen (Lt. Lee); Richard Castle (Kovack); Bruce Cowling (Capt. Marks); Paul Langton (Col. Howe); Art Aragon (Sanchez); Felix Noriego (Swope); Denver Pyle (Thompson); Brett Halsey (Saunders); Susan Kohner (Maria); Anabel Shaw (Helen); Mary Field (Mrs. Murphy); Gordon Gebert (Audie as a boy); Julian Upton (Steiner); Tommy Hart (Klasky); Anthony Green (Lt. Burns); Howard Wright (Ben Houston); Edna Holland (Edna Houston); Maria Costi (Julia); Didi Ramati (Carla); Barbara James (Cleopatra); Joey Costaretta (Street urchin); Rand Brooks (Lt. Harris); Nan Boardman (Maria's mother); Henry Kulky (Sgt. Stack); John Pickard (M.P.); Don Kennedy (Marine Recruit Sergeant); Ralph Sanford (Chief Petty Officer); Rankin Mansfield (Dr. Synder); Madge Meredith (Corinne); Mort Mills (Soldier on ship); John Bryant (Jim); Ashley Cowan (Scottish soldier); Howard Price (Truck driver); Alexander Campbell (Rector); Terry Murphy (Audie's younger brother in childhood scenes); John McIntire (Narrator). Stunts: Bobby Hoy, John Daheim.

RUNNING TIME: 105 minutes

FILMING DATES: Early September 1954 to October 28, 1954

LOCATION: Fort Lewis, Washington; Bakersfield, California; Universal backlot.

BUDGET/COST: Approximately $800,000

With Murphy's assured performance in *Destry* as evidence of his ability, and backed up by favorable critical reaction and a healthy box-office return, Universal decided the time was right for Audie to play himself in *To Hell and Back*, the film version of his own wartime biography. The biggest stumbling block was Murphy himself, who had previously resisted studio efforts to persuade him to allow the film to be made because of the severe emotional strain it might place on him, and because he was wary of Hollywood's well-known penchant for glorification and "phoniness" in making war films. He finally agreed, with the understanding his own exploits were to be played down in favor of a film dedicated more to a group of fighting men than to one man. Even after green-lighting the project, he was reluctant to appear in it, suggesting instead someone like Tony Curtis play him; but Murphy finally agreed, and acted as technical advisor (uncredited) as well as star, working closely with director Jesse Hibbs and writer Gil Doud on the preparation for the film.

Of his book, Murphy once said, "It was a lousy book, because it was a lousy war." But the film that emerged from it was far from "lousy," surprising even those critics who had sneered at the idea of a former hero having the bad taste to glorify his own exploits for the rewards of fame and money. Filmed entirely in the U.S., yet convincingly "European" in its physical aspects, it won unanimous acclaim and went on to become Universal's biggest moneymaker up to that time. Despite elements of Hollywood gloss, it is still regarded as a worthy achievement. The critics agreed.

New York Times: "Gallantry has been glorified more dramatically on film previously but Mr. Murphy, who still seems to be the shy, serious tenderfoot rather than a titan among G. I. heroes, lends stature, credibility and dignity to an autobiography that would be routine and hackneyed without him."

New York Times Guide to Movies on TV: "The impressive, unmannered presence of Audie Murphy and some exceptionally vivid battle scenes give real merit to this dramatization of his autobiography.

In the heat of action, on the front, Murphy and highly-charged heroics are vivid realities."

Australian Women's Weekly: "Murphy brings to the tough job of reliving his own past an agreeable modesty and the lack of pretense of a true combat veteran."

The *Melbourne Herald* (Australia) called the film "...a monument to the courage, steadfastness and self-sacrifice of the infantry soldier. It burns with credibility because Audie Murphy the actor is playing Audie Murphy the foot-slogger.... [O]n the spectacular side the film is splendid."

The *London Daily Mirror* labeled the picture "...inspiring and exciting ... Audie enacts on the screen — modestly and convincingly — the role he played in real life.... [It is] a film of blood, sweat and tears ... well and vividly produced."

Time: "Credibility burns in his mild face and gentle gestures as he moves through scenes of battle raptly, like a man reliving them with wonder and something of reverence."

Picturegoer: "The film is restrained, humorous, searching. What gives it its special quality is the intensely personal feeling. The element of authenticity gives the incredibly rugged battle scenes a vitality rarely seen on the screen. And Murphy, playing himself, provides by far the best performance of his career. It must be just as difficult to relive your own past on the screen as to create an entirely new character. When he goes into action, that baby-face takes on a tenacity you'd hardly credit."

Departing from the book to a large degree, the film condensed Murphy's somewhat rambling and chaotic (yet authentic) reminiscence into a more conventional dramatic format, even though there were times when it did tend to ramble itself, tracing Audie's life from his youth as a Texas farm boy through his enlistment, introduction to battle, the gradual loss of

Audie Murphy, with a wounded Gregg Palmer, is ready for action in *To Hell and Back* (1955).

most of his companions, to his heroic stand against massive odds while manning the machine-gun of a burning tank-destroyer. It closed with a re-creation of his being awarded the Congressional Medal of Honor, America's highest wartime decoration.

Apart from the climactic encounter, the film played down Murphy's exploits, resulting in a sincere, not overly spectacular movie in which the comradeship of men at arms was as important as the action sequences. In this respect it was well served by such dependable players as Charles Drake, Marshall Thompson and Jack Kelly, all of whom gave performances which outstripped anything they had done on film previously, or would do again. But despite Murphy's insistence his own part be minimized, it was on him that the film depended, and he displayed a conviction and deep sense of involvement he would never surpass.

It is this film which is always mentioned in connection with Murphy, and had he retired after completing it (as he several times threatened to do), he would possibly have won a place among the immortals of screen acting. But even so, his portrayal was so truthful that even the sad decline of his last years cannot diminish it. Many scenes took on an added dimension of reality purely through his presence, and even the phony war-movie comedy scenes avoided the clichéd look they might have had without him. In light of later blood-spattered war movies, it was surprisingly restrained, almost dignified in its approach, and never allowed its star to appear the super-hero of so many other flag-waving Hollywood war films.

The rapport between Murphy and his fellow actors, in particular Drake, Kelly and Thompson, was vital and alive, each seeming to draw an added dimension of sensitivity and humanity from Murphy. Charles Drake's death scene took on a poignancy that overrode the inherent sentimentality of the sequence. The scene, reproduced almost exactly from Murphy's account in the book, was a key emotional moment in the film, superbly handled by director Jesse Hibbs and his actors. Murphy and Drake are pinned down on a hillside. Drake, impatient for action, stands up and is shot. Murphy goes virtually berserk, charges up the hill and annihilates the German machine-gunners with ruthless ferocity before returning to sit beside Drake's body. The camera stayed on his sweat-and-grime stained face as the tears welled in his eyes, with the silence only finally broken by Jack Kelly's softly-spoken, "C'mon Murph." Few actors could have conveyed such deep emotion so totally—the grief was so real and believable that the scene came close to being embarrassing, as if the camera had intruded on a man's most private moment—and it is this scene more than any other which remains in the memory. Murphy himself had backed away from it until it could no longer be avoided, inventing excuses to have it postponed. Director Jesse Hibbs said later, "Audie wasn't doing much acting in this. He played it as he felt it." The feeling came through, loud and clear, and suddenly audiences and critics to whom Audie Murphy was just another cowboy star had discovered a shining new screen personality. The modest boy in the cowboy hat, smiling awkwardly at the heroine and confounding the bad guys, was replaced by a movie-selling product of top-shelf magnitude, who had proved he could carry a big-scale, top-budget movie to towering box-office heights.

Unfortunately, forgotten was the fact that *To Hell and Back* was—and had to be—strictly a one-shot winner. The emotions had been real, the dedication and compelling screen presence torn from a man's tortured memories. The Audie Murphy who returned to the job of a working actor was still the same basically untrained, limited personality who came across best in simple, uncomplicated little movies built around his limitations. For

Murphy, this was to be a tragic misconception.

Nevertheless, *To Hell and Back* will remain his memorial. Even today, when it is often fashionable to downgrade the assembly-line movies of the '50s, critical comments are generous and almost totally unanimous in assessing that its elevation above the run-of-the-mill war movie was due entirely to the blazing conviction of Murphy's performance. It was a unique achievement in the life of a man who lived the title not once but many times during his stormy life and film career.

REMEMBRANCES: *Audie Murphy:* "Once I thought I didn't want to act it [the war] out again — because I had been through it and written about it — but now U-I wants to do it as a movie. I've always felt their story [of the infantrymen] should be told. I just play a part in it. This isn't just my story — it's the story of all our company and of the infantry. There's going to be one hell of a jury looking at this film and reviewing it out front. It would have been tough if I hadn't been so busy [during the filming]. I was sort of an assistant technical director on it and I was helping out with these things. If I'd had nothing to do but sit there and do my little part, I'd have gone nuts. I have to admit, I love the damned Army. It was my father, mother, brother to me for years. It made me somebody, gave me self-respect."

Staff Sergeant Audie Murphy, commissioned on the battlefield, has his second lieutenant bars pinned on by his commanding officer, Paul Langton, as another officer, Bruce Cowling, watches in *To Hell and Back*.

Audie considered himself "very lucky" to come out of WWII alive. "I was wounded three times. Bravery under fire sometimes happens because a soldier, particularly an infantryman, is actually safer flat on his belly firing his rifle than running away. He is sure a good target when he's upright. War is a nasty business, to be avoided if possible and to be gotten over with ASAP. It's not the sort of job that deserves medals."

Producer Aaron Rosenberg: "The problem of getting [his childhood] out of Audie I turned over to [scriptwriter] Doud. Doud was weeks talking Murphy out of a deep mood which settled over him as he tried to recall the details of a childhood which was spent hunting rabbits for a twelve-place dinner table which knew no other sustenance but bread and molasses. [On the film,] never once did I get a report [that Audie] had been hard to handle, yet he had more right to be than any star I've known."

Director Jesse Hibbs: "Just getting Audie to talk was like pulling teeth for the first three months when we were planning the picture. Audie had come out of grinding poverty to become the most publicized war hero in history. He was understandably sensitive about both of these factors in creating the picture. He knew he was sticking his neck out trying to recreate the war as he saw it. [In our westerns] he had little to say about the script or the action and did exactly as he was told. In his own story of WWII, I found him tenacious about every point."

Gordon Gebert: "Audie was very low-key, very unassuming, very kind and very friendly. I was about 13 or 14. My parents were clear about who he was. It struck me that his personality would not motivate him to show me how to play himself as a youngster. I remember we shot my scenes in a field in Bakersfield … the heat was pretty much like it was in Texas.

"Director Jesse Hibbs was a fairly hands-on director. I remember flopping down in the field to take a shot at the rabbit, and I remember taking some instruction on how to handle the rifle, which, of course, was important that I knew *exactly* what I was doing and be very comfortable with that. I don't recall if Audie came to Bakersfield, but I don't think so. I did meet him on the Universal set. I have a copy of his *To Hell and Back* book, which he autographed. He was a very retiring, modest fellow."

Stuntman Jack Williams: "Audie was really the nicest guy in the world, but he was deadly. He was capable of killing without blinking an eye. I didn't think *To Hell and Back* did justice to him. I thought it was a terrible picture. It's too bad he didn't have a good director like Sam Fuller. He had Jess Hibbs, who had been an assistant director. Hibbs was a hell of a nice guy, but he was totally unprepared for this big opportunity. That picture just fell apart like a four-dollar suitcase."

Gregg Palmer: "Audie never talked about his war experiences. But in *To Hell and Back*, the way he walked, it was like 'Here we go again' déjà vu. In our dressing rooms, either mine or his, at night we'd play a hand of poker … two dollars or so, just to kill time. But at lunchtime Audie would get out there with the guys shooting dice and he'd throw a hundred dollar bill down. He'd say, 'Cover it.' He'd break the game in nothing flat! If he lost, he'd throw another hundred-dollar bill down. If he hit it, he'd let it ride. They'd try to cover it and pretty soon the game was over with!

"Audie was a deep thinking man, generous man, big heart. Didn't care too much for the executives of Madison Avenue, but he loved the workers, he loved the wranglers. He was to himself quite a bit, but he was loved by the crew.

"He'd caress a pistol — he'd look at it — like petting it. Audie could stand there, put a cartridge on top of his hand, drop it, draw and come up and try to hit or clip the cartridge with the barrel of the gun before the cartridge fell. Very few, if any of us, could do that. He was very fast!"

Regarding Audie's devilish sense of humor, Denver Pyle told writer Robert Nott, "He'd go to great lengths to pull a gag on somebody. On that war picture of his life, *To Hell and Back*, we were shooting up in Oregon, working together running tanks. One night Audie says to me, 'I'm gonna go out and take one of these tanks for a drive. You wanna come?' I said, 'Sure. What if we get caught?' He said, 'Well we'll go to the brig.' [Laughs] God, he made a big thing out of this, and I never realized until years later that it was all set up. So he goes, 'We'll sneak out after we have our dinner. I'll go out first and wait for you, then we'll go on over and get us a tank.' I said, 'Well, you got a key to it?' He said, 'They don't need a key. You just turn it on and go.' So we snuck over and got in a tank, he revved it up and we ran it all over the field where they had 'em parked. We must have played out there until two o'clock in the morning. We put it away, shut it down and got back in our cars, and went back to the hotel. Audie says, 'Now don't you tell a soul about this 'cause they're gonna wanna know who was running them.' So the next day everything was calm. Nothing. I found out later he had gotten permission to go get a tank and run it. He just told them what he was gonna do and they said, 'Hell yes.' He had experience running the thing, but he had the crap scared out of me. He said, 'You know what we'd get if we got caught stealing one of these? This is government stuff!' Anyway, that was kind of his sense of humor."

In talking with Robert Nott about Randolph Scott, Joel McCrea *and* Audie Murphy, Paul Picerni said, "I would have to say I enjoyed working with Audie more because I had a longer relationship with him. I didn't have much to do with Joel, and Randy was a big star and I was under contract and still learning. But Audie and I were closer. We socialized together, played poker and had dinner together. I'll put it to you this way: Audie would remember me. Randy and Joel would never remember me, [Laughs]."

About *To Hell and Back*, Picerni has also stated, "It was a picture about a great American. If Audie ran for president tomorrow, I'd vote for him—that's how powerful he was. Audie was 5' 10", weighed about 150 lbs., but he was powerful, had great strength. If he said something, you knew he meant it. He had tremendous inner strength. When you were in his presence, you just felt it. If you get in a poker game with Audie and he calls you, you think about it, or if he raises, you think about calling him because ... just something about him. That inner strength came across in his acting."

Stuntman Bobby Hoy: "Murph was a great guy. He was one of our heroes. People don't ever think of him that way much anymore. We were gonna do his life story, *To Hell and Back*. We were supposed to go up to Yakima, Washington, but the show was delayed. I happened to run into him in the steam room. I said, 'Murph, what's going on? We're all needing work. We gotta make some money.' He said, 'Well, there's that sequence where I pick up the German machine gun and I kill eight or ten guys.' He was scared they were gonna laugh at him. He said, 'I'll look like Victor McLaglen in *Under Two Flags* from the '30s about the French Foreign Legion fighting the Arabs.' McLaglen comes into the fort, picks up a .30 caliber water-cooled machine gun, lays it over his arm and takes all these guys off the parapet. Audie was afraid the public wouldn't believe it. I said, 'Audie, let me ask you a question. Did you do it?' He said, 'Yeah.' I said, 'Well, screw 'em!' About a week later we went and did the picture. He was very shy, but he wouldn't take any guff from anyone. He was a good man.

"As for stunts, there were really only two or three stuntmen on that show. Johnny Daheim and I went through the whole show. We'd put German uniforms on under American uniforms, take off the American uniforms, jump on the tank and be the Germans. Back and forth, 'cause we had a production manager who was very *frugal*.

"Audie had a stand-in, Volney Peavyhouse. He was somewhat of a war hero in his own right. He was with the 8th Air Force and made more than the qualified trips over Germany. He came back to the States and was teaching guys bomber flying or whatever. Then for some reason [he] never went back in an airplane again. When we went to Washington for *To Hell and Back*, Volney took the train. He wouldn't fly. [His nerves had been wrecked by dangerous night missions over France during the war.] Nice, quiet guy. Audie was his friend. A stand-in is always there on the set. He's the lowest paid guy, but he can never leave the set. When the actors aren't working he's gotta walk it for the camera, he's gotta stand there for the lighting guy. Every time they say, 'Cut. Print. We'll move over here,' he's gotta be that actor while the actor is rehearsing his lines or getting made-up."

Author *W. Lee Cozad:* "My first, last and only role in the movies occurred when I was in the Army. In *To Hell and Back* I am one of the hundreds of soldiers marching on a wet parade ground just prior to Murphy receiving the Congressional Medal of Honor. For this uncredited bit part, I received the grand sum of five dollars in my pay packet the following month."

NOTES AND COMMENTS: The movie rights for *To Hell and Back* were sold to Universal for $25,000, with Audie getting 60 percent of that. In addition, he was paid $100,000 for his role in the film and acting as a technical advisor. In addition, Audie

A muddied and tired Audie Murphy takes a break on movie equipment at Ft. Lewis, Washington, where he re-enacted his WWII exploits for *To Hell and Back*.

received 10 percent of the net profits—which amounted to $387,745, Murphy declared in a 1966 legal statement. With some of his profits from this film Audie purchased a 90-acre farm near Dallas, Texas, in late 1954 for $45,000, as well as an 841-acre ranch near Romoland, California, in 1957. Although Audie quickly sold the Texas property, he did develop the California ranch as A-M Farms. It was here he raised and sold quarter horses, retaining about 30 horses on the ranch at a time. His plan was to go into the ranching business full time and give up filmmaking. However, in need of money by 1963, Audie sold the ranch to Bob Hope for an amount in excess of a million dollars. On July 22, 1963, Hedda Hopper reported: "The place adjoins Del Webb's Sun City for retired people, is warm the year 'round and has no smog. I asked Audie if he was getting out of that business. 'No, I'm buying a smaller place. Spend my weekends watching my horses.' I asked how he was feeling these days—if he still had those terrific pains. 'Nope, I feel better than I did ten years ago. I owed so much money it got where it didn't hurt any more.'" Perhaps Audie should have held onto the ranch though, as Hope's financial statement in 1968 listed the property at 1,004 acres worth $5,000 an acre, totaling $5,020,000.

The famous Colmar Pocket battle scene worried Audie, as he told stuntman Bob Hoy. Audie was concerned he was acting braver in the film war than he was in the real war. But a little humor alleviated a tense situation. As Audie climbed atop the burning tank destroyer, the machine gun jammed, causing Audie to quip to producer Aaron Rosenberg, "Rosie, if that had happened in France, you wouldn't have a picture to make!"

On October 3, 1954, Audie and the first unit left the Fort Lewis, Washington, filming location, leaving the second unit to shoot inserts. The first unit returned to the studio to shoot interior scenes.

The only accident while filming in Washington occurred when a TNT explosion blew a rock into Audie's leg, cutting a deep gash.

The censors at the Breen office objected to a scene between Audie and a street urchin, finding the dialogue about meeting girls unacceptable. Although the censors approved "Hell" in the title, they vetoed the expression "I don't give a damn." A nose-thumbing scene with Charles Drake was deemed "unacceptable," as was the phrase "a silly son of a scratch."

The film premiered in October 1955, but a special showing of *To Hell and Back* was arranged for the top brass at the Pentagon on July 16, 1955.

Audie's quarter horse, Flying John, was again paid for his non-use in this film. Audie had set up a "horse annuity" savings fund for his two sons and put the money Flying John earned into this fund.

Shortly after filming was completed, Audie's 29-year-old brother Richard died of brain cancer in mid–November 1954.

Audie and comedian Doodles Weaver guested on veteran bandleader Horace Heidt's *The Swift Show Wagon* on February 19, 1955. The Saturday night NBC show originated from a different American city each week. Each show included a salute to the personality of the week, someone from the state who had performed a heroic deed. Audie was selected to represent Texas.

Within a month of *To Hell and Back*'s release, to plug the film Audie guested on CBS' popular game show *I've Got a Secret* on September 7, 1955. Under host Don McNeil (subbing for regular Garry Moore), panelists Bill Cullen, Audrey Meadows and Faye Emerson were blindfolded and asked to figure out what Audie was doing with the other regular panelist, Henry Morgan. In the eight-minute segment, Audie had brought (as best he could) Morgan to military attention.

World in My Corner
(UNIVERSAL-INTERNATIONAL, MARCH 1956)

CREDITS: *Producer:* Aaron Rosenberg; *Director:* Jesse Hibbs; *1st Assistant Director:* Joseph E. Kenny; *2nd Assistant Director:* Bill Sheean; *Story:* Joseph Stone, D. D. Beauchamp (treatment), Jack Sher (1st draft), Gil Doud (to complete); *Screenplay:* Jack Sher; *Editor:* Milton Carruth; *Director of Photography:* Maury Gertsman; *Art Di-

rectors: Alexander Golitzen, Bill Newberry; *Set Directors:* Russell Gausman, Julie Heron; *Gowns:* Bill Thomas; *Makeup:* Bud Westmore; *Sound Recording:* Leslie I. Carey, Robert Pritchard; *Dialogue Coach:* Harold Goodwin; *Hair Stylist:* Joan St. Oegger; *Music Supervision:* Joseph Gershenson; *Technical Ad-visors:* Frankie Van, H. Tommy Hart.

CAST: Audie Murphy (Tommy Shea); Barbara Rush (Dorothy Mallinson); Tommy Rall (Ray Kacsmarck); Jeff Morrow (Robert T. Mallinson); John McIntire (Dave Bernstein); Howard St. John (Harry Cram); Chico Vejar (Al Carelli); H. Tommy Hart (Stretch Caplow); Carl Sklover (Tommy's second); Cisco Andrade (Cisco Parker); Baby Ike-Robert Johnson Jr. (Bailey); Dani Crayne (Doris Randall); Sheila Bromley (Mrs. Mallinson); James F. (Jimmy) Lennon (Ring announcer); Steve Ellis (TV announcer); Freddie Herman (Opponent); J. Howard (Girl Guest); Art Aragon (Lynn); Frank Muche (Sparring partner); Stan Farrar (Doctor); Herb Lytton (Doctor); Mushy Callahan (Referee); Ted Thorpe (Photographer); Bob E. Perry (Fight arena timekeeper); John Phillips (Arena man); Frankie Van (Referee); Charlie Perry (Arena man); Jack Gardiner, Pat Miller (Reporters in dressing room); Eddie Parker, Bud Wolfe, Glen Thompson (Hotel thugs); Joey Barum (Sparring partner); Volney Peavyhouse (Cab driver); George Lynn (Butler); Russ Vincent (Man in club lounge); Gisele Verlaine (Woman in club lounge); Tony Garcen (Boy in club lounge); Myrna Hansen (Girl in club lounge); Wally Rose, Bud Winters, Jim Wilson, Sailor Vincent, Paul Weber, Harold Floyd (Men in arena audience); Larry McGrath, Wallace Rooney (Men); Sammy Shack (Fighter).

RUNNING TIME: 82 minutes.

Audie Murphy ready for prizefight action in *World in My Corner* (1956).

FILMING DATES: May 31–June 27; July 7,8; August 29; December 30, 1955

LOCATION: Universal backlot; Mrs. William Rains estate, 603 Doheny Rd., Beverly Hills, California; Union City, New Jersey; Hoboken Dock, New Jersey; Jackson and Alameda streets in Los Angeles, California. Pickup shots filmed in a "squalid section of New York City."

BUDGET/COST: $664,118

Following the massive success of *To Hell and Back*, Universal tried to repeat the formula by casting Murphy in another non-western role in a semi-prestige movie seemingly more suited than a western to his elevated status as a top box-office commodity. Universal reunited Murphy with his *Hell* producer-director team of Aaron Rosenberg and Jesse Hibbs, and co-starred him with Barbara Rush, a talented actress who had served her apprenticeship in sec-

World in My Corner

ond features and was now regarded as a leading lady of some stature.

Unfortunately, the elements did not jell, and the result was a disappointment on all counts. The primary fault lay in the initial choice of material—a familiar rehash of just about every cliché in the prizefight movie book. Movie history has proven the only really successful films about boxing have been those that approached the subject with passion, dedication and often savagery. Universal, with its bland, assembly line outlook, was not the studio to produce another *Set-Up*, *Champion*, or *Body and Soul*. Consequently, the finished product looked like a poor imitation of these illustrious predecessors. The script, predictable almost to the point of boredom, offered the kid from the "wrong side of the tracks" making it big in the boxing world, the romance with the upper-crust girl, the gangsters out to make a killing, the corrupting influences of sudden fame and wealth, the big fight on which everything depends, and the final realization of the "true values" of life. It would have taxed John Garfield to make them acceptable, and Murphy was just not up to the job. Though many of the fight sequences were quite realistic, in other scenes Murphy was his usual pleasant self, but lacked the inner fire necessary to make the character believable in his passionate desire to escape from his property-stricken beginnings. The rest of the cast seemed content to act out their standard roles with a shallowness matching that of the script. Only John McIntire,

Audie Murphy delivers a telling right hook to his opponent in *World in My Corner*.

as the inevitable world-weary and wise trainer, managed to transcend the dullness. Tommy Rall, the vital, young dancer of *Seven Brides for Seven Brothers* and other musicals, tried his hand at a dramatic role as Murphy's boyhood friend, a hustler on the fringe of gangsterdom, but had little success.

Despite an impressively-mounted publicity campaign, trading heavily on Murphy's *To Hell and Back* success, the film failed to ignite any corresponding enthusiasm with paying customers. The critic for *Picturegoer* summed it up: "...[T]he fight scenes are good and the dialogue is crisp.... Likable Audie Murphy has too much explaining to do to be convincing in an unsympathetic role." Even Audie himself chimed in, "People can sit home and see four or five fights a week on TV. Why would they go to the movies to see a phony fight and skimpy story?"

REMEMBRANCES: *Director Jesse Hibbs:* "Audie is the most conscientious screen actor I've ever known. He trained like a pro for eight weeks for this part because he was determined to look like an expert in the ring; so many hard punches he had to take in order to deliver one."

Cisco Andrade: "That Audie. He really isn't faking. He's the first actor I ever saw who wasn't afraid of getting hit hard in a prize fight scene."

NOTES AND COMMENTS: Audie's salary rose to $51,500 for *World in My Corner*, commensurate with his elevated "stardom" following *To Hell and Back*. John McIntire earned $15,000, while Barbara Rush took home $8,500. In addition, in what today would be termed a "perk," Audie's horse,

John McIntire bandages Audie's hands in preparation for another bout.

Flying John, earned $300 for *World in My Corner*—in which, of course, he does not appear. Three hundred dollars worth of Broadway theater tickets and massages for Audie were also included in the film's budget.

Before the film, Audie trained strenuously for three hours a day for eight weeks in Terry Hunt's gym to get himself to welterweight condition for the film.

Top-ranking welterweight Chico Vejar played Carelli in the film, as well as helping Audie train for his role. Vejar was a dramatic arts major at New York University, although his only other billed role came in Universal's *The Midnight Story* a year later.

Actor William Campbell was considered for the role eventually played by Tommy Rall.

U-I contract player Clint Eastwood was to have played a bit part as "Bruce at the Mallison home." The role was either eliminated before filming or ended up on the cutting room floor.

Volney Peavyhouse, the cab driver in one sequence, was a frequent stand-in at Universal for Audie.

Art Aragon was an ex-fighter known in the boxing world as "the Golden Boy." He earlier played himself in *The Ring* (1952, United Artists). Aragon is also in Audie's *To Hell and Back*.

Audie joined the Masonic Lodge in February 1955 and became a Master Mason on June 27, 1955. He retained membership in the organization for the rest of his life.

On July 9, 1955, Audie guested on master mentalist Joseph Dunninger's Saturday night *The Dunninger Show* on NBC. A reward of $10,000 was offered each week to anyone who could prove Dunninger was a fake. The money was never claimed. This night, Dunninger attempted to match two keys, selected from a group of 100, to their specific locks, of which there were over 100.

Audie also guested on ABC's one-hour Thursday night military talent show *Soldier Parade* (formerly *Talent Patrol*) in the summer of 1955. Singer Richard Hayes, in the Army himself at the time, acted as co-host with Arlene Francis.

Walk the Proud Land

(UNIVERSAL-INTERNATIONAL, SEPTEMBER 1956)

CREDITS: *Producer:* Aaron Rosenberg; *Director:* Jesse Hibbs; *1st Assistant Director:* Phil Bowles; *2nd Assistant Directors:* James Welch, Ray De Camp; *Story Source: Apache Agent: The Story of John P. Clum* by Woodworth Clum; *Screenplay:* Gil Doud, Jack Sher; *Editor:* Sherman Todd; *Director of Photography:* Harold Lipstein; *Special Photography:* Clifford Stine; *Art Directors:* Alexander Golitzen, Bill Newberry; *Set Decorators:* Russell A. Gausman, Ray Jeffers; *Costume Designer:* Bill Thomas; *Makeup:* Bud Westmore; *Sound Recording:* Leslie I. Carey, Frank H. Wilkinson; *Dialogue Coach:* Harold Goodwin; *Hair Stylist:* Joan St. Oegger; *Music Supervision:* Joseph Gershenson. CinemaScope. Color by Technicolor.

CAST: Audie Murphy (John P. Clum); Anne Bancroft (Tianay); Pat Crowley (Mary Dennison); Charles Drake (Sgt. Tom Sweeney); Tommy Rall (Taglito); Robert Warwick (Eskiminzin); Jay Silverheels (Geronimo); Eugene Mazzola (Tono); Anthony Caruso (Disalin); Victor Millan (Santos); Ainslee Pryor (Capt. Larsen); Eugene Iglesias (Chato); Morris Ankrum (Gen. Wade); Addison Richards (Governor Safford); Maurice Jara (Alchise); Frank Chase (Stone); Ed Hinton (Naylor);

Marty Carrizasa (Pica); Francis McDonald (Indian Shaman); John Pickard (Sheriff); Clem Fuller (Stage Driver); George Keymas (Ponce); Natividad Vacio (Compos); Harold Goodwin (Telegrapher); Cliff Burdette (Driver); Paul McGuire, Tyler McVey, Jack Tomas, Jack Mather, William O'Neal, Rankin Mansfield, Jean Andrew, William Forrest, Vi Ingram, Jerry Eskow, Bernie Gozier, F. Fowler, Ray Narcho, Joshua Pancho (Townspeople/Cavalry/Officials). Stunts: Al Wyatt, Jimmy Van Horn, Willard Willingham, Reg Parton, Jack Carey, Billy Williams, Clem Fuller, Carey Loftin, G. Thompson, Loren Janes, Ken Terrell, Sailor Vincent, Bob Hoy, L. McMahon, F. McDougall, Walt LaRue, Joe Yrigoyen, E. Avery, Bobby Herron, Carol Henry, Don Happy, B. Gozier, Jerry Eskow.

RUNNING TIME: 88 minutes

FILMING DATES: November 21, 1955–January 6, 1956. Pickup shots March 12, March 20, April 6, 1956

LOCATION: Old Tucson, Arizona; Bear Canyon, Elephant Butte, Rattlesnake Pass, Arizona; Universal backlot, California.

BUDGET/COST: $1,140,497

In the years since its almost-unnoticed initial release, this film has come to be warmly regarded by many film writers for its quiet integrity and sincere attempt at something different in the field of Wild West biographies. Apparently a project in which Murphy himself was strongly involved, *Walk the Proud Land* was a long, leisurely tribute to real-life Indian agent John Philip Clum, who was involved with Apache rebel Geronimo, and later published a pro–Earp newspaper in Tombstone at the time of Wyatt Earp and Doc Holliday. Originally called *Apache Agent*, the film traced Clum's career from his ac-

Audie Murphy with Anne Bancroft and Eugene Mazzola.

Audie Murphy is Indian Agent John P. Clum in *Walk the Proud Land* (1956).

ceptance of the post, through difficulties with Indian-hating white men and suspicious tribesmen, to the final proving of his integrity to both sides. Romance was introduced via Anne Bancroft, as an Indian girl presented to Clum, and some mild drama was generated through the jealousy this aroused with Clum's Eastern fiancée (Pat Crowley).

With no real villains and only minor action sequences, the film relied on human relationships, atmosphere, and a muted evocation of frontier life. Although successful in this, the picture was another misfire with audiences—possibly because it was so far removed from the usual action-filled light-weight Murphy westerns that had preceded it. Around the time of its production, Murphy announced his interest in filming a similar biographical tribute to western painter Frederick Remington, but the project never materialized. One can only assume the luke-warm audience reception to *Walk the Proud Land* caused the studio to shelve the idea, which is unfortunate, since Murphy obviously had considerable respect for men such as Clum and Remington.

Written by Gil Doud and Jack Sher, and again directed by Jesse Hibbs, the film made good use of the CinemaScope process in its depiction of Indian rituals and wide-open locations, and the low-key performances were in tune with the sober treatment. Charles Drake, teamed for the third time with Murphy, was again dependable (as Clum's only supporter); but Bancroft, her acting potential as yet untapped, was little more than the Hollywood stereotype of the Indian maiden, although she came off as more interesting than Pat Crowley. Tommy Rall, still trying his luck as a straight actor, was conspicuously unsuccessful as a young Indian, and was overshadowed by Tony Caruso and Jay Silverheels, the latter repeating the role of Geronimo he'd played in the 1952 Universal western *Battle at Apache Pass*. Murphy himself gave the film a solid center with a quietly commanding performance.

Some historical reports indicate Clum was far from the man of principle presented by Murphy, but as a fictionalized biography, marred only by a tendency to plod heavily at times, *Walk the Proud Land* was a credit to Murphy and director Hibbs. As with *World in My Corner,* the studio was still chasing the elusive pot of gold at the end of the *To Hell and Back* rainbow, but was heading in the wrong direction. By casting Murphy in bigger-budgeted, weightier and more "respectable" movies, they were moving away from the qualities that had built up his popularity, and even Murphy's most laudable efforts could not overcome his material.

REMEMBRANCES: *Tommy Rall:* "I had a role as Audie Murphy's fight manager in *World in My Corner*, and as an Indian in *Walk the Proud Land* with Anne Bancroft. Bancroft and I were both on location in Arizona and we both got very sick. I came back to L.A. and had to rest for several months. Universal dropped my contract when I was in the hospital, and I went back to New York [to do musicals on Broadway]."

Anthony Caruso: "Audie was kind of a loner. I didn't associate with him much except to work with him. As far as I knew, he was a great guy. As an actor, I don't think he was too good, honestly, but I give him an A for trying, and he did learn while he was trying. He was out of his element with *Walk the Proud Land*. I do remember we were on location in Arizona for such a damn long time, and it was hot and miserable. Audie played cards in between shots with somebody — maybe his stand-in."

NOTES AND COMMENTS: Audie received $50,000 for his role, while Anne Bancroft earned $15,000, Pat Crowley $8,000, Tommy Rall $7,500 and Charles Drake $6,750. U-I once again forgave Murphy $1,500 indebtedness and paid him $300 for the use of his horse.

William Campbell was originally scheduled to play the Santos role eventually acted by Victor Millan. David Janssen was also tested for a role.

Audie Murphy is at odds with the Governor (Addison Richards, left) and the General (Morris Ankrum) on the treatment of reservation Indians.

Anne Bancroft took ill only a day or so after arriving on location in Arizona and required x-rays back in L.A. Her illness caused many filming delays, and very little of her work in the finished film was shot on location. Tommy Rall, Robert Warwick, Eugene Iglesias, Anthony Caruso and Charles Drake also suffered from the same mysterious illness, causing further delays. Many pickup shots were filmed in March and April back at the studio.

Six gallons of body makeup and four gallons of stain were ordered — and used — for Indian makeup.

Audie spent Thanksgiving eating turkey with Apache Indians on location.

Audie appeared in a suit and tie in the trailer, or preview, for *Walk the Proud Land*, and spoke a few introductory words about the historic man he portrayed, John P. Clum.

Audie appeared on NBC's *Colgate Variety Hour* sometime either in October or November of 1955. The Sunday evening variety hour was formerly known as the *Colgate Comedy Hour*. During the short-lived variety version of the long-running show (it began in 1950), scenes from a new film were shown and the stars from the movie appeared. Audie, interviewed by his friend and gossip columnist Hedda Hopper, was there to promote *To Hell and Back*, which was released in October 1955.

The Guns of Fort Petticoat
(COLUMBIA, APRIL 1957)

CREDITS: *Producer:* Harry Joe Brown; *Director:* George Marshall; *Assistant Director:* Abner E. Singer; *Source Novel: The Petticoat Brigade* by C. William Harrison; *Screenplay:* Walter Doniger; *Editor:* Al Clark; *Director of Photography:* Ray Rennahan; *Art Director:* George Brooks; *Set Decorators:* William Kiernan, Frank A. Tuttle; *Sound Recording:* Franklin Hansen Jr.; *Music:* Mischa Bakaleinikoff. Print by Technicolor.

CAST: Audie Murphy (Lt. Frank Hewitt); Kathryn Grant (Ann Martin); Hope Emerson (Hannah Lacey); Jeff Donnell (Mary Wheeler); Sean McClory (Kettle); Jeanette Nolan (Cora Melavan); Patricia Livingston (Stella Leatham); Kim Charney (Bax Leatham); Ernestine Wade (Hetty); Peggy Maley (Lucy Conover); Isobel Elsom (Charlotte Ogden); Ray Teal (Salt Pork); Nestor Paiva (Tortilla); James Griffith (Kipper); Charles Horvath (Indian Chief); Ainslie Pryor (Colonel Chivington); Dorothy Crider (Jane Gibbons); Madge Meredith (Hazel McCasslin); Francis MacDonald, George DeNormand, Reed Howes (Cavalry officers); Hugh Sanders (Sgt. Webber); John Dierkes (Storekeeper); Charles Meredith (General); Iron Eyes Cody (Medicine Man).

RUNNING TIME: 82 minutes

FILMING DATES: Mid-April 1956–May 16, 1956 (plus two other days in late May)

LOCATION: Old Tucson, Arizona.

If his home studio had erred in judgement with Murphy's films following *To Hell and Back*, Murphy himself compounded the error with his first film as an independent producer. Under the terms of his new contract with Universal, he was allowed to make occasional films away from the studio, so he teamed up with producer Harry Joe Brown, a long-time associate of Randolph Scott, to produce and star in the film version of a western novel called *The Petticoat Brigade*. The plot was an intriguing one — an army officer, appalled at his commanding officer's slaughter of an Indian village, deserts in order to warn an outpost of women of expected Indian reprisals, forms them into a crack fighting unit, and repulses the savages. The women later rally to his aid and help him win a pardon for his desertion.

Murphy and Brown engaged George Marshall to direct. With their *Destry* collaboration in mind, the end result should have been a return to form for Murphy. Sadly, it was not. The picture had none of the *Destry* style and vigor, the script was notably lacking in humor, and the pace was sluggish. Murphy, in a very routine western-hero role, was adequate but not much more, and most of the film's interest was generated by the formidable Hope Emerson in another of her big, tough pioneer women roles.

On the credit side, there was a degree of enjoyment in Murphy's efforts to teach the women the rudiments of combat, and the battle scenes were well staged, but overall it was a disappointment and marked the beginning of a series of very patchy Murphy films. The slick, professional gloss of the Universal western, though often derided, was badly needed in a film in which even the color seemed flat and uninteresting. Whether due to poor judgement or poor advice, Murphy's initial outing as a producer was a flop.

REMEMBRANCES: *Audie Murphy:* "My rugged role in the film was nothing compared to the tedious job of training 42 women how to become soldiers."

Sean McClory: "I was the dirty villain, so to speak. Audie was very quiet. Very serious. He didn't drink with the boys, so to speak. He stayed to himself most of the time. Very nice, sweet. I never heard him

Director George Marshall shows Audie Murphy how to grab Kathryn Grant for a scene.

raise his voice in anger ... wanted to be open to everybody. Other than that he was locked into himself. We were at Old Tucson before the rest of the main cast came down, so there were the two of us with all those women. But he didn't go trawling like I did. Being Irish, we spoke about the fighting heritage of the Irish. He was really interested in the old historic stories. But not a word about the war, and I didn't ask him. I made a reference to it at the beginning and he ignored me, so I thought, best leave it alone."

Left: Audie Murphy instructs Dorothy Crider in the proper use of a rifle in *Guns of Fort Petticoat* (1957). *Below:* Audie Murphy watches while tough Hope Emerson levels her weapon on "dirty villain" Sean McClory. Patricia Livingston and Kim Charney are just to the left of Emerson, while Jeff Donnell stands behind McClory.

NOTES AND COMMENTS: His ulcers finally flaring to a point where serious medical attention was needed, Audie (as reported by motion picture columnist Louella Parsons) went to Cedars of Lebanon Hospital on May 18 and was scheduled to be operated on that morning by Dr. Stanley Imelman. Audie had left the Old Tucson shooting location with two days filming left on the picture. Parsons reported, "As soon as he is able, he will go before cameras for the windup."

Kathryn Grant, borrowed from Columbia by Universal-International for *Mister Cory* (1957), was to "somehow work into her schedule the extra days needed to complete *Guns of Fort Petticoat*." (Grant married singer Bing Crosby in 1957.)

Exercising his contract option to make pictures outside Universal, in November 1955 Audie formed the Audie Murphy Company, a production company with producer Harry Joe Brown. Though they purchased three film properties, *The Guns of Fort Petticoat* was the first — and the last — produced by the pair. After one picture, quarrels between the two ensued, and Brown filed a $1,000,000 suit on September 18, 1957, against Audie. Audie was exercising a clause in their contract that gave him the right to choose which film to make next. Possibly because Audie simply wanted out of the deal with Brown, he publicly chose two impossible projects, one of them being Ibsen's *Peer Gynt*. Brown's complaint asserted, "these characterizations would be wholly unsuited to Murphy's talents." Murphy countered with, "I resent Harry Joe Brown's attempt to dictate my future in the industry." The contract was dissolved out of court.

About this time, Audie purchased the rights to *The Woods Colt*, a novel by Thames Williamson that Audie liked and tried to develop with writer Marion Hargrove at Universal. Audie apparently saw a lot of himself in the story, but for a variety of reasons the film never progressed beyond the scripting stage, and Audie eventually sold the story rights. Several Williamson stories were turned into films, including *Savage Horde* (Republic, 1950) with William Elliott and *A Bullet Is Waiting* (Columbia, 1954) with Rory Calhoun.

Joe Butterfly
(UNIVERSAL-INTERNATIONAL, JULY 1957)

CREDITS: *Producer:* Aaron Rosenberg; *Director:* Jesse Hibbs; *Assistant Director:* Phil Bowles; *Story:* Based on a three-act play by Evan Wylie and Jack Ruge; *Screenplay:* Sy Gomberg, Jack Sher, Marion Hargrove; *Editor:* Milton Carruth; *Director of Photography:* Irving Glassberg; *Art Directors:* Alex Golitzen, Alfred Sweeney; *Set Decorator:* Russell A. Gausman; *Makeup:* Bud Westmore; *Sound Recording:* Leslie I. Carey, Joe Lapis; *Music Director:* Joseph Gershenson. Color by Technicolor. CinemaScope.

CAST: Audie Murphy (Pvt. John Woodley); George Nader (Sgt. Ed Kennedy); Keenan Wynn (Henry Hathaway); Burgess Meredith (Joe Butterfly); Keiko Shima (Cheiko); Fred Clark (Col. E. E. Fuller); Charles McGraw (Sgt. Jim McNulty); Shinpei Shimazki (Little Boy); Reiko Haga (False Tokyo Rose); Tatsuo Saito (Father); Chizu Shimazki (Mother); Herbert Anderson (Major Ferguson); Eddie Firestone (Sgt. Oscar Hulick); Frank Chase (Chief Yeoman Saul Bernheim); Harold Goodwin (Col. Hopper); John

Joe Butterfly

Audie Murphy in a "light" moment from *Joe Butterfly* (1957), with Charles McGraw (left) and Fred Clark (center).

Agar (Sgt. Dick Mason); Willard Willingham (Soldier).

RUNNING TIME: 90 minutes

FILMING DATES: Mid-July, 1956–August 31, 1956

LOCATION: Japan; on board the U.S.S. Los Angeles.

"Spare us from the new Audie Murphy," wrote *Picturegoer* magazine. "If this is the new Audie Murphy, please give us back the old! As a comic, Murphy certainly takes his pleasures sadly. Even the overfrantic larking of such polished light comedians as Burgess Meredith and Keenan Wynn can't cast a reflected twinkle into Murphy's eye. The film is verbose and confused ... the script has a hasty look."

This cute, over-sentimental, quite embarrassingly awful film must rate as one of the worst attempts at screen comedy ever perpetrated, and mention of it is enough to make even the most ardent Murphy admirer squirm. Almost nauseating in its patronizing attitude towards the Japanese people and their culture, and totally tasteless in its "love thy former enemy" theme, it compounded the insult by miscasting fine actor Burgess Meredith (in grotesque Asian makeup) in the title role, rather than a genuine Japanese actor, surrounding him with a bunch of players (including Murphy) who were either insufferably dull or grossly caricatured.

The pathetic and predictable plot revolved around a group of correspondents from an Army magazine called *Yank* attempting to get out the first issue in postwar Japan. Murphy played Private John Woodley, the unit's ace photographer, a rebel who arouses the ire of his superior

Burgess Meredith and Audie Murphy on the set of *Joe Butterfly*.

officers and causes disaster wherever he goes. Meredith's title character is an oriental con-man who latches onto the magazine team for his own profit. Director Jesse Hibbs must shoulder the blame for the film's leaden pace, but he was poorly supported by a cast that should have done much better, even with such bad material. Fred Clark overplayed outrageously, as did Keenan Wynn as the semi-heavy of the piece, while George Nader, a reliable leading man of Universal crime dramas and romantic epics, was wooden, and the rest of the cast provided a line-up of cardboard cut-outs who frantically thrashed about trying to be funny in front of the over-emphasized Japanese locations. Murphy looked self-conscious and obviously out of his depth, even though in terms of actual screen time he had less to do than Nader.

Universal obviously hoped to cash in on Burgess Meredith's stage success in *Teahouse of the August Moon*, but what was effective on stage came over as excessively phony on the screen. While Murphy had always displayed a pleasing sense of comedy in his best westerns, he was hopeless in an outright comedic role. This was to be his last chance at carrying a major Universal production, and his only other "prestige" movie for the studio would find him covered by the proven box-office strength of James Stewart.

REMEMBRANCES: Screenwriter *Sy Gomberg*: "Audie shouldn't have been playing comedy."

Frank Chase: "When you were around a guy like Burgess Meredith, Keenan Wynn or Fred Clark, you were in very fast company. Nobody ever tried to steal scenes

Director Jesse Hibbs gives last-minute instructions to leading lady Keiko Shima before filming a scene with Audie Murphy (dressed in ancient Japanese warrior garb) for *Joe Butterfly*, shot on location in Japan.

from Audie, but I just don't think he ever got into the flow of the humor of it."

John Agar: "My contract with Universal ended after I did *Joe Butterfly*. Audie and Burgess Meredith both had a percentage of the movie. The cast used to get together to play poker. Audie would get into the game with so much money we couldn't play against him! The Japanese people were very supportive of this movie and showered Audie with gifts, including crickets, which are good luck in Japan."

NOTES AND COMMENTS: Screenwriter Marion Hargrove wrote a best seller about his humorous experiences as a draftee prior to Pearl Harbor—*See Here, Private Hargrove.*

On June 27, 1956, just prior to filming, Audie was presented two more WWII medals by King Baudouim I of Belgium.

While making the film, Audie heard of a 13-year-old Japanese-American girl, Caroline Kido, and her eagerness to come to America, so he helped her and her mother work out arrangements to do so. Caroline lived for three and a half years with the Murphy family while she attended school. She made her film debut in *The Nun and the Sergeant* (1962, United Artists), and was also in *Kronos* (1957, 20th Century–Fox) and *Confessions of an Opium Eater* (1962, Allied Artists), as well as TV episodes of *That Girl* (1967), *My Three Sons*

(1962, 1964) and *Bachelor Father* (1962). On June 17, 1961, Caroline said of the Murphys, "They treated me like their own daughter." At that time Caroline was living with her mother, who had recently come to the U.S. from Japan.

On July 22, 1956, while Audie was in Japan, through his lawyers he purchased the Mack Ranch on Benson Highway at Mountain View, Arizona. A working cattle ranch, the sale included over 400 head of cattle and five horses. What Audie paid for the ranch was not disclosed, but the ranch was listed at $180,000.

After only a couple of days in Japan, Audie sent Hollywood columnist Hedda Hopper a typical postcard (dated 7/25/56) which read, "Dear Hedda, I've been through a lot of experiences in my life, but never one like a trip in a Tokyo taxicab. Give me the Hollywood freeway anytime. Finally got our *Joe Butterfly* going after a solid week of smog. (They've got it here too!) Everybody's enchanted with our leading lady, Keiko Shima—a real Japanese doll. Audie"

In mid–1957 Universal nixed a picture called *Night Riders* Audie wanted to do with Robert Mitchum.

Night Passage
(UNIVERSAL-INTERNATIONAL, AUGUST 1957)

CREDITS: *Producer:* Aaron Rosenberg; *Director:* James Neilson; *Assistant Director:* Marshall Green; *Second Unit Director:* James C. Havens; *Source Novel: Night Passage* by Norman Fox; *Screenplay:* Borden Chase; *Editor:* Sherman Todd; *Director of Photography:* William Daniels; *Special Photography:* Clifford Stine; *Art Directors:* Alexander Golitzen, Robert Clatworthy; *Set Decorations:* Russell A. Gausman, Oliver Emert; *Costume Designer:* Bill Thomas; *Makeup:* Bud Westmore; *Sound Recording:* Leslie I. Carey, Frank H. Wilkinson; *Music Composer and Conductor:* Dimitri Tiomkin; *Songs:* "Follow the River" and "You Can't Get Far Without a Railroad." Music and lyrics: Ned Washington and Dimitri Tiomkin. Sung by James Stewart. Carl Fortuna — accordionist/musician. Technirama. Technicolor.

CAST: James Stewart (Grant McLaine); Audie Murphy (Utica Kid, Lee McLaine); Dan Duryea (Whitey Harbin); Dianne Foster (Charlotte "Charlie" Drew); Elaine Stewart (Verna Kimball); Brandon De Wilde (Joey); Jay C. Flippen (Ben Kimball); Herb Anderson (Will Renner); Robert J. Wilke (Concho); Hugh Beaumont (Jeff Kurth); John Day (Latigo); Jack Elam (Shotgun); Tommy Cook (Howdy Sladen); Paul Fix (Feeney); Ellen Corby (Mrs. Feeney); Olive Carey (Miss Vittles); James Flavin (Tim Riley); Donald Curtis (Jubilee); William Phillips (Barley); Kenny Williams (O'Brien); Ben Weldon (Pete); Jack Williams (Dusty); Boyd Stockman (Torgenson); Frank Chase (Trinidad); Chuck Roberson (Roan); Henry Wills (Pache); Harold Goodwin (Pick Gannon); Polly Burson (Rosa); Patsy Novak (Linda); Willard Willingham (Click); Harold Tommy Hart (Shannon); Ted Mapes (Leary); Clem Fuller (Trainman in baggage car); John McKee (Man); Mrs. Connolly, Mrs. Wyatt, Mrs. Defermando, C. Woods (Local extras in dance scene). Stunts: Boyd Stockman, Jack Williams, Reg Parton, Bill Williams, Willard Willingham, Polly Burson, Ted Mapes, Chuck Roberson. Stand-ins: Ted Mapes (for Stewart), Volney Peavyhouse (for Murphy).

RUNNING TIME: 94 minutes

FILMING DATES: September 14, 1956–

Night Passage

Audie Murphy watches as badman John Day taunts Elaine Stewart, while her husband Jay C. Flippen appears vexed in *Night Passage* (1957).

November 28, 1956; pickup shots with Murphy and Stewart on March 8, 1957

LOCATION: Durango, Colorado, on Durango-Silverton Railroad; Estelle Mine in Sierra Nevada Canyon, Colorado; Second unit stunt work at Lone Pine and Bishop, California; Universal backlot.

BUDGET/COST: $1,674,140

Universal's gamble on Murphy as a big-budget crowd-pleaser had not paid off. He'd been tried out in drama, in comedy, and in a "thinking" western, and had failed to repeat his *To Hell and Back* success in any of them. Belatedly, the studio acknowledged what Murphy fans had known all along—he belonged in straight westerns.

The credentials for his return to the saddle were impressive. A top-selling western novel, a script by Borden Chase (who'd already given the studio such western successes as *Winchester 73*, *Bend of the River* and *The Far Country*), and a top-drawer cast headed by James Stewart, who'd starred in the three Chase westerns and provided the studio with one of its all-time-great moneymakers, *The Glenn Miller Story*. Anthony Mann, director of the Chase-Stewart westerns, was signed to make *Night Passage*, but, reportedly, production delays clashed with another commitment (for *The Tin Star* at Paramount), and James Neilson replaced him. Without Mann's special talent as a western director, what emerged was a handsomely-mounted, large-scale entertainment that promised much but delivered little more than routine western action and performances. Stewart played Grant McLaine, a former railroad trouble-shooter fired because he let the Utica Kid, a bandit, escape. Re-hired some years later, he is given the task of getting a payroll through to the end-of-track construction crew, but fails when the train he is riding is ambushed by Whitey Harbin (Dan Duryea) and the Utica Kid (Murphy). Grant trails the gang, reveals the Utica Kid is his younger brother Lee, escapes and is finally trapped by Harbin's gang. The Kid, in a change of heart, joins his brother and dies protecting him from Harbin's bullet.

Filmed on location in Colorado, the movie was the first in Technirama, and was visually quite magnificent, with great clarity and depth in its many scenes of mountain ranges and deep gorges. Unfortunately, the action didn't match the magnificence of its setting. Both James Stewart and Dan Duryea seemed content to trade on previous successes—Stewart affecting a too-casual re-working of his *Bend of the River* character, and Duryea almost playing a parody of his Waco Johnny in *Winchester 73* and Whitey Kincaid in *Ride Clear of Diablo*. By contrast, Murphy, given the best lines and an impressive all-black outfit, seemed a better actor than either, although he only first appeared some 30 minutes into the film and gave his usual self-contained, unemotional performance. Audie's downplaying favored him over the roaring Duryea. Both Audie and Stewart managed to generate some emotion in a quiet little scene in which Stewart sang a boyhood song, with Murphy gradually, unwillingly, joining in. But it was an isolated moment in the general pattern of straightforward western situations. It does suggest, however, what the film might have become if Anthony Mann had been able to direct it. Borden Chase's dialogue was good, and Dmitri Tiomkin provided an excellent score, well suited to the grandeur of the locations, but the film's limited time span, with all the action taking place in the space of less than two days, seemed to work against the epic feel it was aiming for, leaving the final impression of a B-western struggling to fill out a large frame.

Among the supporting cast, Dianne Foster was good company as the girl loved by both brothers, and Jay C. Flippen was dependable as the railroad president, but Elaine Stewart seemed glamorously out of place as Flippen's wife. Brandon De Wilde, the talented boy who'd won fame in *Shane*, was unfortunately required to virtually repeat the character, even to using the same name, Joey, and the calculation was too blatant for comfort—nor was he required to put his talent to any more use than as a standard teenager. James Stewart singing two songs to his "own" accordion accompaniment (actually Carl Fortuna) provided some gimmick value, and they were logically integrated into the action. The final gunfight was handled with dash and vigor.

REMEMBRANCES: Regarding his co-starring rather than sole-starring role in this film, Audie said, "The only thing important is to stay on the screen, and I'm here through the whole story. So what's the fuss? I hate to use a cliché, but variety is the spice of life. I've been in a rut. Too much sweetness and light. In *Night Passage* I'm a bad boy and I love it."

Dianne Foster: "The fun of that picture was working with Audie. He was just such a special person. He had a great sense of humor; the little boy in him was constantly visible. He was very accessible as an actor and a person. He wanted very much to have his career. He wanted to be good at it. He didn't fool around when he was working—he worked. He was always prepared, always professional, he never messed up. He was charming, warm and gracious. I can't say enough lovely things about him.

"He seemed to work well with [James] Stewart. I was always in awe of Stewart. I thought he was the greatest movie idol—romantic and warm and genuine. But working with him at this time, he tended to keep more to himself. I don't mean he was unpleasant in any way, he was not, but he isolated himself a little more from the cast and crew, whereas Audie just bounced

Terry, Pamela and "Skipper" Murphy relax on a Sunday around Durango, Colorado's famous narrow gauge railroad engine, while Audie was filming *Night Passage*.

right in there and flowed. Audie was a lot more accessible. I think Jimmy had more of the production crew around him, but I always felt he wasn't that happy.

"Audie was one of the guys—he played cards with the fellows, the crew. He was more comfortable with the crew than with the fellow actors, and he didn't seem comfortable thinking of himself as a movie star. I knew he was this great war hero, but in real life, he was a mild mannered, easy going country boy. It didn't match the war hero I had heard about.

"One thing gave me an insight into what Audie must have been like in the war. He had his own horse, a big, beautiful animal that was trained. Anyway, this horse wouldn't do something, and there were several takes. Audie got tighter and tighter; the horse got tighter and tighter. Audie got angrier and angrier. Audie hauled back and smacked his fist hard on the side of the horse's face, just below the jaw! I thought, 'Oh my God.' But the horse just kind of shook its head. It didn't seem to be hurt at all. [Laughs] This horse weighed 1,000 pounds. Audie was lucky he didn't break his hand. He had a powerful punch, but the horse had a harder head. He was mad and just ... pow! At least Audie wasn't too tall, and he couldn't reach too high! This scourge of activity really surprised me, but now I put the two—the shy country boy and the macho war hero—together. The trainer came over and took the reins, and Audie said, 'Get rid of him!' Audie didn't think about it — if he had hurt himself, the shoot would have been halted. He just did it — he reacted. This instantaneous reaction, this rage, you saw that he had it in him. It was controlled while we were working, but it was always there. That's the only time I saw that side of him — the war hero who didn't know what he was doing but just did it.

"I think Audie was a limited actor. What he did was good. He was believable because he had an honesty to him and he projected that honesty on the screen. He had a personality that was quite winning. And the accent and the voice were great. In the movies I saw him in, he was pretty much always Audie, but he was believable in the scenes because he was honest. Audie had a sweetness to him that was very, very winning, a smile that could charm anybody.

"We were shooting in Durango, at a high altitude in the mountains [11,000 feet]. They had trucks with oxygen masks, cots, all that stuff set up like a mini-hospital. We would do a sequence and get so winded that we'd have to go lay down and rest; get some oxygen, then go act some more. It was tiring. It stretched from weeks into over two months. It was a difficult location. We'd get up early in the morning, load up and go on location — 90 minutes out. They were long days and everybody was tired. We just had time to get back, have a meal, learn our new lines for the next day's shoot. And they were always changing the script.

"Dan Duryea had a great sense of humor, almost a leprechaun's sense of humor. He was always saying something funny to keep the spirit going on the film set. He wasn't anything like the characters he portrayed.

"Here's a funny Dan Duryea story. We went on locale one day, a day that looked threatening, and we were out there shooting. You could just watch as the sky changed right in front of you. This big storm came in and snow started falling so fast and hard. I never saw a crew work so fast to get us out of there. There was only one road in, and if we had been delayed another hour, we wouldn't have gotten out of there. It was a horrendous ride back. We were in a limo and I don't even think we had chains on the tires. We were slipping and sliding down this icy road all the way back, and the snow kept coming down. Dan was a nervous wreck. I mean, everybody was frightened, but it was funny to see this brave movie villain cringing. We kind of slid down the mountain, but we got out safely."

Jack Elam: "We'd play liar's poker all the time. Everybody in Hollywood plays it with dollar bills. [Audie and I would] play it between times on the sets while we were waiting around. Everybody always says, let's go for five-dollar bills or let's go for ten-dollar bills. I wouldn't do it. I don't like to play with them because they'll cheat you. They'll bring in planted bills. But Audie and I, every time we met, we'd play for hundred-dollar bills. Only with Audie would I play with hundreds. Because Audie was a gambler who wouldn't cheat. I *knew*. And he knew I wouldn't either. We had the same feeling about each other. So we always played at least one game with hundred-dollar bills. I remember one time in the commissary at Universal, we went to the cashier and got, I don't know, I guess he got $500 and I had $200 on me. But we sat in the commissary and everybody in the commissary came around. They never heard of anybody playing with hundred-dollar bills. There was no way he was going to beat me, and there was no way I was going to beat him. We could play all day and end up even, so what the hell's the difference. He was very good at it and so am I. My reputation was the champion of Hollywood, but I didn't beat him.

"He was underrated as an actor and a very interesting guy, but he had a dynamite temper if you did him some wrong. I saw him flare up three or four times when he thought there was an injustice around him, and believe me, he was like a coiled rattlesnake when he flared up, but never unreasonably. It was always in line, such as if he didn't like some smartass on the set who was getting smart with a gal or something like that."

Jack Williams: "Funny thing the way the photograph of Audie and I came about. We were up in Durango. I'd just had a double-page spread in the Toronto newspaper about me as a stuntman about where I damn near got killed at Universal driving a wagon on *The Second Greatest Sex* and had a terrible wreck. I had to have about 30 stitches in my head. This got written up. I never did see it, but Universal saw it so they sent word to get pictures of me with the stars. Everybody thought I was gonna be the next big star at Universal, and all the stuntmen were trying to butter me up so when I got to be a star they'd get to double me. So that's where the picture of Audie and I came from.

"I was hired to double Dan Duryea. They didn't have a double for Jack Elam. I didn't even charge 'em, just did all those chases and stuff for Elam."

"James Havens, the second unit director, only had one camera. In the scene where they pulled down that water tower, they thought my horse had blocked the shot, but he didn't. [Laughs]"

"Actually, the 'big thing' up there was the leading lady ... the blonde, Elaine Stewart. Both Dan Duryea and Bob Wilke were trying to ... you know ... pursuing her.

"The main thing wrong with the picture was the fact they had Jimmy Neilson directing instead of Anthony Mann. They lost Tony somehow, but I don't think Jimmy ever did very good as a director. Tony had a touch."

Tommy Cook: "Previously I'd done *Bad Boy* with Audie. Now I was in New York, and they brought me to Durango, Colorado, where they headquartered *Night Passage*. We had terrible weather, certain days when we couldn't even shoot. We had some fine character actors, from Dan Duryea to Bob Wilke — who was carrying on with Elaine Stewart.

"Audie was very well liked. I don't know of anyone who didn't like Audie. And I don't know of anyone Audie didn't respect. He was just a genuine, down to earth guy. I think he realized his talents as an actor were limited, but he made the best of it. Audie was usually with the wranglers, the real men of the crew. My relationship with Audie, on the set shooting, and off the set, was always on the positive side. I will always remember Audie as being someone who was so well liked, never gave anyone any trouble at all, eager to learn.

"What's interesting, when we had those days with inclement weather, the dice would come out and we would shoot craps in a makeshift area against a shed. I had never really gambled in my life, and I was 26. Willard Willingham, Audie's great buddy, was there. I'm watching them shoot dice. I'm a total neophyte but I have some cash on me, so I decide when Audie is shooting the dice to play against him. I'm with the house. I end up over the period of time winning about $600 to $700. I sent it home! Audie could have taken offense at me playing against him and winning while he was losing, but he didn't, he was very good natured about it. So [Laughs], I consider Audie taught me the world of gambling — and I haven't stopped since. [Laughs] With Audie, and others, gambling is a matter of living on the edge.

"Every time I was with Audie, I would sorta look through him, and I'd think, 'Look at this guy, he's just a medium build, he's so innocent looking and anything but ferocious. But here's a guy that was the most decorated hero — the extraordinary guts this guy must have had.' It's just a source of interest to me to wonder what was his make-up, why was he so distinguished on the battlefield and so courageous?"

NOTES AND COMMENTS: James Stewart made $50,000 for the film, while Audie received $35,000 and was "forgiven indebtedness" to Universal. Brandon De Wilde earned $23,400; Dianne Foster, borrowed from Columbia, made $17,000; Elaine Stewart $10,000; Jay C. Flippen $10,500.

Even though Dianne Foster recalls getting to the location took up to 90 minutes, the assistant director's daily notes on *Night Passage* indicates that many times it took as much as two hours and forty-five minutes to get to their location. Once on location, the cast and crew were provided 10 gallons of coffee and 10 dozen doughnuts.

Actor Frank Chase, seen in many of Audie's films, is the son of screenwriter Borden Chase.

A lot of time on this shoot was lost due to clouds and inclement weather. On top of that, the crew experienced generator problems, and nearly everyone became ill at one time or another. Audie had a bad cold, as did Frank Chase and Elaine Stewart. James Stewart wrenched his neck. Dianne Foster suffered from an ear infection. Even Audie's son, Terry, caused some concern when he swallowed a penny while visiting the location with his mother, Pamela. Added delays came from James Stewart's dissatisfaction with the script and lengthy story conferences with director Neilson.

Universal wanted Mara Corday, who had worked with Audie in *Drums Across the River*, to be in *Night Passage*, but her husband, actor Richard Long, took the call from her agent and turned down the job offer. According to Mara, Long really didn't want her working and did this to her on several occasions.

Elaine Stewart was arrested for "delaying and impeding" traffic in downtown Durango while posing for stills, wanting to get some publicity shots with a Rocky Mountain background. Stewart was arrested for insisting on continuing her

Stuntman Jack Williams and Audie Murphy pose beside the track in Durango, Colorado.

cheesecake poses on the rocks of the Animas River when a policeman tried to stop her because traffic was jamming up as drivers sought a bumper to bumper look-see. All charges were later dismissed.

Norman Fox's novel answers many of the questions the film poses, such as "Why is it called 'Night Passage'?" In the novel, the entire story takes place between late afternoon one day and early morning the next. The work train is making its supply run overnight, with all of the characters on personal passages. But Hollywood doesn't spend big bucks to make a film in Colorado at night when you can't see the pretty scenery. The change to a daytime story obscured the title.

Stewart and Murphy's first names, "Grant" and "Lee," are obvious Civil War references. As explained in the novel, they were born in Missouri during the war and were both in their mid–20s when the story takes place in 1888 Montana (not Colorado, where the movie is set because that's where Universal found the trains they used).

Murphy's character nickname of "Utica Kid" is a reference to Utica, Montana, not Utica, New York. Both Murphy and Stewart were a bit old for the parts as outlined in the novel, and not anywhere near close enough in age. Murphy could just about have been Stewart's son.

Actor Sean McClory was hired to play the part of one of the train engineers, but after three days on location (September 26–29), he was sent back to Los Angeles due to "improper conduct," and the parts were reshuffled.

Suspicion: "The Flight"
(NBC, November 25, 1957)

CREDITS: *Producer:* Frank P. Rosenberg; *Director:* James Neilson; *Assistant Director:* Willard Shelton; *Screenplay:* Halsted Welles, Gene L. Coon; *Editor:* Lee Huntington; *Editorial Supervisor:* Richard G. Wray; *Director of Photography:* Ernest Haller; *Art Director:* John Lloyd; *Set Decorations:* James Walters; *Costume Designer:* Vincent Dee; *Makeup:* Jack Barron; *Sound Recording:* Steve Bass; *Hair Stylist:* Florence Bush; *Music Supervisor:* Stanley Wilson.

CAST: Audie Murphy (Steve Gordon); Jack Warden (Charlie Hake); Everett Sloane (Col. Migel Del Seguiras); Henry

TV Guide ad for "The Flight."

Brandon (Col. Polendo); Susan Kohner (Gina Obregon); Vladimir Sokoloff (Enrique Bartogas); Joe Perry (Rafael); Vito Scotti (Jose); Harold Goodwin (Charlie); Freddy Roberto (Fatso); Susan Ridgway (Newsstand girl); Albert Carrier (Doctor); Louis Zito (Bartender); Alan Lee (Soldier); Host: Dennis O'Keefe.

RUNNING TIME: 60 minutes

There's nothing special about Audie's first dramatic role on TV, for the one-hour *Suspicion* episode "The Flight," which casts him as an adventurous free-lance pilot unknowingly hired out to transport a kidnapped politically important professor to a South American country. Once there, Audie is forced to remain by corrupt politicians until, with the aid of the local underground and a stranded newspaperman, he is able to facilitate the rescue of the aged professor.

A love interest between Audie and Susan Kohner, who turns out to be the leader of the underground and the professor's daughter, is woven into the proceedings. But with only 50 minutes of real story-time, there's not sufficient space to fully develop the various plots, giving the production an unfulfilled feel. Direction by James Neilson (*Night Passage*) is flat and unexciting, even in the final shootout.

G.E. Theatre: "Incident"
(CBS, FEBRUARY 9, 1958)

CAST: Audie Murphy; Darryl Hickman; Russell Thorson.

RUNNING TIME: 30 minutes

Audie's second dramatic appearance on network television was in "Incident," a half-hour Civil War drama on Sunday night's *General Electric Theatre*. Audie played a Confederate soldier captured by another soldier, Darryl Hickman. The written synopsis for the episode (unavailable for viewing) reads: "Returning with his prisoner, a Civil War soldier is accused of desertion and arrested. The prisoner, who has become his friend, then helps him escape."

Although Audie had stated he wouldn't make any further war films, he liked the *G.E. Theatre* drama because of its simplicity and fidelity to basic human emotions.

Audie Murphy as a Confederate soldier struggles with Union soldier Darryl Hickman in the *G.E. Theatre* presentation of "Incident."

The Quiet American
(UNITED ARTISTS, FEBRUARY 1958)

CREDITS: *Producer:* Joseph L. Mankiewicz; *Associate Producer and Technical Director:* Vinh Noan; *Director:* Joseph L. Mankiewicz; *Assistant Director:* Piero Mussetta; *Story Source: The Quiet American* novel by Graham Greene; *Screenplay:* Joseph L. Mankiewicz; *Editor:* William Hornbeck; *Director of Photography:* Robert Krasker; *Art Director:* Rino Mondellino *Set Decorator:* Dario Simoni; *Makeup:* George Frost; *Sound Recording:* Bail Fenton-Smith; *Hair Stylist:* Ida Mills; *Special Effects:* Roscoe "Rocky" Cline, George Schlicklin; *Music:* Mario Nascimbene; *Conducted by:* Franco Ferrara.

CAST: Audie Murphy (the American); Michael Redgrave (Thomas Fowler); Claude Dauphin (Inspector Vigot); Giorgia Moll (Phuong); Bruce Cabot (Bill Granger); Fred Sadoff (Dominguez); Kermia (Miss Hei); Richard Loo (Mister Heng); Peter Trent (Eliot Wilkins); Clinton Anderson (Joe Morton); Yoko Tani (Hostess); Sonia Moser (Yvette); Phyng-Thi Nghiep (Isabelle); Vo Doan Chau (Cao-Dai Commandant); Le Van Le (Cao-Dai Pope's Deputy); Le Quynh (Masked Man); Georges Brehat (French Colonel). Stunts: Willard Willingham.

RUNNING TIME: 121 minutes

FILMING DATES: January 28, 1957–March 6; March 20–June 5, 1957

Michael Redgrave, Giorgia Moll and Audie Murphy in *The Quiet American* (1958)

LOCATION: Saigon, Vietnam; and Cinecitta Studios in Rome, Italy.

Novelist Graham Greene's scathing denunciation of American involvement in Vietnam (prior to the actual war) was toned down considerably for the screen, even to the extent of altering the ending to one more palatable to American feelings at the time. Perhaps in the light of these changes, Murphy's failure in the central role is not quite so total. Certainly his portrayal of the young American whose well-meaning interference in Asian affairs leads to his own death was a brave try, but he was up against stiff acting competition from Michael Redgrave and Claude Dauphin, with most critics making unfavorable comparisons.

Not only was the production plagued by illnesses (Murphy's and Redgrave's), cost overruns, adverse filming conditions and a lack of respect for each other by the two stars, in retrospect it's possible to consider that the film's failure was purely a matter of timing—audiences were not quite ready for even such mild anti–American fare. Viewed today, the picture tends to take on some of the mythology of *The Red Badge of Courage*—a flawed masterpiece plagued by interference, with Murphy again the main sufferer. Whether it would have been as well-regarded as director Mankiewicz's other triumphs, like *All About Eve*, is unanswerable. By no means lively entertainment, *The Quiet American* certainly was not the dull, talky melodrama many dismissed as worthless at the time of its release (when such introspective cinema was not the order of the day). Although Murphy was in no way a match for Redgrave's superb study of cynicism, or Claude Dauphin's equally effective portrayal of a knowing policeman, Audie's blandly non-involved characterization of the unwitting catalyst in an explosive situation was perhaps exactly what Mankiewicz intended. Indeed, taking Redgrave's performance as part of an overall pattern, and not as the tour-de-force hailed by most critics, this seems more than likely, and it's doubtful whether such a strongly individualistic filmmaker as Mankiewicz would have cast Murphy purely as box-office insurance.

Looking at the care and obvious commitment put into the film (which did, unfortunately, lead to some overstatement), it would appear the director wisely used both Murphy's strengths and limitations to maximum effect. Due to Murphy's narrow range, and his lack of practical experience in handling subtle, double-edged dialogue with the control of nuances and inflections of a Redgrave, the American emerged as a somewhat remote, self-contained figure existing in his own enclosed area and not really relating to the other characters—which is really what Greene's original 'Quiet American' was all about: a man so convinced of the rightness of his own actions that he remained blind to the chaos his well-meaning but totally uninformed interference caused.

Murphy's American was, in fact, closer to Greene's character than to the altered American of the film, who ultimately emerged as a nice guy duped by the wicked Communists—an innocent unjustly sent to his death by the spiteful British journalist—rather than a dangerously righteous man justifiably destroyed as a necessary safety measure. But such hindsight, while it might justify Murphy's failure to come to grips with a seriously muddled conception of his character, and explain the initial failure of the film, cannot alter the fact that fail it did, disastrously. Redgrave was praised, but Murphy and the film were soundly panned.

Audie tried to improve his status and become a better actor, but he picked the wrong vehicle. With *The Quiet American* a dismal failure and a forgotten film, Murphy never again aspired to such dramatic heights outside the sphere of the western.

REMEMBRANCES: *Audie Murphy:* "The biggest artistic flop of my career. The main reason I wanted to do this picture was to

Michael Redgrave (center) and Audie Murphy (right) were not on the best of terms while filming *The Quiet American*.

get away from the bread and butter stories UI's been putting me in. The pictures I make there are cheapies—but that's the kind of thing I have to do until I finish my contract."

Joseph Mankiewicz: "A bad movie made at a bad time in my life."

William Russo (author of *A Thinker's Damn*, a definitive examination of all the problems that beset the film, from inception to editing): "Willard Willingham said, '*The Quiet American* was a microcosm of everything that happened to Audie. This film explained things about Audie that nothing else would ever tell you. So this film bears looking at very closely. Here's a man who knew Audie all of his adult life and he's saying, this is the story, if you want to know who Audie Murphy is, examine what happened during this film and you'll have the answers.' According to Willingham, it was not widely known in those days, Michael Redgrave was suffering from the beginnings of Alzheimer's disease. Even though he was a brilliant actor he was muffing lines, 30 to 40 times in a take. Now, after 20 to 30 times anyone would start to get impatient trying to do a scene. According to Willingham, Audie knew his lines, knew his motivation, hit his marks and was ready to do that film. It was Redgrave who caused all kinds of problems. And the director took the side of Audie."

Jan Merlin: "Audie had a chance in *Quiet American* to do an extraordinary part that nobody would have ever given him to begin with. Can you imagine what a tremendous thing Audie faced to begin with to do this film? He was willing to take a crack at it. That film had many flaws in it, many problems and many reasons for

A barroom scene from *The Quiet American*, with Audie Murphy (left) and Michael Redgrave (right).

why it failed ... they weren't Audie's fault. But this guy, with all his fame, could not bring this thing together ... he didn't have the capacity to do the part ... but he was gonna do the best he could. But there were other problems involved in the making of the film. I wish the picture would have worked for him because it could have changed what he was doing. Maybe he could become a character actor. But things happened with this picture that were always against him. The chemistry between Audie and Redgrave was never right."

NOTES AND COMMENTS: Mankiewicz originally wanted Montgomery Clift and Laurence Olivier for the lead roles; but when they were not available, he went with Murphy and Redgrave.

After suffering for a time, on February 5, 1957, Audie was flown from Saigon to Hong Kong; on February 7 he was operated on for a ruptured appendix. Although Murphy's recovery was predicted to take up to five weeks, Audie miraculously returned to Saigon on February 18. Upon his return, already displeased with the script and unkept promises by Mankiewicz about proposed changes, Audie's zest, health and commitment to the film weakened.

It's now realized Michael Redgrave was suffering from the early effects of Alzheimer's during the production, taking as many as 30 takes to get a scene. By then Audie's concentration had wandered. Redgrave and Murphy were diametrically opposed actors and frequently clashed in scenes shot in Rome. Redgrave's contempt for Audie was quite outspoken. Then Redgrave became quite ill with the flu by March 26, and by the time the company arrived in Rome, he sensed the production was in trouble and lost interest in the film.

Ride a Crooked Trail
(UNIVERSAL-INTERNATIONAL, SEPTEMBER 1958)

CREDITS: *Producer:* Howard Pine; *Director:* Jesse Hibbs; *1st Assistant Director:* William Holland; *2nd Assistant Director:* Ray De Camp; *Story:* George Bruce; *Screenplay:* Borden Chase; *Editor:* Edward Curtis; *Director of Photography:* Harold Lipstein; *Art Directors:* Alexander Golitzen, Bill Newberry; *Set Decorators:* Russell A. Gausman; Ray A. Jeffers; *Costume Designer:* Bill Thomas; *Makeup:* Bud Westmore; *Sound Recording:* Leslie I. Carey, Donald McKay; *Hair Stylist:* S. Kirkpatrick; *Music Supervision:* Joseph Gershenson. CinemaScope; Eastman Color by Pathe.

CAST: Audie Murphy (Joe Maybe); Gia Scala (Tessa Milotte); Walter Matthau (Judge Kyle); Henry Silva (Sam Teeler); Joanna Moore (Little Brandy); Eddie Little (Jimmy); Mary Field (Mrs. Curtis); Mort Mills (Pecos); Frank Chase (Deputy Ben); Leo Gordon (Sam Mason); Bill Walker (Jackson); Ned Wever (Attorney Clark); Richard H. Cutting (Banker Curtis); Morgan Woodward (Durgen); Rayford Barnes (Big Jim); Bill Grant (Powers); Harold Goodwin (Doctor); Henry Wills (Clovis); John Truey (Yuma); Glen Thompson (Marshal Noonan); Tony Jochim (Counselor Hutchins); Tom Hart (Dan Watson); Richard Crane (Madigan); Clem Fuller (Sam/Tom, wagon driver);

In *Ride a Crooked Trail* (1958), Audie Murphy (far left) confronts the Teeler gang (left to right): Bill Grant, Mort Mills, Morgan Woodward, Henry Silva (as Teeler) and Rayford Barnes.

Bob Steele (Jed Blunt); Butch Letheridge (Shorty); Don Gamble (Red); Bob Candee (Bucktooth); Eddie Parker (Excited man at dance); Lillian Culver (Mrs. Weller at dock); Ken Patterson (Gambler at dock); Helen Jay (Fancy girl at dock); Paul Newlan (Riverboat captain); Doug Wilson (Sam at dock); Ann Cornwall (Mrs. Ray at dock); Charles Sherlock (Man at dock); Sailor Vincent (Bag handler at dock); Sally Olds (Mrs. Nugent); Beulah Christian (Mrs. Adams); Ed Randolph (Bartender); Paul McGuire, Maria Janine Clement, Vincent Perry, Rusty Lane, Jimmy Fields, Gene Martin, Gerry Hartlenben, Danny Dunbar, Bobby Middlestead, Howard Wendell, Amzie Strickland, Kay Stewart, Mary Newton, Kathy Garver, Kenneth MacDonald, Steve Dunhill, John Truex, Bobby Herron (Townspeople). Dog: Paddlefoot. Stunts: Jack Williams, Glen Thompson, Jack Carey, Willard Willingham, Bobby Herron, Reg Parton, Don Happy, D. Hudkins.

RUNNING TIME: 88 minutes

FILMING DATES: August 28, 1957–October 1, 1957; October 4, 7, 1957

LOCATION: Janss Ranch, California; Universal backlot.

BUDGET/COST: $832,082

Murphy's next Universal western occupied a middle ground somewhere between the full-scale quality of *Night Passage* and the medium-budget but thoroughly professional standard of his early westerns. Production values, with color and CinemaScope, were impressive. Jesse Hibbs, still a prestige director, was again in charge, and Murphy's co-stars were recognized second-level performers normally associated with top supporting roles in important features. Universal cunningly hedged its bets by giving the film an aura of importance, but also maintained its links with the earlier Murphy films. The result was sound entertainment, light and cheerful, a shade too glossy and studio-bound, but firmly in the tradition of the best Murphy westerns, despite the slight feeling of pretentiousness. Murphy was again an anti-hero—a bank-robbing bandit with the unlikely name of Joe Maybe who is mistaken for a famous lawman and given control of a tough town. His initial plan to use his position for unlawful purposes is thwarted when an old girlfriend arrives (Gia Scala); to protect himself, he pretends she is his wife. The couple are made foster-parents of an orphan, and Murphy's change of heart is complete when he routs an attempted bank robbery by a former comrade, confesses all to the local judge (Walter Matthau), and is pardoned for his past sins.

Murphy played for wry comedy most of the time (even including an amusing hangover scene after a night of drunken carousing), and received solid support from the cool and beautiful Gia Scala as the shady lady whose respectable instincts are aroused by the fake marriage. The genuinely witty screenplay (again by Borden Chase) allowed Murphy and Scala to make the most of the sly innuendoes surrounding their setting up house together. Future Oscar-winner Walter Matthau was still polishing his craft in this Murphy western, and gave an over-the-top, rip-roaring performance as the shoot-first frontier judge, carving the ham in rich but enjoyably edible chunks. The bleak-eyed, blank-faced Henry Silva was a most satisfactory badman.

The film was short on action, and the characters all too neatly dressed to engender any particular feel of realism, but its abundant good humor and free-wheeling performances carried it through.

REMEMBRANCES: *Morgan Woodward:* "I'm a veteran of World War II and the Korean War. Back in those days, if you were a Texan you were a big shot with a fellow Texan. We were brothers. We really felt that way about our fellow Texans. I was well aware of Audie. I couldn't believe a guy that looked like a matinee idol could have been the most decorated soldier in WWII. Anyway, I was very, very proud of him. When he came to Hollywood I was hoping he'd do very well, but I knew it would be a terrible adjustment for him.

"I was working frequently at Universal. When I got the opportunity to do *Ride a Crooked Trail* I was real excited to be a dirty dog heavy in the picture against Audie Murphy. I was really looking forward to meeting him. Sure enough, the first day on the set I walked up to Audie and I said, 'Audie, I'm Morgan Woodward and I'm from Arlington, Texas! I'm sure happy to meet a fellow Texan. I've always admired what you did in the war and I like what you're making of yourself in pictures.' He looked at me with those funny eyes that kinda never held a steady gaze, they darted all the time. I held out my hand and he shook my hand very weakly. I remember his hands looked like a man 60 years old, and he was only in his early thirties. Wrinkled hands. Liver spots. He just kinda mumbled something, I'm not even sure what he mumbled, then turned and walked away. [Chuckles] I thought he's not one of those guys who's crazy about his fellow Texans.

"Audie was a practical joker. I don't think he played practical jokes on people he didn't know or didn't like very well. While we were on location he threw a sack of rattlesnakes in a room of one of his buddies. They thought that was quite funny. [Laughs]

"I was six foot three inches tall then, weighed 220 pounds, but, as small as he was, I got the idea I would not want to cross this man if I'd weighted 400 pounds and been seven feet tall. There was just something about him — I wouldn't have wanted to cross him. He was wound very tight."

Frank Chase (upon seeing Audie's

Always a gentleman, Audie Murphy shades Gia Scala from the sun between takes on *Ride a Crooked Trail.*

temper flare up after a meeting at the front office): "Audie said, 'You know there are some guys I would *really* like to do in.' Here is a guy that means what he says." Chase, who didn't like to gamble, did, on occasion, with Audie. "I'd lose $16 and he'd want that right now. I had to go and borrow it."

Jack Williams: "Audie got along with everybody, but he had a terrible gambling habit. He and Walter Matthau — Matthau was a hell of a gambler — they'd bet $2,000 to $5,000 a card or whatever it was. Audie was just absolutely addicted to gambling. His friend Willard Willingham *was* a poker player. Anytime you get in a poker game and you find people who are better than you, you better get out of the game. But Audie wanted to play every hand. Audie wanted action. But in poker you gotta sit there and wait. Audie was about instant gratification.

"I can't help but think all that killing and everything Audie saw just … they say people that have seen that kind of bloodshed are never the same."

NOTES AND COMMENTS: Audie was paid $50,000, as well as being forgiven $1,383 indebtedness to the studio. Walter Matthau earned $20,000; Gia Scala $6,850; Frank Chase $1,800; Henry Silva $3,750; Eddie Little $3,000; Joanna Moore $2,500; Mary Field $3,600; Leo Gordon $2,000. The dog, Paddlefoot, was paid $40 a week plus $35 a week for his trainer. Producer Howard Pine received $11,700; director Jesse Hibbs earned $32,300 and screenwriter Borden Chase made $30,000.

Walter Matthau apparently wasn't sure what wagon driver Clem Fuller's screen name was supposed to be. As Matthau confronts him he first calls him Sam, then a minute later refers to him as Tom. Fuller (1909–1961), seen in several of Audie's westerns, began working in westerns as a stuntman circa 1931 and wound up his career as Clem, the original bartender on TV's *Gunsmoke*.

Audie's sons, Terry, age six, and Shannon, age four, visited Audie on the set of *Ride a Crooked Trail*. Asked whether they wanted to be western stars when they grew up, Terry answered, "We like to watch the movies, but we wouldn't want to be a movie star—there are too many girls in the movies."

On August 18, 1957, just prior to filming, Audie led the parade at the 13th annual Los Angeles Sheriff's Championship Rodeo, riding his quarter horse, Joe Queen.

Audie's two sons, Terry and Jim, visit him at the riverboat on the Universal backlot during *Ride a Crooked Trail*.

The Gun Runners
(SEVEN ARTS PRODUCTIONS/ UNITED ARTISTS, SEPTEMBER 1958)

CREDITS: *Producer:* Clarence Greene; *Director:* Donald Siegel; *Assistant Director:* Willard Reineck; *Story Source: One Trip Across* by Ernest Hemingway; *Screenplay:* Daniel Mainwaring, Paul Monash; *Editor:* Chester Schaeffer; *Director of Photography:* Hal Mohr; *Art Director:* Howard Richmond; *Set Decorator:* Darrell Silvera; *Cos-

The Gun Runners

tume Designers: Bernice Pontrelli, Morris Friedman; *Makeup:* Frank Fitz-Gibbon, Vince Romaine; *Sound Recording:* Frank Goodwin, Roger Heman; *Hair Stylist:* Lillian Shore; *Music:* Leith Stevens; *Song:* "Havana Holiday" by Joe Lubin and Jerome Howard.

CAST: Audie Murphy (Sam Martin); Eddie Albert (Hannagan); Patricia Owens (Lucy Martin); Everett Sloane (Harvey); Gita Hall (Eva Walstrom); Richard Jaeckel (Buzurki); Paul Birch (Sy Phillips); Jack Elam (Arnold); John Qualen (Pop); Carlos Romero (Carlos); Edward Colmans (Juan); Carl Rogers (Woody); Herb Vigran (Freddy); Roy Engel (Cass); Steven Peck (Pepito); Lita Leon (Pepita); Ted Jacques (Commander Walsh); Freddie Roberto (Berenguer).

RUNNING TIME: 83 minutes

FILMING DATES: January 28, 1958–February 26, 1958

LOCATION: Balboa and Newport Bay, California.

Audie Murphy and Gita Hall co-star in *The Gun Runners* (1958).

No crystal ball would have been needed to predict Audie Murphy and Ernest Hemingway were not compatible in terms of cinema, so it was no real surprise when this third screen version of Hemingway's *One Trip Across* proved pallid. What is surprising is that it should have been made at all, since Hollywood had already presented Hemingway addicts with two excellent versions—*To Have and Have Not* (with its memorable introduction of the Bogart-Bacall duo) and *The Breaking Point* (with John Garfield in one of his last, and best, roles). Murphy was certainly no Bogart, and had already proved his limitations in a Garfield-type role in *World in My Corner*. Although Audie made a brave stab at it, and was acceptable on a surface level (and very good in the pure action areas), the cynicism and passionate bitterness of the Hemingway-style hero evaded him.

Murphy played Sam Martin, a small-time charter boat operator on the verge of insolvency, who becomes embroiled in a plot to smuggle guns to Cuban rebels. (In Australia the film was called *Guns for the Rebels,* since the title *The Gun Runners* had been used for an earlier Alan Ladd movie, *Santiago* in America). Sam's conscience, prompted by the imminent death of his best friend, forces him into the role of crimefighter, and he turns the tables on his "employers" and is reunited with his long-suffering wife. Director Don Siegel drew sharp performances from Eddie Albert and Everett Sloane, but Murphy's blandness robbed the film of a solid center. His performance proved so uninteresting, in fact, that even leading lady Patricia Owens, whose short-lived Hollywood career seemed to have stemmed more from her impeccable British accent than from any claims to special talent or screen presence, overshadowed Murphy.

On one level, the film was satisfactory as a minor-key adventure

Top: Gita Hall and Audie Murphy in Hemingway's *The Gun Runners*. *Right:* Audie Murphy becomes entangled with gun-runner Eddie Albert and his girlfriend Gita Hall in *The Gun Runners*.

thriller for the second feature market, but the portrayals of Albert and Sloane hinted at the possibility that without Murphy it might have earned the same critical acclaim as Siegel's other films of the '50s. Murphy's failure in yet another modern role compounded his unfortunate showing in *The Quiet American*, and, despite the good qualities of *Ride a Crooked Trail*, 1958 was not a good year for him.

REMEMBRANCES: *Jack Elam:* "I am a tremendous admirer of Audie Murphy. He was an underrated actor and a very interesting guy. I think our friendship was cemented one day on *The Gun Runners*. Shooting that Don Siegel picture, we were working down at Laguna Beach somewhere and Audie said, 'Come on Jack. I want to show you my boat.' He had a 60-foot motor sailor. So we went over, and it was a beauty. It was docked somewhere around Newport. And we're sitting on the deck having a drink. Audie wasn't drinking, but he fixed me a drink. Audie said, 'Look at that Luders coming in.' That's a little racing boat, a sailboat. I said, 'Where?' He said, 'Right out there beyond the breakwater.' And I said, 'What the hell are you talking about? There's no boat out there.' He said, 'Yes there is. You just watch. You'll see it come in.' Pretty soon it got closer and closer and pretty soon I could see the boat. I said, 'By God that *is* a Luders, Audie.' He said, 'I told you it was, for chrissake. I saw it half an hour ago.' And I said, 'Well, that's why you're a hero. Because you can see better than anybody else.' And he laughed for half an hour. He really did. He thought that was the funniest thing he'd ever heard. I could never do anything wrong after that. I just said, 'The only thing you could do is see better than anybody.' He did. He had eyesight like a hawk. I mean really. That thing with the boat cemented our relationship for life. I think I used the words, 'You're no f— hero, you just see better than anybody.' You see, that didn't offend him at all, because the truth is he really was a hero. So he didn't have to defend anything. He saw the joke. Some guys who really weren't heroes, they would have to defend that. But not Audie. You had to know Audie. The guy I knew early on is the same guy I knew at the very end of our relationship after we'd done pictures together. There was no change in him. Not even the slightest, from before he'd ever done pictures, before he became a star. Not even the tiniest change in his personality. Because he was what he was. He was Audie Murphy. It had nothing to do with whether he was a movie star or a horse player. There was only one Audie Murphy and there will never be another. I'm certain about that."

Director Don Siegel: "Audie didn't drink, was on time, and caused very little trouble as long as you didn't tread on his temper. He was incredibly shy and strange, and there was a problem reaching him to get a good performance. Something was bothering him. He carried a loaded gun, and one time jumped across the boat at a member of the crew. I had to pull him off. Even the tough guys on the set, the stuntmen, would take detours so they didn't have to walk past him. But he was always polite to me."

Audie Murphy once told screenwriter Jack Lewis, for his book, *White Horse, Black Hat*, "I've done this picture 30 times, only it was with horses instead of boats."

No Name on the Bullet
(UNIVERSAL-INTERNATIONAL, FEBRUARY 1959)

CREDITS: *Producers:* Howard Christie, Jack Arnold; *Director:* Jack Arnold; *Assistant Director:* John Sherwood; *Story:* Howard Amacker; *Screenplay:* Gene L. Coon; *Editor:* Frank Gross; *Director of Photography:* Harold Lipstein; *Art Directors:* Alexander Golitzen, Robert E. Smith; *Set Decorators:* Russell A. Gausman, Theodore Driscoll; *Costume Designer:* Bill Thomas; *Makeup:* Bud Westmore; *Sound Recording:* Leslie I. Carey, Frank Wilkerson; *Hair Stylist:* Larry Germain; *Music:* Herman Stein; *Music Supervisor:* Joseph Gershenson. Eastman Color by Pathé; CinemaScope.

CAST: Audie Murphy (John Gant); Joan Evans (Anne Benson); Charles Drake

(Dr. Luke Canfield); Virginia Grey (Roseanne Fraden); Warren Stevens (Lou Fraden); R. G. Armstrong (Asa Canfield); Willis Bouchey (Sheriff Buck Hastings); Edgar Stehli (Judge Benson); Simon Scott (Henry Reeger); Karl Swenson (Earl Stricker); Whit Bissell (Thad Pierce); Charles Watts (Sid); John Alderson (Ben Chaffee); Jerry Paris (Harold Miller); Russ Bender (Jim Mertz); Jim Ryland (Hugo Mott); Guy Wilkerson (Farmer); Hank Patterson (Charlie, chess player); Harold Goodwin (Wilson, bank teller); Bob Steele (Poker player); Verna Felton (Lady in store).

RUNNING TIME: 77 minutes

FILMING DATES: Late August 1958–September 26, 1958

LOCATION: Universal backlot; Conejo Valley, California.

BUDGET/COST: Approximately $550,000.

This film was the closest Murphy came to a classic western, and, like *Walk the Proud Land*, has been the subject of favorable reassessment by a number of film writers in recent years, mainly in relation to the other work of director Jack Arnold. Arnold was responsible for some of the most interesting and stylish science-fiction dramas in the boom years of the 1950s, and is now generally regarded as the foremost director in that area. He also received high praise for his modern western *Man in the Shadow*, with Jeff Chandler and Orson Welles, and directed the best of Rory Calhoun's Universal westerns, *Red Sundown*. His ability to suggest dark forces lurking beneath a calm surface, and skillful building of tension, were vital elements of his sci-fi work. He brought the same qualities to bear on the Murphy film.

Audie Murphy instructed Joan Evans on how to handle a gun for *No Name on the Bullet* (1959).

The plot centered around John Gant (Murphy), a feared hired assassin who executed his victims without mercy — but only after legally goading them into a fight. When Gant arrives in the town of Lordsburg, his very appearance is enough to cause panic among all those hiding a guilty secret, even though he refuses to divulge the name of his intended victim. Only after the town has been torn apart by gunfights, lynch law and suicide does Gant reveal his intentions, but is thwarted in his task when the victim, a retired Judge (Edgar Stehli), dies from a heart attack while attempting to kill Gant. The local physician (Charles Drake), who has befriended the gunman, smashes Gant's gun arm with a blacksmith's hammer, thus ending his career by making him an easy target for the inevitable challenger. "A lot of men would like to kill John Gant," Audie says, painfully mounting his horse. "But it took a healer with a hammer to make it easy for them."

Gant is one of the most unusual and interesting leading characters ever to appear in a western — a man of considerable intelligence and psychological insight, aware and unashamed of the nature of his calling, totally without moral scruples in the achievement of his ends. He acknowledges his function in society as the tool of evil, feels only contempt for his employers, but refuses to compromise his professional ethics. Murphy, in a surprising departure from his standard western persona, brought striking credibility to the role, clearly delineating the complexity of the character and maintaining an air of frightening invincibility. His success was due, in no small part, to the intelligent script and the superior performances of the supporting cast — in particular, Charles Drake as the doctor who shares chess games and philosophical discussions with Gant. But, in the final analysis, it was Murphy who gave the film its special feeling of inevitable tragedy and simmering tension. There is no stopping John Gant. When the sheriff (Willis Bouchey) challenges him, Gant wounds him with almost contemptuous ease. Humiliated, the lawman asks, "Why didn't you kill me?" "I wasn't paid to," is the gunman's cool and logical reply. When a lynch mob confronts him, Gant disperses them by coldly naming the men he will kill before they kill him; and when a frightened, guilty store clerk (Warren Stevens) challenges him to draw, Gant calmly sips coffee, watching with a mocking smile as the man crumbles before his eyes and runs.

For most of the film Murphy did little but sit and talk, but his presence was felt in every scene. His performance was without question the most mature and impressive of his entire career, and Jack Arnold deserves equal credit for making full use of his star's personality, background and dramatic limitations in a role that embraced them completely within its own structure.

It is not too presumptuous to compare Murphy's John Gant with Alan Ladd's immortal Shane — in each case the actor and the role were in total accord; and if *Bullet* missed out on the stature of *Shane*, it is mainly due to the familiarity of the Universal backlot location, the inevitable surface gloss, and a degree of shallowness in the drawing of the minor characters by writer Gene L. Coon.

From the point of view of the "serious" moviegoer, of course, the lack of regard for the film is understandable — it was released without fanfare, and generally thought of as 'just another Audie Murphy western.' It deserves recognition as one of the best serious westerns of the 1950s, and, in some quarters at least, is finally achieving it.

REMEMBRANCES: *Joan Evans:* "In *No Name on the Bullet* we had some really fine people. R. G. Armstrong is an accomplished actor and an absolutely wonderful man. The man who played my father ... wonderful old character man ... Edgar Stehli. Charlie Drake was a darling. Charlie could get along with anybody and

How it's done: The smoke from Audie Murphy's six-gun still hangs in the air as the camera films a *No Name on the Bullet* action scene.

everybody—and did. Charlie was funny and delightful. Charlie and Audie got along very well. Charlie was cute and funny and was certainly not intimidating in any way. Charlie was an asset to any movie set.

"Jack Arnold, the director, seemed to take it more seriously than Fred DeCordova [who directed Joan's earlier film with Audie]. Jack had a wonderful sense of humor, but, actually, *No Name on the Bullet* was a much more interesting picture. The material was more serious than *Column South*. It was really an allegory."

Virginia Grey: "I had no scenes with Audie. I didn't know him at all. I'd work, go home and not socialize with these people."

R. G. Armstrong: "Audie was a small man fully charged ... you got the feeling he was the real thing. [Chuckles] He'd use those pistols if he had to. He kept 'em loaded when he carried 'em around. He manifested [his war experience] in his personality. He had an inner reality. A lot of good actors have an inner reality. They draw their characters off of that—like Brando does. That's where I got it. I was on that picture and observed Audie.

"I was a blacksmith on that film. [Laughs] They had a paper maché anvil. I had to pick it up—I said get a real one! They did. I had to struggle carrying that thing one place to another. It was about 250 to 300 pounds."

John Alderson: "I did like Audie. Two

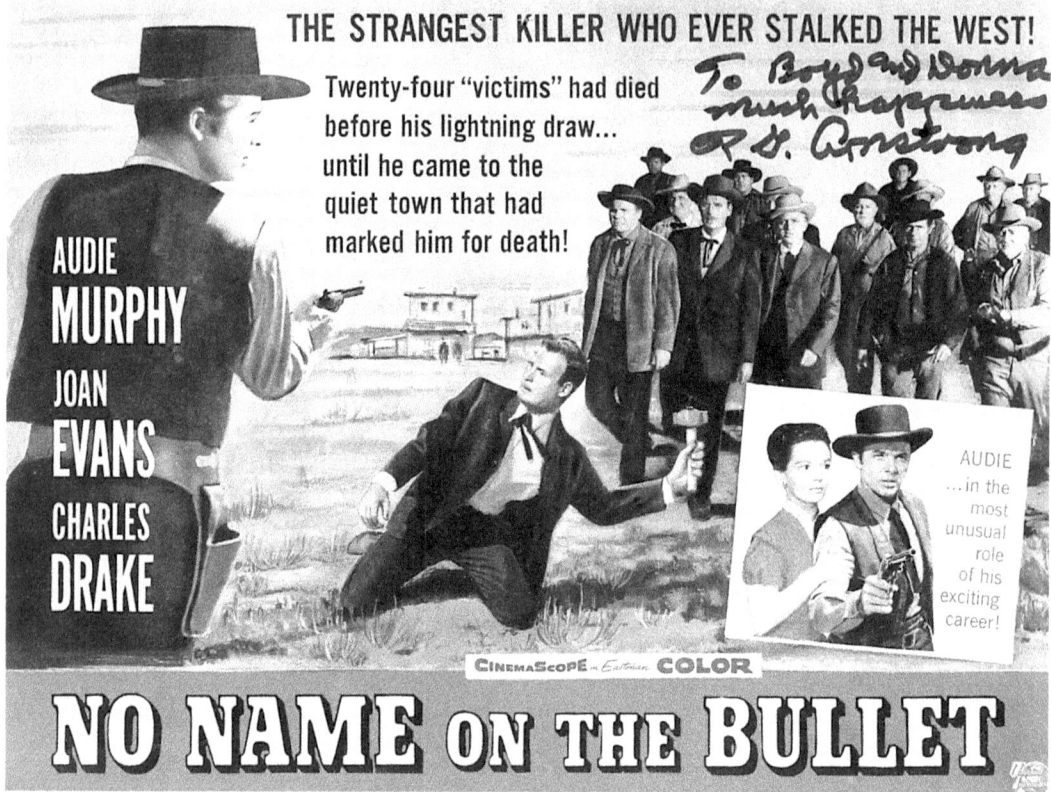

Title lobby card autographed by R. G. Armstrong, who is on the far left of the group of townspeople. In the middle stands Karl Swenson. Charles Drake holds the blacksmith hammer. The inset photo shows Joan Evans and Murphy.

soldiers together from sad environments that found Army life a welcome change for the better. Also, two guys [who], as if by mutual consent, deliberately avoided any chat about war experiences. In fact, you can avoid any blowhards that brag about their feats as being just plain bullshitters. Practically every conversation I had with Audie was about gambling on horses. To us, trainers and their cheating jockeys and their tricks, plus boneheaded touts, was enough to amuse us both. Also, both of us had little time for the movie crowd. His contempt for the bigwigs of Hollywood was colossal.

"By far his closest friend was Casey Tibbs. We all three, for quite a long time, were members of a gym on Cahuenga run by an ex-champ boxer, Mushy Callahan. The place was full of actors, but all the chat was about jokes and mostly odd extras and crazy stuntmen. The language matched Army scuff. The real attraction was for all of us to get the champ talking about his best fights. I think Casey helped Audie enormously with all the tricks of riding and handling pistols.

"Producer Gordon Kay said he thought Audie was banned from Hollywood Park because he was making all his bets by phone with outside bookies. I doubt the authenticity of that. There were no pocket phones available in those days, and phones at the track were always closed during racing. I used to sit with Audie at Santa Anita, Los Alamitos and Pomona, but rarely went to Hollywood because I didn't like the place. You could, of course, run into bookies at any track, but it was always on credit bets when you went broke. Audie was very obstinate. I used to know [jockey] Bill Shoemaker very well, but he was always on heavy favorites; and the few times he wasn't, Audie always knew something that would beat him. I think it's safe for me to say that gambling was Audie's nemesis.

"There is a biography named after the film I did with Audie, *No Name on the Bullet*. It's been years since I read it so my memory is a little hazy, but I didn't like it. I think what the author did was to go back to where Audie spent his school days and talk to people and relatives who knew him there. So a lot of it could be classified as fairytale gossip. Gordon Kay might be right about him hating the world, but I think Audie was just by nature as closed as an oyster. Didn't think he was overly educated. A complex human being, but you could trust him."

Audie's good friend and horse racing buddy, World Champion rodeo cowboy *Casey Tibbs*: "Of all the actors I saw ride a horse, Ben Johnson is the best. I'd have to rate Joel McCrea second, followed by Audie Murphy, Dale Robertson and James Caan."

NOTES AND COMMENTS: Charles Drake checked into the studio for his role in *No Name on the Bullet* and was outfitted for his part with a Stetson Jimmy Stewart once wore, a jacket first worn by Joel McCrea and a pair of boots that were made for Arthur Kennedy. "If they give me Hoot Gibson's horse to ride," Drake told director Jack Arnold, "you'll have to get yourself another boy."

The Wild and the Innocent
(UNIVERSAL-INTERNATIONAL, MAY 1959)

CREDITS: *Producer:* Sy Gomberg; *Director:* Jack Sher; *Assistant Directors:* William Holland, Frank Shaw; *Story:* Sy Gomberg; *Screenplay:* Sy Gomberg, Jack Sher; *Editor:* George Gittens; *Director of Photography:* Harold Lipstein; *Special Photography:* Clifford Stine; *Art Directors:* Alexander Golitzen; Robert Clatworthy; *Set Decorators:* Russell A. Gausman; William F. Taff; *Costume Designer:* Bill Thomas; *Makeup:* Bud Westmore; *Sound Recording:* Leslie I. Carey, Joe Lapis; *Hair Stylist:* Larry Germain; *Music Supervision:* Joseph Gershenson; *Original Music:* Hans J. Salter; *Song:* "A Touch of Pink" by Diane Lampert and Richard Loring, sung by George Mitchell and Audie Murphy. CinemaScope. Eastman Color by Pathe.

CAST: Audie Murphy (Yancey); Joanne Dru (Marcy Howard); Gilbert Roland (Sheriff Paul Bartell); Jim Backus (Cecil Forbes); Sandra Dee (Rosalie Stocker); George Mitchell (Uncle Lije); Peter Breck (Chip Miller); Strother Martin (Ben Stocker); Wesley Marie Tackitt (Ma Ransome); Betty Harford (Mrs. Forbes); Mel Leonard (Pitchman); Lillian Adams (Kiri); Val Benedict (Richie); Jim Sheppard, Ed Stroll, John Qualls, Frank Wolff (Henchmen); Stephen Roberts (Bouncer); Tammy Windsor (Townswoman); William Fawcett (Mountain Man); Rosemary Eliot, Barbara Morris, Louise Glenn (Dancehall girls). Stunts: Jimmy Sheppard, Hal Needham.

RUNNING TIME: 84 minutes

FILMING DATES: Late October 1958–November 13, 1958

LOCATION: Big Bear, California area; Universal backlot.

Murphy's next Universal film fell far short of the standard set by *No Name on the Bullet*, but for once it was not his fault.

Audie Murphy helps Joanne Dru stave off the unwanted advances of Peter Breck in *The Wild and the Innocent* (1959).

The direction (by writer Jack Sher) and script lacked the substance of the Jack Arnold film, and Murphy, though convincing, was too old for the character he was required to play.

A lightweight backwoods comedy-romance, the film had Murphy as a young mountain-bred fur trapper who unexpectedly hooks up with an orphaned teenage waif (Sandra Dee) during his annual fur-selling trek to town. In the town, both youngsters fall prey to the corrupt attractions of city life until the young man, seeing the error of his ways, rescues the girl from the clutches of the evil sheriff (Gilbert Roland), and the two "innocents" return to the untainted air of the mountains.

Although Murphy still retained his youthful appearance, there was a maturity in his playing that worked against the script's depiction of his character as a raw youth, and he seemed to have more in common with Joanne Dru as the scheming "older woman" of the piece than with Sandra Dee. Murphy was quietly effective throughout, and particularly so in the film's two excursions into violence — one in which he brutally crushes gunman Peter Breck's hand with his boot heel, and the other in which he reluctantly kills Gilbert Roland. His self-disgust after the killing was expressed with considerable feeling. Overall, the impression was of a good performance wasted on poor material.

Released at a time when Murphy's movies were receiving less and less prominence, the film was generally ignored and

Audie Murphy grins at the "look-alike" doll of his co-star Sandra Dee.

shunted into supporting spots; but it ambled pleasantly along at a sedate pace, gaining authority from the sharp playing of Gilbert Roland and Joanne Dru. It was pleasing, if entirely forgettable, entertainment.

REMEMBRANCES: *Peter Breck:* "It was the third feature I'd done. I hadn't worked with any of these people at Universal at all. I'd heard that fantastic story about Audie and Tony Curtis. (See *Kansas Raiders.*) (Laughs) Audie definitely had a dark sense of humor. Audie and I were friendly — as much as Audie would let people in to be his friend. He was very guarded. I don't think he could get used to the spectacular way publicity was handled and all of that. Nothing was private, and he was a very private man. At times watching Audie, I thought he was uncomfortable (in the role). It was silly, and he didn't want (to do) silly. He was a very quiet man, but when he got upset, it flashed. Then he'd come back down, very quiet."

"Sandra Dee was very quiet and withdrawn. I had a good role, a very loud, boisterous type of guy and I don't think she was ready for that kind of atmosphere around her. It was loud and brash in the scenes and I think it jarred her whole image. She and Audie worked well together."

"The scene where Audie throws me in the horse trough I did myself. I could have had Hal Needham or someone do it, but I was agile and capable. Same with the fight at the dance."

"I thought it was a good, light western. It wasn't earth-shattering. It was a good exposure for me and for a lot of others who were in it. Jack Sher had directed episodes of *Gilligan's Island* with Jim Backus."

NOTES AND COMMENTS: The produc-

The camera has been placed on a ski lift at Big Bear to follow Audie Murphy and Sandra Dee up a winding mountain trail for *The Wild and the Innocent*.

tion carried the working titles *The Buckskin Kid and the Calico Gal* and *The Wild Innocents*.

Screenwriter-director Jack Sher normally wrote comedies (*My Favorite Spy*, 1951; *Kid from Left Field*, 1953), but was co-writer on one of the most famous westerns of all time, Shane (1953) with Alan Ladd. Sher also wrote Audie's *World in My Corner* and *Joe Butterfly*.

This seems to be the first of a dozen or so movies on which stuntman Jimmy Sheppard doubled for Audie. Stuntman Bobby Hoy said, "He made a great double for Audie. Sheppard later got killed on *Comes a Horseman* (1978). He got drug to death doubling Jason Robards. Broke his neck when the horse ducked off through the gate, swung him around on the rope and he was knocked out. He was a good stuntman, a good guy and a good friend of Audie's ... and mine."

Cast a Long Shadow
(UNITED ARTISTS, JULY 1959)

CREDITS: *Producer:* Walter M. Mirisch (a Mirisch–Murphy Company Production); *Director:* Thomas Carr; *Assistant Director:* Austen Jewell; *Source Novel: Cast a Long Shadow* by Wayne D. Overholser; *Screenplay:* Martin M. Goldsmith, John McGreevey; *Editor:* Richard Heermance; *Director of Photography:* Wilfrid M. Cline; *Art Director:* David Milton; *Set Decorator:* Joseph Kish; *Costume Designer:* Sid Mintz; *Makeup:* Vincent Romaine; *Sound Recording:* John Kean; *Sound Editor:* Bruce Schoengarth; *Special Effects:* Milt Rice; *Music:* Gerald Fried.

CAST: Audie Murphy (Matt Brown); Terry Moore (Janet Calvert); John Dehner (Chip Donohue); James Best (Sam Mullen); Rita Lynn (Hortensia); Denver Pyle (Harrison); Ann Doran (Charlotte Calvert); Stacy Harris (Eph Brown); Robert Foulk (Hugh Rigdon); Wright King (Noah Pringle); Mason Alan Dinehart (Dick Calvert); Terry Frost (Wade); Rusty Westcoatt (Man in church); Nacho Galindo (Mexican hotel clerk); Jack Dodson (Charlie Bowles); Claire Carleton (Saloon floozy); Dale Van Sickel (Poker player); Ray Jones (Man in church); Kermit Maynard (Man at bar). Stunts: Dale Van Sickel.

RUNNING TIME: 82 minutes

FILMING DATES: December 1, 1958–December 19, 1958

LOCATION: Janss Ranch; Fox Century Ranch, both California.

BUDGET/COST: Approximately $500,000

Murphy's first western away from Universal since *Fort Petticoat*, but more significantly his first western in black and white, was a below-par reworking of his earlier *Gunsmoke*, made on an obviously limited budget and directed by Thomas Carr, a prolific maker of B-features with stars like Sunset Carson, Whip Wilson and Wayne Morris. Murphy played a derelict wanderer who unexpectedly inherits a large cattle ranch, since he is believed to be the illegitimate son of the former owner. Forced to undertake a cattle drive to save the ranch from ruin, he overcomes all manner of opposition and succeeds, in the process learning the ranch foreman (John Dehner) is actually his father.

Murphy's performance was competent and suitably rugged, but he lacked the edge required to be totally convincing once the character had assumed the role of a bullying tyrant; and although he conveyed well the initial bitterness of the down-and-out drifter wallowing in self-pity, he was

Audie Murphy receives a message of caution from Rita Lynn in *Cast a Long Shadow* (1959).

out-acted by the more consistent playing of John Dehner. Dehner's compassionate and authoritative performance was further proof of a fine talent that had languished for many years in cheap western and costume melodramas, and was, in fact, too good for the film. Terry Moore, a glamour starlet in some of the early 20th Century–Fox CinemaScope films, made for a mature and strong-willed heroine; and the chief heavy, a double-crossing cowboy, gave James Best a stronger role than in any of his earlier Murphy westerns.

Dehner, Moore and Best can easily be recognized as slightly rearranged versions of the characters played by Paul Kelly, Susan Cabot and Jack Kelly in *Gunsmoke*, and the second-hand look of the film was emphasized even further by the use of stock footage from the Howard Hawks classic *Red River*. Both the stampede and the river crossing from that film were cribbed and combined with occasional cut-in shots of Murphy, making the end result a flat, routine second-feature cheapie that clearly marked the beginning of Murphy's decline as an important personality in the eyes of Hollywood and the public.

REMEMBRANCES: *Terry Moore:* "I had lived in Lubbock, Texas, previously. People would stand around the block waiting for an Audie Murphy picture. When I started working with Audie, he said, 'I hate the script, I hate the director, everything's terrible.' He was just gonna walk through it. I said, 'Audie, all those people in Lubbock stand around the block for you. You're gonna rehearse! Come to my dressing room — we're gonna make this picture good, whether it's a good script or not.' He said okay. We didn't, but we did our best. I thought Audie gave one of his best per-

Co-stars Terry Moore and Audie Murphy relax between scenes of *Cast a Long Shadow*.

formances because I made him rehearse and rehearse. I said you can't go and tell everybody you didn't have a script, you didn't have a good director, it was too hot and all of these things.

"He was very exciting to work with. I know why he was a hero in WWII because I never saw anybody with the reflexes Audie had. Anybody come up behind him … [Terry makes a quick motion] he had his gun out ready to go. He had eyes behind him and he was very jumpy. But he moved like a tiger … like a cat."

Wright King: "I think you'll find I'm pretty 'up' about acting and all the actors. I don't like knocking actors, there's only two or three that ever bothered me, and Audie was one of them. This film wasn't at the top of his career, but he was just incommunicado. I had a role that was set with him quite a bit, but I just didn't have any communication at all with him. He just didn't care about communicating. Just kind of a grouch. Now, Terry Moore is a fervent, passionate actress; passionate in the sense she really likes acting, and is a good actress. She's a dear, wonderful person. Later, we became very good friends. She is a Mormon. She had a lot of great Mormon stories. One of them was, being very close to Howard Hughes, is that Hughes worked with Mormons and then he refused to work with anybody but Mormons. Terry is a ball of fire. But Audie—I was doing good in New York and went up to see John Huston about *Red Badge of Courage*, that Audie got. I later saw it and thought he was so good. He came across very nicely.

"The director of *Cast a Long Shadow*, Tommy Carr, was a typical B movie director. He was good, he could get the product out. He was the son of a character woman, Mary Carr."

Ann Doran: "Audie was a nice boy. Very shy, but very eager to do a good job."

Mason Alan Dinehart III: "Audie was a prankster! What he loved to do is pull me over to the side and say, 'Now in this scene I'm gonna hit you and what I want you to do is jump straight up in the air and land on your back.' Of course, I did that and the director would say, 'What in the … Cut! What in the hell is going on?' Then Audie would stand there sheepishly, looking like 'What are you doing, Mason?' [Laughs] As if it was my idea. He loved to do pranks like that. I know he owned horses, and we played cards on the set … I think we played Hearts rather than poker. Basically, he kept to himself, he never really socialized.

"Now, Jim Best was kind of a psycho. The heavyset guy—Robert Foulk, who played a character part—got on the wrong side of Jimmy. And Best just terrorized him. His eyes would get big and he'd just look at him. Foulk was just in terror of him. I'd never met Jim Best before—he seemed like just a regular guy until this happened. He was just gonna tear this guy apart. And for no real reason. Foulk was an unassuming, simple guy. Best just showed himself to be so irate … he just wanted to terrorize Foulk. I always respected Best's acting, he was a good actor, but that was so surprising that he would take on, probably, the weakest guy on the set. Foulk was a guy who didn't want any trouble from anybody, didn't really talk to anybody, and Best just terrorized him.

"Denver Pyle I knew from being on *Wyatt Earp* with him. [Dinehart played Bat Masterson on the series.] Denver was a fun guy, always cutting up. John Dehner pretty much kept to himself."

NOTES AND COMMENTS: Although divorced, Audie went to bat to cast former wife Wanda Hendrix in the role eventually played by Terry Moore.

Since Audie's partnership with Harry Joe Brown did not work out on *The Guns of Fort Petticoat*, he formed a partnership with producer Walter M. Mirisch, who had been successfully producing medium-range westerns with Joel McCrea for release through United Artists. But Audie dissolved the Mirisch partnership also when *Cast* ended up produced on the cheap in black and white.

Ford Startime: "The Man"
(NBC, JANUARY 5, 1960)

CREDITS: *Producer:* Robert Northshield; *Executive Producer:* Hubbell Robinson; *Director:* Robert Stevens; *Associate Director:* Hugh McPhillips; *Story Source:* Adapted from Mel Dinelli's 1950 Broadway melodrama; *Screenplay:* James P. Cavanaugh; *Technical Director:* Walter Miller; *Lighting Director:* William Knight; *Scenic Designer:* Don Shirley Jr.; *Costume Designer:* Guy Kent; *Audio:* Phil Falcone; *Video:* Tony Nelle; *Stage Manager:* Chuck Stamps; *Unit Manager:* Sigmund Bajax; *Music Composer:* Frank Denning; *Music Conducted by:* Al Fanelli. In color.

CAST: Audie Murphy (Howard Wilson); Thelma Ritter (Mrs. Grace Gillis); Michael J. Pollard (Doug); Joseph Campanella (Repairman); Joseph Sullivan (Joe, Bartender); William Hickey (Bill); Renne Jarrett (Judy); John McGovern (Mr. Franks); Phil Adams (Bowler).

RUNNING TIME: 60 minutes

DATE: Broadcast live (and kinescoped) January 5, 1960

In a real departure from his heroic roles, Audie played against type and was quite frightening at times in this suspenseful adaptation of a Broadway melodrama (which had also once been adapted on radio for Frank Sinatra). Widow Thelma Ritter takes pity on and hires Murphy, who appears at first to be just a lonely young man, as a handyman in her large house. She does not let his odd remarks upset her, as he seems to have known her deceased son. Slowly, Ritter begins to realize that Murphy is a very troubled man. Suspicion and terror begin to build as he locks the doors, draws the drapes and turns away callers, even Ritter's niece. Murphy is quite good at portraying a man tormented by his inner self.

REMEMBRANCES: *Joseph Campanella:* "Audie was very quiet, very calm. He wasn't distant, just reserved. He didn't make demands, he was very professional. Within a certain context, I thought it was a very good performance too. He brought something different than anybody else would have done. Most people would have been more menacing, but in his own quiet way, it didn't have to be.

"I'll never forget, his luggage was stolen when he got to New York and he had

Audie Murphy and Thelma Ritter in a tense moment from "The Man."

to get some suits and things. He had them made in a big quick hurry. But [chuckles] they had to make room for the suits to carry his gun, so he had to have a readjustment. I enjoyed meeting him ... very unassuming for a man who won every medal in the world.

"We rehearsed about six days at the old catering house down at 2nd Avenue and 7th Street in New York. The director, Bob Stevens, had done *Suspense* on live TV for years. The part I played was played on Broadway by Richard Boone."

Hell Bent for Leather
(UNIVERSAL-INTERNATIONAL, FEBRUARY 1960)

CREDITS: *Producer:* Gordon Kay; *Director:* George Sherman; *Assistant Director:* Phil Bowles; *Source Novel: Outlaw Marshal* by Ray Hogan; *Screenplay:* Christopher Knopf; *Editor:* Milton Carruth; *Director of Photography:* Clifford Stine; *Art Director:* Richard H. Riedel; *Set Decorators:* Russell A. Gausman, Julia Heron; *Makeup:* Bud Westmore; *Sound Recording:* Waldon O. Watson, Joe Lapis; *Hair Stylist:* Larry Germain; *Music:* William Lava, Irving Gertz; *Music Supervisor:* Joseph Gershenson. CinemaScope. Eastman Color by Pathé.

CAST: Audie Murphy (Clay Santell); Felicia Farr (Janet); Stephen McNally (Harry Deckett); Jan Merlin (Travers); Robert Middleton (Ambrose); Rad Fulton (Moon); Herbert Rudley (Nate Perrick); Malcolm Atterbury (Gamble); Joseph Ruskin (Shad); Allan Lane (Kelsey); John Qualen (Old Ben); Bob Steele (Jared); Eddie Little Sky (William); Steve Gravers (Grover); Olan Soule (Paradise bartender); Tom Tully (Thom Moore); Beau Gentry (Stone); Mike Ragan (Drunken cowboy in Paradise); Kermit Maynard (Man in Paradise bar). Stuntmen: Willard Willingham, Polly Burson, Joe Yrigoyen, Walt LaRue.

RUNNING TIME: 82 minutes

FILMING DATES: August 17, 1959–September 11, 1959

LOCATION: Lone Pine, California; Universal backlot.

BUDGET/COST: Approximately $600,000

Despite a number of promising elements, Murphy's next Universal western was little more than a routine chase drama that fell below the standard of his earlier Universal work (although several rungs higher on the scale than *Cast a Long Shadow*). Filmed in CinemaScope and color in quite spectacular desert and mountain locations around Lone Pine, California, it was directed by George Sherman, who had been responsible for a large number of good Republic Bs in the 1930s and '40s, as well as several above average Universal westerns in the early '50s with Joel McCrea, Jeff Chandler and others. Murphy's co-star was Felicia Farr, an excellent actress who had won considerable praise for her work in the Delmer Daves westerns *Jubal, The Last Wagon* and the classic *3:10 to Yuma*. But *Hell Bent for Leather*'s small cast and lack of dramatic development gave it a hasty, tight-budgeted appearance, and Murphy was required to do little but exude rugged authority, which he did quite well. The role could have been played by any one of a dozen run-of-the-mill cowboy heroes, and was totally undeveloped in the screenplay.

Murphy played Clay Santell, a horse trader deliberately mistaken for a wanted bandit by a reward-and-glory-hungry lawman (Stephen McNally), who plans to kill him on the way to prison. Santell escapes, takes schoolteacher Janet Gifford (Felicia

Lawman Stephen McNally restrains Audie Murphy while townspeople Herbert Rudley, Allan Lane and Rad Fulton watch in *Hell Bent for Leather* (1960). It was Murphy who brought former B-western star Allan Lane into his films, only to regret his decision later.

Farr) hostage, and makes for a town where he believes the real bandit, the excellently vicious Jan Merlin, may be hiding. Hotly pursued by the psychotic lawman, the pair finally locate the real bandit, and both he and the lawman are killed. Santell proves his innocence and prepares to live happily ever after with his former hostage, now his staunchest defender.

Stephen McNally, normally dependable as either hero or villain, was allowed to rant and rave to a near-ludicrous degree as the corrupt Marshal; while Farr's acting ability was hardly put to the test in a role which required little more than a lot of clambering over rocks, panting and screaming in terror.

Robert Middleton, another semi-prestige actor with an impressive list of credits, appeared as an outlaw leader in a pointless sequence that had little to do with the plot. One of the primary points of interest for western fans was the appearance of two former cowboy heroes in small roles. Allan "Rocky" Lane played a townsman, and Bob Steele was a rancher. The film's original title was *Hell Bent for Paradise*—Paradise being the ironic name of the tiny desert township in which Murphy finally locates the real bandit.

REMEMBRANCES: *Jan Merlin:* "I didn't approach Audie as a hero. I went into the picture facing another actor. Audie and I were about the same size ... I was a little taller than him but I wasn't towering over him ... so we were pretty well matched. Whatever chemistry there was, we liked each other. Oddly enough, here's a guy doing parts I wanted to play ... Billy the Kid and all of those guys. I was now going to be a heavy in *his* heroic picture. It was kinda fun for me to discover I was gonna be a real crazy. Here was the hero of the United States who was now an actor who was going to be the brunt of my antagonism. The very first thing I did to him was hit him with my shotgun butt, steal his horse, off I went. That was my introduction to Audie. People often ask me if I talked to Audie about the war. I didn't. Maybe that's another reason we got along.

"Audie wasn't going to play Hamlet ... he wasn't an actor-actor. He was Audie and he knew his limitations, and sometimes he'd stand up to the director, 'Listen, I can't do *that*. I wanna do it like this.' And he'd do it his way, so that he felt comfortable. Once he was comfortable, he was believable. And it was a pleasure to watch him do that. This was a guy who knew his own craft, his self-taught craft. He wasn't taught to be an actor. That was something they were trying to force him into. Audie did what he always did, he did his best. And he came off very well. The best word for Audie is still. He would do things and accomplish a great deal, yet you were never aware he was doing these things. He did some things in pictures that were wonderful to watch.

"Audie was sometimes short-tempered with some people on the set, but it was for good reason. Either because it involved the scene he was doing and maybe it wasn't going right, and he knew it was going to affect his performance. He would complain about that. All actors do that. Audie was sometimes a difficult person. Audie was a quiet person. He wasn't the kind of a guy who'd sit around spending the night telling

Audie Murphy prepares for a scene in *Hell Bent for Leather*.

stories. He *loved* to sit down and play poker. Play poker til the end of time. Problem was, he was a lousy poker player. [Laughs] Willard Willingham, who was a marvelous poker player, tried to teach him how to play poker, and said, 'You know, I couldn't do it!' Audie just couldn't understand the game. Audie lost a lot of money. Willard said it was hair-raising the amounts the man would lose. But he loved to play the game. Audie and Willard, the two of them, were about as close as you could possibly get. They even looked alike. If you saw Willard at a distance, you thought that was Audie walking away. That's why Willard made such a good double for Audie. Willard was also like Audie, quiet ... unwilling to sit around and tell stories. He refused interview after interview.

Audie Murphy and Felicia Farr form an uneasy alliance as they're *Hell Bent for Leather*.

"And the stuntmen, I couldn't believe the things they did. I was always in awe of them — and grateful when they accomplish something and nobody gets hurt. I remember being almost terrified when two stuntmen [Joe Yrigoyen and Polly Burson] doubling Audie and Felicia Farr went over a small cliff in a wagon and rolled down the hill.

"As for [director] George Sherman, he knew his stuff. You never had a question about what it was he wanted you to do or how to do it. He was good about letting you play it pretty much as you, as an actor, saw it. He made it easier up in that rough Lone Pine location."

Stuntlady Polly Burson: "There was one time in the business when I literally froze. Up in Lone Pine — Willard Willingham and I were doubling Audie and Felicia Farr, Jack Lemmon's wife, climbing over those rocks. We got to a point, now I had this wig and long skirt on, and the wind was whipping this long skirt over my head, and the wig-hair too. We had to jump over several rocks. Willard had jumped from one point to another, but I couldn't hardly see. I can hear Willard, 'Come on, Polly. Come one, take my hand. Jump!' I finally got where I could see his hand with all that in my face. If he hadn't jerked me I might still be standing there. [Laughs]"

NOTES AND COMMENTS: Audie enjoyed flying and learned to fly himself in the mid–1950s, eventually buying a plane, which he flew to the Lone Pine location. He and director George Sherman did an aerial scouting flight looking for unique locations. What really sold Audie on owning a plane was the ease with which he could travel to his working cattle ranch near Tucson, Arizona, a spread of over

Eddy Arnold, Roy Rogers and Audie Murphy made a rare appearance singing together on NBC's *Chevy Show* in September 1959.

16,000 acres which he bought for approximately $150,000 in 1956, as well as his 800-acre horse ranch near Romoland, California, which he purchased in 1957. He'd put an airstrip in there in August 1958.

On September 27, 1959, Audie guested on a color Sunday night one-hour NBC special *Chevy Show*, a summer replacement for *The Dinah Shore Chevy Show*. Roy Rogers and his wife Dale Evans hosted the color program from their Double R Ranch in Chatsworth, California. Besides Audie, who sang with Roy and country singer Eddy Arnold, the guests were singer-comedienne Edie Adams, pop singer Connie Francis, trumpeter Rafael Mendez, the Sons of the Pioneers, the Hollywood Square Dancers and the Rudells, trampoline performers. The Rogers children also joined in. Roy Rogers stated, "Audie was a terrific person. He had a lot of guts."

On October 12, 1959, the *Los Angeles Times* reported Audie was being sued for $775,000 by Paul Kazear, an underwater expert who claimed Audie failed to complete a movie deal with him. Kazear claimed he was orally commissioned to write a script about skin diving, and that Marina Orschel, Miss Germany in the 1957 Miss Universe contest, was to have a role in the film, which was to be shot in Mexico. Kazear gave some photos of Orschel to Audie, which were not returned when the picture deal fell through. Audie refused to pay Kazear for the script. The case was settled in 1962 with the court ordering Audie to simply return the script and the photos.

Although not shown until 1961, Audie started filming his TV series, *Whispering Smith*, in June of 1959. During a production shake-up on the show, Audie filmed *Hell Bent for Leather*.

The Unforgiven
(UNITED ARTISTS, APRIL 1960)

CREDITS: *Producer:* James Hill, a Hecht-Hill-Lancaster Presentation; *Executive Production Manager:* Gilbert Kurland; *Director:* John Huston; *Assistant Director:* Tom Shaw; *Screenplay:* Ben Maddow, based on a 1957 novel by Alan Le May; *Editor:* Russell Lloyd; *Director of Photography:* Franz Planer; *Art Director:* Stephen Grimes; *Costume Designer:* Dorothy Jeakins; *Makeup:* Frank McCoy, Frank LaRue; *Sound Recording:* Basil Fenton-Smith; *Sound Editor:* Leslie Hodgson; *Special Effects:* Dave Koehler; *Music:* Dimitri Tiomkin, recorded in Rome, Italy, with the Santa Cecilia Orchestra. Panavision, Technicolor.

CAST: Burt Lancaster (Ben Zachary); Audrey Hepburn (Rachel Zachary); Audie Murphy (Cash Zachary); John Saxon (Johnny Portugal); Doug McClure (Andy Zachary); Charles Bickford (Zeb Rawlins); Lillian Gish (Mattilda Zachary); Albert Salmi (Charlie Rawlins); Joseph Wiseman (Abe Kelsey); June Walker (Hagar Rawlins); Kipp Hamilton (Georgia Rawlins); Arnold Merritt (Jude Rawlins); Carlos Rivas (Lost Bird). Stunts: Bobby Herron.

RUNNING TIME: 121 Minutes
FILMING DATES: February 1, 1959–May 20, 1959
LOCATION: Durango, Mexico.
BUDGET/COST: $5.5 million

In terms of budget, co-stars and director, *The Unforgiven* was Murphy's most prestigious western; and his performance—in a character rather than a star role—was one of his best, and good enough to rank alongside his work in *The Red Badge of Courage* and *No Name on the Bullet*. (His performance in *To Hell and Back* must inevitably stand apart from his other work because of the intensely personal nature of the film—it was "being" rather than "acting," and cannot fairly be compared with his more objective portrayals.) John Huston's epic-scale drama of life on the Texas frontier offered not only action but also the controversial aspect of racial prejudice—in this case against the Indian.

The central characters are the Zachary family—Ben, the eldest son (Burt Lancaster), Cash and Andy, the younger brothers (Murphy and Doug McClure), Mattilda, the mother (Lillian Gish); and Rachel, the adopted daughter (Audrey Hepburn). The family is torn apart by emotional and physical violence when it is revealed Rachel is actually an Indian, and the film's theme revolves around the efforts of Ben to protect the family from the prejudice of its neighbors and the efforts of a band of Kiowa Indians to claim Rachel as

Audie Murphy played a fervent Indian hater in *The Unforgiven* (1960).

their own. Cash, nursing a psychotic hatred of Indians, deserts the family, but returns to assist in the final battle against the Indians, during which Mattilda is killed, Rachel kills her own Indian brother, and Ben and Rachel realize their love for each other.

An offbeat, somber-hued melodrama of human relationships and social pressures set against a harsh background, the film was perhaps a little too different for its time, and was not the box-office success it should have been, although critical reception was unanimously favorable. It was rich in powerful images and emotional climaxes, its characters complex and in some cases bizarre, and its performances complemented Huston's direction and the superbly-evoked period sense.

Murphy, for the first time taking less than top billing, was listed under the title, with Lancaster and Audrey Hepburn above it; but unlike his other departures and standard western hero roles, this was a personal and critical success. With a mustache and long hair, Audie played his first unsympathetic character (even John Gant had his own code of honor), a man whose uncontrollable hatred of Indians overrides even family ties, and was required to both break down and cry and get roaring drunk—both of which he accomplished with total conviction under Huston's guidance. The scene in which he goes berserk during an Indian attack, feverishly firing shot after shot at the retreating savages before breaking down and sobbing in Lancaster's arms is only matched during his career by his reaction to Charles Drake's death in *To Hell and Back*. Critics praised his *Unforgiven* performance in terms of an actor doing a good job, rather than as a low-budget westerner trying to change his image (as they had with his previous break-away roles). Working as a member of an ensemble of seasoned professional performers, and not as an out-front hero figure, Murphy surprised many critics with his emotional depth, his rapport with his fellow actors, and total affinity with Huston's concept of the film.

But there were few directors of Huston's caliber prepared to offer top roles to a low-budget western actor, and the "new" Audie Murphy, a character actor of considerable potential, again stepped aside for the old, familiar and now almost out-of-date western hero to return to the well-known rut of formula horse operas. Once more, as with *To Hell and Back*, the possibility of taking on more prestigious and rewarding roles had presented itself, but again the opportunity had been missed. There would be no third chance.

REMEMBRANCES: *John Huston:* "Audie is afraid of making a fool out of himself in front of the camera, so he tightens up. I assure him that I'll protect him. He believes me and gives his all."

John Saxon: "Down in Mexico, on *The Unforgiven*, I knocked on Audie's door and first thing he did, he opened the door and he had a .38 [gestures as if pointing a gun]: 'How are ya?' [Chuckles] Then later, one day, Doug McClure and myself were on one side of a small river about ready to leave. I don't know what we said or did to Audie, but he started target shooting over our heads with a .22 pistol. I guess he thought he was that good of a shot that he wasn't gonna injure us. [Laughs] Audie was a good actor. I remember John Huston saying on the set that few people understood how good Audie was. I could see that he had a great deal of facility in just relaxing into a certain degree of honesty in playing the scenes. I think his biggest problem was he didn't know how good he was. His ability as an actor was maybe confined or limited, but I think there was a great deal of truth to the way he did things. I don't think he took acting seriously, that hampered his development in a way. The majority of his films were westerns, because he got identified with being a western type — soft-spoken but lethal — then westerns started fading out in the 1960s. Audie wouldn't be good in a horror film, and I think that was

The Unforgiven was Audie Murphy's second film for director John Huston.

part of the problem that began to develop in terms of his career. He was good at it—a natural. Like Elvis Presley. But I don't think either of them thought of it enough to delve into the characters or try a different voice or whatever.

"[In *The Unforgiven*] I was supposed to be a great horseman. John Huston invented a scene one day about transfers. It was a story where Audrey Hepburn's favorite pony was stolen by Joseph Wiseman, and it was such a fast pony—how were we gonna track it down? I was to ride one horse bareback, lead three others on a hackamore. I'd never ridden bareback in my life. I walked up to Huston and said, 'You want me just to get on and go beyond camera range?' He looked at me, 'No, son. You see those rocks....' They were about two miles away. I'd done about 10 pictures and I knew—was he gonna film me going into those rocks? I knew he was giving me a challenge. So I jumped up on the horse, Burt Lancaster hands me the three ropes with the other horses. I kick this horse and it goes and the others stay—I jackknifed off and I hit and there was a silence. When I got up everybody was laughing—because I was alright. Huston wasn't visible, he was sitting back and he says, 'How are you, son?' I said, 'I'm okay.' He said, 'Good, let's try it again. This time lead 'em out a little slower.' [Laughs] So I get on the horse and I know he's really giving me a chance. I start real soft and I get 'em into a nice little cantor. I'm thinkin', 'Okay, I'm gonna do this!' And suddenly, the horse I'm on spurts forward ... I don't know why, but I didn't have time to think. I'm holdin' on to the other ones and—[whistles and motions upwards] I go off again! This time I see three sets of hooves go over my head. I get up, and I'm okay. So I started walking back in—I'm half a mile away from the camera. As I approach the camera, I'm about 30 or 40 yards away, I hear Huston's voice again, 'How are you, son?' I said, 'I'm okay.' 'Good. Let's do it again!' [Laughs] 'Okay!' I did it four times and I couldn't get beyond a certain point because I realized at that time what was happening — I was riding a mare and the other horses were nipping at her backside. Every time that spread occurred, I couldn't hold on, so after the fourth time, I let go and stayed on [my horse]. Then it was no more fun for Huston with me and he put the stuntman on. I felt good, because the stuntman was Bobby Herron and he couldn't get any further than I did! So they decided let's get these horses trained to ride together and we'll do it at another time."

NOTES AND COMMENTS: John Huston originally wanted Richard Burton for the role Audie eventually played, but Burton insisted on equal billing to Lancaster — to which co-producer Lancaster would not agree. In retrospect, it was a wise decision, as Burton would have been totally miscast.

Ray Stricklyn was originally set for the role eventually played by Doug McClure. Again, Lancaster objected to Stricklyn.

Susan Kohner, Ina Balin, Gloria Talbott and Suzanne Lloyd were all tested for the role of adopted daughter Rachel. Unexpectedly, a major star in Audrey Hepburn was announced. Obviously cast for her star power, she was just as obviously miscast.

John Huston remarked in his 1980 autobiography *An Open Book* that *The Unforgiven* was the one film he disliked making in his long career. Instead of an authentic depiction of the west and a harsh frontier racial theme, the picture was commercially loaded with action and heroics. Apparently it was also quite heavily edited as well — note the way John Saxon's character seems to just disappear.

The production was fraught with behind-the-scenes problems. Hepburn, who had not told anyone she was pregnant, took a fall from a horse, breaking four bones in her back and suffering a miscarriage. Murphy was one of the first to reach her and provide aid. With great fortitude, she returned to work after only three weeks off. Murphy nearly drowned on March 3, 1959, when the small rowboat in which he and airplane pilot Bill Pickens were duck hunting capsized. Because of a war injury to his hip, Murphy could not swim and was caught beneath the boat momentarily. Then he clung to the edge of the boat, along with Pickens, who wouldn't leave him. A German still photographer, Inga Moroth, spotted the men through her telephoto lens, stripped down to bra and panties, and swam out to rescue them. Some newspapers regarded the incident as a publicity stunt. Later, three technicians working on *The Unforgiven* died when their plane crashed.

Charles Affron, in his book *Lillian Gish, Her Legend and Life*, reports, "There were problems even with the usually obliging Lillian Gish during the making of *The Unforgiven*. She couldn't bear Audie Murphy, who played one of her three sons. She claimed Murphy was trigger happy, that he would shoot any animal that moved, or would plug a beer can thrown across a bar or a fly-specked light bulb if he was in the mood. She refused to ride with Murphy in the car to and from location. Then there was the struggle to break Lillian of what John Huston considered old acting habits. Screenwriter Ben Maddow reported that on the first day of shooting Lillian was 'still stuck in the era of silent films. She came out with pancake-white makeup, made her look like a clown. It took quite a while to get her to peel off that stuff.' Huston put Lillian through endless repetitions. Assistant director Tom Shaw, who thought she was 'a terrible actress,' described the excruciating process. 'Every time we did it he would say to her, "Absolutely wonderful, but we're just going to do it once more." That was his method of just breaking the woman down where she had no energy at all. She was just *whipped!* And so was I! He got her so worn out she wasn't looking for D. W. Griffith anymore.'"

Audie Murphy, Burt Lancaster and Doug McClure laugh as the still cameraman catches them in their long johns during the filming of *The Unforgiven*.

This was Hecht-Hill-Lancaster's costliest film; originally budgeted at $3 million, the final tally was $5.5 million. A commercial flop, it put an end to Hecht-Hill-Lancaster's production company.

The Zachary family sod house built for the film in Mexico reportedly cost $300,000. The salaries of Hepburn, Lancaster and Huston were also in this range. Murphy received $75,000.

Novelist and screenwriter Alan LeMay also wrote the 1954 novel on which the 1956 John Wayne film *The Searchers* was based.

Seven Ways from Sundown
(UNIVERSAL-INTERNATIONAL, SEPTEMBER 1960)

CREDITS: *Producer:* Gordon Kay; *Executive Producer:* Edward Muhl; *Director:* Harry Keller (some scenes: George Sherman); *Assistant Director:* Thomas J. Connors Jr.; *Source Novel: Seven Ways from Sundown* by Clair Huffaker; *Screenplay:*

Clair Huffaker; *Editor:* Tony Martinelli; *Director of Photography:* Ellis Carter; *Art Directors:* Alexander Golitzen, William Newberry; *Set Decorator:* George Milo; *Makeup:* Bud Westmore; *Sound Recording:* Waldon O. Watson, William Russell; *Hair Stylist:* Larry Germain; *Music:* William Lava, Irving Gertz; *Music Supervisor:* Joseph Gershenson. Eastman Color by Pathé.

CAST: Audie Murphy (Seven Jones); Barry Sullivan (Jim Flood); Venetia Stevenson (Joy Karrington); John McIntire (Sgt. Hennessey); Kenneth Tobey (Lt. Herly); Mary Field (Mary Karrington); Ken Lynch (Graves); Suzanne Lloyd (Lucinda); Claudia Barrett (Gilda); Teddy Rooney (Jody); Jack Kruschen (Beeker); Robert Burton (Eavens); Ward Ramsey (Fogarty); Don Collier (Duncan); Don Haggerty (Dorton); Fred Graham (Wagon man #1); Dale Van Sickel (Wagon man #2); Henry Rowland (Sam); Bill Henry (Hobbs bartender); Charles Horvath (Jake Hanley); Henry Wills (Wagon driver); Guy Wilkerson (Buckley townsman). Stunts: Jim Sheppard, Henry Wills, Fred Graham, Dale Van Sickel, LeRoy Johnson, Joe Yrigoyen, Bobby Herron, Dean Smith, Bob Terhune.

RUNNING TIME: 87 minutes

FILMING DATES: May 2, 1960–May 26, 1960

LOCATION: Red Rock Canyon, west of Las Vegas, Nevada; Valley of Fire State Park, northeast of Las Vegas, Nevada; Universal backlot, California.

BUDGET/COST: Approximately $600,000

A comparison between the plot of this film and that of *Ride Clear of Diablo* is re-

John McIntire (left) played new Texas Ranger Audie Murphy's mentor in *Seven Ways from Sundown* (1960).

vealing. In *Diablo* Murphy was intent on finding the killer of his father and brother, and was steered in the direction of a notorious gunman by a crooked superior hoping to have him killed. In *Sundown* he was looking for the killer of his brother, a Texas Ranger, and was given the job of arresting a legendary bandit by a devious Ranger captain who, like the sheriff in *Diablo*, was actually responsible for his brother's death. In *Diablo* he captured the bandit, and the two became uneasy allies against common foes until the gunman sacrificed his life to save Murphy. In *Sundown* he also captured his prey and was forced to frequently enlist his help until the bandit sacrificed his life. The only difference in the ending was that in *Sundown* it was Murphy who killed the bandit—after the other drew but slowed his draw on purpose. Yet despite the plot similarity, or perhaps because of it, the later film was able to stand on its own feet as a well-constructed, fast-moving and thoroughly entertaining western that could bear comparison with the best films of Murphy's peak era.

Beautifully photographed, *Seven Ways from Sundown*'s success rested equally on the crisp direction of the underrated Harry Keller and the professional performances of the cast, who all responded admirably to a well-written screenplay by Clair Huffaker who had adapted his own novel for *Sundown*, and would later write such westerns as *Flaming Star, The Comancheros* and Murphy's *Posse from Hell*. Murphy combined the gentle humor of his earlier films with the easy authority of his later work, providing a perfect contrast to Barry Sullivan's bravura display of smooth charm and cool savagery. The rapport between the two stars was skillfully developed through laconic dialogue exchanges and tense action sequences. Sullivan's was perhaps the better acting performance, but it did not overshadow Murphy's solid contribution, although character actor John McIntire came close to stealing the film from both stars with his appealing portrayal of a grizzled veteran Ranger who trains the green young recruit (Murphy) for his daunting task, only to be shot from ambush by Sullivan early in the story. Venetia Stevenson, the girl back home, and Murphy shared an obvious chemistry, but she appeared only in the opening and closing sequences—and so was not around long enough to slow the action down.

A wide range of well-photographed locations, from prairies to pine covered mountains, gave a fine outdoor feeling to the action without dwarfing the actors, and the early part of the film included some excellent, detailed episodes in which McIntire taught Murphy to use a handgun. The script made a point of the fact that although Murphy was very good with a rifle, Sullivan was his superior with a pistol, thus adding an edge to the final man-to-man confrontation. The growing respect and affection between the two men was achieved without resorting to sticky sentimentality, and the final shot of Murphy kneeling beside Sullivan's body as the camera pulls back held genuine emotional power.

A thoroughly satisfying piece of entertainment, this was to be the last of Murphy's starring westerns to approach the standard of his best films of the 1952–1955 era, although a few of his remaining films as a traditional western star would offer varying degrees of merit.

REMEMBRANCES: *Gordon Kay* produced seven films with Audie from 1960 to 1966. *Seven Ways from Sundown* was the second. Kay spoke of Audie's volatile personality: "He *was* a problem. He'd get these obsessions against certain people ... and he didn't like them at all. It was a helluva job getting him to not get nasty with people. I can't think of any specific thing, because people were *gone* by the time he got in the middle of his hate. He wasn't difficult with the scripts; those, basically, seemed to be all right. He was erratic. The second picture I made with him, *Seven Ways from Sundown*, was started by [director] Georgie Sherman. He was well liked by everyone, had shot hundreds of films. George had an attitude of 'let's shoot this shit and get it over with,' pardon my French, but that's the way he used to talk. He and Audie were somewhat alike in that respect. So, you had a conflict of Georgie's tough, disinterested personality and Murphy, who got furious with George when George said something like that. George was out–Audieing Audie! In a squabble over a line reading on the second day of the picture, Audie picked him up out of the director's chair and threw him back in. George almost broke his back, falling around in the chair. George came tearing down to me and said, 'I'm scared, I'm afraid to go back on the set....' Now, George was a little teeny guy and I didn't want him to go back. He said, 'I can't, I'm scared.' I said, 'All right, go home, Georgie, forget it.' He started, then turned and cried, 'Oh my God, I'm under contract here. What are they going to do with me?' I said, 'Look, just go home and forget it. Nobody's going to do anything to you. Nobody's certainly going to ask you to walk back in that lion's den.' He finally relaxed, and in the meantime, I went over and talked to another producer, Mel Tucker ... he agreed with me. We couldn't send George back. God knows, Audie could have shot him! So that was a *little* problem. [Harry Keller took over the picture.] Lots of gray hair! I figure that's part of the producer's job, try to make the

Claudia Barrett (left) found Audie Murphy "playful" in her scenes with him and Barry Sullivan.

thing go. Once you've bought it, you've bought it.

"[Leading lady] Venetia Stevenson thought Audie was marvelous. She wrote a book or something about how wonderful he was.

"[As for the Universal executives], they wanted to know what the basic story was. Generally, they were satisfied with a synopsis. If they had suggestions, we'd incorporate them. It got to the point where I had to ask the fellows to at least screen the pictures. They said, 'We know it's good.'"

Love scenes were a bit of a problem for Audie. "He was uncomfortable. It was best for him to play an uncomfortable guy in a love scene. We tried to make him a cowpoke who wished he could disappear. You can't force someone.

"The shooting schedules ran up around 20 days, some a little longer. We tried to make Audie's films for $600,000 and under. Never made 'em much under! That was the deal when I took them on.

"Director Harry Keller and I started back at Republic. I knew him a little in the cutting room. Harry had been a film editor, then began directing. We got to know each other better, worked together, so when I got to Universal, I was working with a guy I was very fond of. We worked together so much they called us the Gold Dust Twins at Universal. We just kept making picture after picture together. Universal finally said, 'We got to break you two up.' I said, 'Why?' 'Because, you're always working together.' I said, 'Don't you like our pictures?' They said, 'Yes, but we got to mix things up a little.' Jack Arnold and William Alland, a director and producer respectively, had been working together, so they gave Jack to me and Harry went over to Alland. Then what happened was, my script, whatever it was, was ready and Bill was having trouble with his and wanted Jack back because they used to work together on the scripts. So Bill came crying, saying, 'I want Jack Arnold.' So Universal gave Jack back to him and Harry back to me and away we went. Then Universal gave up. [Laughs]"

Suzanne Lloyd: "I just came in to do one scene, and I can remember being curious as to what type of man this decorated war hero was. In my own head, without even meeting Audie, I was thinking he would have to be very powerful, his presence would be very powerful, and he would be very commanding and kind of a take charge human being. That's sort of what I was expecting. I was curious about it. When I actually got on the set and met this man, I thought, this is a man that charged up a hill and saved all those lives. And he was just sitting there very quietly, very unassuming. He surprised me. Then we did the scene, and I left. I did that film when I was first getting started."

Screenwriter *Clair Huffaker* (to author Don Graham): "Audie fit in well with the two characters I wrote in those two books [*Seven Ways from Sundown* and *Posse from Hell*]. In both scripts he was a young guy with a sense of humor, a wry quality about him, and put in a situation where he has to do something bigger than life. So it really kind of fit him."

Claudia Barrett: "On *Seven Ways from Sundown* Audie Murphy was playful. When I was trying to do my clasps he was making faces at me and it was very difficult to concentrate. [Laughs] I don't think I rehearsed with Audie until we actually did the take."

Dean Smith: "We were out somewhere near Las Vegas and I did a nice saddle fall. Willard Willingham doubled Audie at the beginning [of Audie's career], then he and his wife started writing some screenplays. Then Jimmy Sheppard was young, he came in and started doing Audie's stunts. Audie kinda moved Willard into writing and doin' other stuff for him.

"Jimmy was killed. He was doing *Comes a Horseman* [1978]. Jim had to do a drag for Jason Robards. They had it fixed where Jimmy would be drug through this gate. Evidently, something went wrong being drug through the gate, and he was slammed up against a post … and it killed him. Jimmy made a good double for Audie. Sheppard was a horseman, more athletic, a real daring kind of guy.

"Audie was a nice guy. He was hard to get to know, but he was nice to me. Audie would appreciate you for what you were and who you were, but he wasn't much to run around with a bunch of people. But I'll tell you what, he did love running around with Casey Tibbs. They'd go to a horse track and bet on the horses. Audie did love to gamble. Between Casey and Audie's gambling, if they hadn't lost so much, it might have helped them have a few more material things than what they ended up with.

"But what's impressive to me, go down to the rotunda at the state capitol of Texas and see Audie Murphy's picture hanging there, and by God, I can truthfully say I worked with one of the greatest WWII heroes of all time."

NOTES AND COMMENTS: Audie and his wife Pam separated in late March 1960, just about six weeks before production began on *Seven Ways from Sundown*. She remained with their two sons at their North Hollywood home (4201 Toluca Road) while Audie stayed at his horse breeding ranch near Perris, California.

Co-star Venetia Stevenson, by her own admission, hated acting and got out of it as soon as she could. In fact, this was her last film. She married singer Don Everly in 1962. But during the film, and for about a year afterward, she and the now separated Audie carried on a torrid, well-publicized love affair. She told author Don Graham, "I

Audie Murphy and leading lady Venetia Stevenson enjoyed good chemistry together — on and off the screen.

really liked him. I would imagine that most women he was involved with would say the same thing. He was just a nice, sweet, gentle kind of guy. A super guy. He had a kind of gentle quality about him." Apparently, Audie and Venetia established a bond through their mutual love of horses. Her experience was gained with show jumpers, and she was an expert rider.

In June and early July of 1960, Audie donated his time and talent toward making a 45-minute color documentary about the Army missile program, *The Broken Bridge*, in Europe for the U.S. State Department. Some of the film was also lensed at White Sands Missile Range in New Mexico. The picture was first shown on the U.S. Army's TV show *The Big Picture* in May 1961, and was then released in theaters as a short subject. For his participation, Audie was presented the highest civilian decoration the U.S. Army gives, the Civilian Service Medal, on November 9, 1961. Completing the documentary, Audie went to Hong Kong for a rest, and was due home around July 15.

The boy in the film, Teddy Rooney, is the son of actor Mickey Rooney. The younger Rooney's film career was quite brief, lasting only from 1958 to 1960.

Posse from Hell
(UNIVERSAL-INTERNATIONAL, MAY 1961)

CREDITS: *Producer:* Gordon Kay; *Associate Producer:* Willard Willingham; *Executive Producer:* Edward Muhl; *Director:* Herbert Coleman; *Assistant Director:* Ray Gosnell Jr.; *Source Novel: Posse from Hell* by Clair Huffaker; *Screenplay:* Clair Huffaker; *Editor:* Frederic Knudtson; *Director of Photography:* Clifford Stine; *Art Directors:* Alexander Golitzen, Alfred Sweeney; *Set Decorator:* Oliver Emert; *Makeup:* Bud Westmore; *Sound Recording:* Waldon O. Watson, Joe Lapis; *Hair Stylist:* Larry Germain; *Music Supervision:* Joseph Gershenson. Eastman Color by Pathe.

CAST: Audie Murphy (Banner Cole); John Saxon (Seymour Kern); Zohra Lampert (Helen Caldwell); Vic Morrow (Crip); Robert Keith (Capt. Brown); Rudolph Acosta (Johnny Caddo); Royal Dano (Uncle Billy Caldwell); Frank Overton (Burt Hogan); James Bell (Benson); Paul Carr (Jack Wiley); Ward Ramsey (Marshal Isaac Webb); Lee Van Cleef (Leo); Ray Teal (Banker Larson); Forrest Lewis (Dr. Welles); Charles Horvath (Hash); Harry Lauter (Russell); Henry Wills (Chunk); Stuart Randall (Luke Gorman); Allan Lane (Burl Hogan); Walter Reed (Frightened townsman in saloon); Kenneth MacDonald (Posse instigator #1); Rand Brooks (Posse instigator #2); Don C. Harvey (Town councilman); I. Stanford Jolley (Undertaker); Ralph Moody (Livery stable owner); Steve Darrell (Cowhand); Steve Terrell (Brash town youngster); Howard J. Negley (Joe, bartender); Billy Hughes (Jackie). Stunts: Jimmy Sheppard, Jerry Gatlin, Joe Yrigoyen.

RUNNING TIME: 89 minutes

FILMING DATES: October 31, 1960–November 29, 1960

LOCATION: Lone Pine, California; 20th Century–Fox Ranch.

BUDGET/COST: Approximately $600,000

Novelist-screenwriter Clair Huffaker again adapted one of his own novels for the screen, and the result, though less satisfactory than *Seven Ways from Sundown*, was a commendable, if flawed, attempt at something deeper in western drama, with Murphy, in the role of a gunslinger named Banner Cole, leading a diminishing posse in pursuit of a quartet of particularly brutal escaped convicts who have massacred a large portion of the population of a small town, including the Sheriff, a close friend of Cole's. The posse, split by personal differences, gradually loses interest until only Cole, a green Easterner (John Saxon) and an Indian (Rudy Acosta) remain. By the time they have dealt with the convicts, only Cole is left on his feet, and he returns to castigate the townspeople for their lack of support before agreeing to their request to take on the job of Sheriff.

The film veered towards heavy drama, hinting darkly at thematic depths it never fully embraced, and included such strong meat as anti–Indian racial prejudice and the gang-rape of a girl taken hostage by the fugitives, although only the aftermath was seen in the somewhat battered shape of intriguing New York actress Zohra Lampert, who gave further impetus to the film's offbeat qualities. The heavy dramatics seemed overstated at times, with the posse populated by a contrived collection of psychotic misfits (the arrogant two-gun youngster out to make a reputation, the glory-seeking ex-officer intent on reliving old campaigns, the young Easterner questioning the values of the West), but the performances possessed a richness that might have lifted the film above the realm of melodrama if the script had not tried to cram so many complexities into the action.

Frank Overton, Robert Keith, Vic Morrow and Royal Dano were all experienced and highly individual performers. Rudy Acosta exuded a quiet dignity as the Indian who ultimately proves a better man than the white men who despise him. Ward Ramsey and Paul Carr provided competent new faces on the western scene, and John Saxon again showed he was an actor of more ability than his early pin-up roles had suggested. But despite this formidable act-

John Saxon and Audie Murphy are the only two left of the *Posse from Hell* (1961) when the film ends.

ing weight in supporting roles, Murphy remained in command, offering a hard-bitten, no-nonsense performance. With his features now taking on the lined, leathery look of the habitual outdoorsman, he had progressed from the deceptive youth with the gentle manners to the mature westerner whose authority in matters of action and survival was never in question. He was no more versatile as an actor, but he now possessed a solidity and confidence that overrode his dramatic limitations.

Although ultimately shot down by its own pretensions, *Posse from Hell*, with its impressive use of the daunting desert and mountain locations at Lone Pine, California, and its atmosphere of continually impending doom, had much to recommend it.

REMEMBRANCES: *Royal Dano:* "On these pictures I would often take my bow and arrow. While others were working, I went over, put a box out there at about 75 yards and I was plunking arrows into it. Murph came over and said, 'I never tried one of those things before, how do you shoot it?' I explained to him he had to anchor in the same place every time so he'd still have the same amount of throw for every arrow. Then you can put your point on whatever you want — use that for an aiming point. He pulled back on it and went a little bit over the box on the first try. He was in line with it, he didn't go off to the side, he went over it. Then he dropped short on the next one. The third arrow was in this box. He just had the kind of coordination that he could learn these things so quickly."

John Saxon: "I remember hearing a story about Audie before I met him. Hugh O'Brian once liked to think he was a fast draw. He was Wyatt Earp on TV. He put out a challenge in Hollywood — $1,000 for whoever could outdraw him. Audie wasn't interested, but O'Brian kept after him until Audie said, 'Okay, let's make it $2,000 and use real bullets!'

"I did two films with Audie. One night he was suffering a bit, he was in between loves with two women ... one was his wife. He asked me if I'd ever been in that kind of situation. He said, 'You ever been in love with two women?' I said, 'No.' But it was something that was really hurting him a great deal."

Producer Gordon Kay had previously produced a series of Allan "Rocky" Lane starrers at Republic. "Audie knew Allan and we used him on one, *Hell Bent for Leather*, then Audie came to me on *Posse*

Audie Murphy (left) is Zohra Lampert's sole comforter after a vicious gang has defiled her in *Posse from Hell*. Her father is played by noted character actor Royal Dano (right).

from Hell and said why don't we use Allan again? I said, 'He was a problem the last time, Audie.' Audie said, 'I didn't have any problems.' I said, 'You didn't, but I did. Allan was pushing the assistant directors around. I didn't like it.' But I agreed, we'd try it once more. And the second time, he crossed Audie. So … I have no idea where Audie knew Allan from. I was perfectly willing to help him, but Allan, God, he came over there like the Queen of the May, wanted to know where his portable dressing room was and, you know, he was playing a nothing, little bitty thing…. I said, Allan, cut it out, you're not at Republic, you're not the star anymore. The director, Herbie Coleman, was a production manager for Hitchcock, and had directed some Hitchcock TV shows. Whether he directed with credit or not, I don't know, and I don't know who agitated the thing about Herbie directing one of Audie's pictures. Seems to me Audie was in on that. Anyhow, there was a thing about having Herb direct a picture. I met with Herb and talked to him. Helluva nice person, lovely guy. He said, 'I'm not being egotistical, but I think I can handle it for you. I would appreciate all the help you can give me.' We went ahead and did *Posse from Hell* with Herb and he did very nicely." (Coleman also directed Audie's *Battle at Bloody Beach* later that year at Fox.)

Now, as to Zohra Lampert, "What a gal! Judas priest! That's one person that absolutely threw Audie for a loop. 'Cause she was this real method actress. She came on and boy, cues meant nothing to Zohra. She'd give you the gist of her lines … and that was about it. Audie had to wait until

Audie Murphy recruits the *Posse from Hell* (left-to-right): Stuart Randall, Rudolph Acosta (behind Randall), Audie, Royal Dano, James Bell (back to camera), Frank Overton, Robert Keith, unknown, John Saxon.

she took a breath before he could get his line in. He was really kind of bewildered by her. She was really something. I got a big kick out of Zohra, but I didn't think I'd better try it too many times. Audie told me, 'She sure is different!'"

Zohra Lampert: "My participation in *Posse from Hell* makes me of some interest. But, frankly, I never quite thought of it as a western, rather merely as another story. John Saxon is a likable fellow whom I barely knew. Audie was a sort of sad fellow whom I knew even less well ... and that was, perhaps, for the best. At least from all the stories I've heard."

Stuntman Whitey Hughes: "They were rehearsing the scene between Audie and my nephew, Billy Hughes, coming into town on the buckboard. As the buckboard pulls in, Billy has a bandage on his eyes and he's supposed to step down off the buckboard. Audie is supposed to help him down. Audie reaches up to take ahold of Billy's arm. Just as Billy let go to come down, Audie just backed off and let him go. Billy was off balance, of course, and he fell right flat on his face. Audie and the whole group, Willard Willingham and the rest, just Ha-Ha'd. They got a big kick out of that. I said, 'I fail to see the comedy in that. That don't strike me as funny.' I mouthed off a bit about it. Audie just stepped out from under Billy instead of helping him down. He just let Billy fall. Bill could have broke an arm or hurt himself and ruined the scene. After I said something, the group just backed off from it. I think it kinda embarrassed Audie after I said that. He probably thought I was Billy's Dad. But I was just babysitting him. He was only 12. I'm sure Audie didn't mean to hurt Billy, but he saw a lot of humor in it."

Rand Brooks: "I not only admired Audie for his service, because you don't do what he did without admiration for the guy, but he wasn't a show-off. I don't think he had the education to be a conversationalist or raconteur but I think he had some basic business instincts. I looked at his films, he had a presence. The camera liked him. And he was easy. Audie didn't know a damn thing about 'acting.' He just naturally had a presence. He put his heart into his lines. I think [James] Cagney must have given him some awful good advice in the beginning. 'Don't worry about height, it doesn't mean a damn thing. Just do that thing and believe what you say.'"

Steve Terrell: "My part was only a day's work. I admired Audie. I thought he was a big star. I was kinda in awe of him because of who he was, but I didn't think he was much of an actor. He didn't seem to be really into it. He was very subdued with whatever he was doing. When I've seen him in other things, he seemed subdued too. But Universal was doing everything they could to make him look good."

NOTES AND COMMENTS: Lee Van Cleef later expressed disdain for *Posse from Hell*, but never elaborated.

Whispering Smith (TV Series)
(NBC, MAY 29, 1961)

CREDITS: *Executive Producer:* Dick Lewis; *Producer:* Joseph Hoffman; *Director:* Christian Nyby; *Assistant Director:* Willard Shelton; *Story:* Borden Chase, Harold Swanton; *Teleplay:* Harold Swanton; *Editor:* Budd Small; *Editorial Supervisor:* Richard G. Wray; *Director of Photography:* Bud Thackery; *Art Director:* George

Patrick; *Set Director:* Perry Murdock; *Costume Supervisor:* Vincent Dee; *Makeup:* Jack Barron; *Sound Recording:* Melvin M. Metcalf Sr.; *Hair Stylist:* Florence Bush; *Music:* Gerald Fried; *Musical Supervisor:* Stanley Wilson.

CAST: Audie Murphy (Tom "Whispering" Smith); Guy Mitchell (George Romack); Sam Buffington (Chief John Richards); Joyce Taylor (Edie Romack); Richard Devon (Duggan); John Cliff (Mike Garrity); Lyn Thomas (Laura); Billy McLean (Corky — Bartender); Bob Hoy (Fallon); Troy Melton, Bill Catching (Outlaws); Hal Needham (Barney Hennessey). Stuntmen: Joe Yrigoyen, Jack Connors, Hal Needham, Bill Catching, Bob Hoy, Troy Melton.

RUNNING TIME: 26 minutes.

FILMING DATES: Summer 1959

LOCATION: Universal/Revue backlot, in particular Denver Street.

BUDGET/COST: Approximately $45,000

Unfortunately, "Stakeout" is the only episode of Audie's short-lived TV series, *Whispering Smith*, available for viewing today. Nothing went right from the get-go with the series. Murphy, hoping to transfer his western screen image onto the small screen, went into production for Revue with *Whispering Smith* (loosely based on the Alan Ladd film) in June, July and August of 1959 on the Universal backlot. The first episode didn't air until nearly two years later! The series was being produced by Revue, the TV arm of MCA, the giant talent agency that had purchased Universal. In a five-day week, two episodes were filmed. Each episode shot two days on sound stages and a half day on the backlot's Denver Street. Calling it "Dragnet on horseback," Murphy told *TV Guide*, "When they said this series could be made cheap my immediate reaction was that we wouldn't make it cheap at all. I fought with them constantly [over scripts, budgets, directors, etc.]." Headaches arose at every turn. Three different producers worked on the show. Costs (initially $45,000 per episode) soared. Even Audie's horse, Joe Queen, was a problem — he was so fast he outran all the other mounts. Finally, Audie was forced to use a double horse. The beleaguered show hit another snag after filming seven episodes when co-star Guy Mitchell (as Audie's partner George Romack) broke his shoulder in a horsefall stunt, halting production for six weeks. Then actor Sam Buffington, who played Chief John Richards, Audie's superior in the series, committed suicide. "I guess he must have seen the rushes," Audie sarcastically remarked. After eight episodes had been produced under Joseph Hoffman, Alan "Pinky" Miller, president of Revue Productions, called in Herbert Coleman, who had first worked as an assistant director with Audie on *Beyond Glory*. Miller explained to Coleman how Audie was unhappy with the episodes thus far produced, and offered Coleman a contract to save the eight programs via rewrites and retakes, and a separate contract as producer/director/writer — whatever it took — for another fifteen episodes, with a total of 23 to be produced. At Audie's suggestion, Coleman brought in Willard Willingham to help with the scripts. Different directors including Coleman himself, helmed each episode.

While this production set-up was being put in place, Audie made *Hell Bent for Leather* in August and September of 1959.

Production on *Whispering Smith* resumed in late 1959. In his book *The Hollywood I Knew*, Coleman explained that the executives at Revue "were satisfied with the shows I was turning out. But unexpected trouble was soon to be upon us. The Writers Guild of America called a strike. Of the twenty-three shows we were to deliver to the network, sixteen were completed. I had three scripts ready to go before the cameras, and guild writers were at work on the final four but were forbidden to continue to work for us. The studio offered to provide non-union writers to complete the work on the four. Audie agreed we should

Whispering Smith (TV Series)

Audie Murphy filmed TV episodes of *Whispering Smith* in 1959, but they didn't air until 1961.

produce the three and postpone the final four until the strike was over. I told Pinky of our decision. 'You'll have to select someone to produce those three,' Pinky said, 'We have something else for you. The Writers Guild has approved an independent company, J&M Productions, to produce a series, *Checkmate*, here at Universal, using the members of their guild.' I turned the final three *Whispering Smith* shows over to Willard Willingham. He would produce them, and I would supervise his work."

The series, about the exploits of 1870s Denver police detective Tom "Whispering" Smith, usually called Smitty, finally was scheduled to debut (when an ill-fated *Acapulco* was scrapped) on Monday, May 8, 1961. "It's like the Redstone rocket — obsolete, but they're going to fire it anyway," Audie joked.

Misfortune struck again as the premiere episode was preempted for an NBC special on astronaut Allan Shepard. The first episode of *Whispering Smith* aired on May 15, 1961. Episodes produced by Coleman were interspersed with some of the eight Hoffman turned out.

Again speaking to *TV Guide*, Murphy said if the series was a success he was "hooked to go back. I'm not really looking forward to its being a smashing success either. My contract is firm for something like 86 episodes. I just don't think I could stand that." Murphy got his wish. The show debuted to critical dismissal, earned poor ratings (opposite proven ratings winners *Surfside 6* and *The Danny Thomas Show*) and was even lambasted by the Senate Juvenile Delinquency Subcommittee in Washington. Sen. John Carroll (D) of Colorado said the show was "not only bad for children, it's bad for adults." The statement completely soured Audie on television, who retorted, "My feeling is [the show] had an extremely high moral value, which has been overlooked. The story was about a policeman who was willing to risk his life [for law and order] and avoided violence for violence's sake. In a half-hour TV show, the bad must be established fast and with impact or the entire show would dwell on this subject. Unfortunately, I have learned that a half-hour TV program cannot present drama at its best." Only 20 episodes aired through September 18, 1961, before the show was cancelled due to its violent content and low ratings, and replaced by *87th Precinct*. The violence NBC and the Senate Subcommittee worried about in 1961 pales by today's savage, profane standards. We'd all be better off with Audie's morals back on TV.

Audie estimated *Whispering Smith* cost him $250,000 in income, figuring the time he lost and offers he had to turn down while waiting to see if the series would be sold.

The following is a TVography of the 20 *Whispering Smith* episodes that aired and the *known* information about them:

Blind Gun. (5/8/61) (Scheduled but preempted; shown later.) *Director:* Pete Lyons; *Screenplay:* Tom Seller. Bandit Thad Janeck, sightless as the result of a gunfight in which he was captured, agrees to turn over his booty in exchange for reward money, which he intends to spend for an operation on his eyes. CAST: Jan Merlin (Thad Janeck); Robert Osterloh (Ben Avery); Earl Hansen; Carol Byron (Mary); Herbert Lytton (Henderson); Harry Strang (Jake).

The Grudge. (5/15/61) *Director:* Herb Coleman. Revenge has a long memory, as Smith seems destined to learn when Ma Gates, widow of an outlaw he once brought to justice, arrives in town with a plan to kill him. To this end, Ma enlists her trigger-happy son Johnny and her daughter Cora in the plan, with Cora as the bait for her lethal trap. CAST: Robert Redford (Johnny Gates); June Walker (Ma Gates); Gloria Talbott (Cora Gates).

The Devil's Share. (5/22/61) Frank Whalen has just proposed to Marjanne Gaul, a gesture which nettles his brother Jeff, a one-time suitor of Marjanne's. Jeff, in fact, works himself up into such a state that he kills his brother. CAST: Clu Gulager (Jeff Whalen); Rosemary Day (Marjanne Gaul); James Lydon (Frank Whalen); Otto Waldis; Kathie Browne.

Stakeout. (5/29/61) (See above for credits and cast.) Detective Romack is approached by a pair of old friends, outlaws Garrity and Duggan. They remind him that he was once a member of their gang, and if he wants to keep that little secret from his present employer, he had better play along on a robbery they have lined up.

Safety Valve. (6/5/61) Several Army officers were shot in the back during skirmishes with the Indians, but there were no Indians behind them, only their own men. CAST: Della Sharman; Harry Carey Jr.; Les Tremayne.

Stain of Justice. (6/12/61) Judge Wilbur Harrington puts an end to Stella Dean's blackmailing—permanently. But shortly after he leaves Stella's house, his son Chris comes calling, and when Smith arrives there, it is Chris holding the murder weapon. CAST: Richard Chamberlain (Chris Harrington); Patric Knowles (Judge Wilbur Harrington); Nancy Valentine (Stella Dean).

The Deadliest Weapon. (6/19/61) Businessman Ralph Miller gets an unexpected reaction to his announcement that he is issuing some gold-mine stock—a death threat. Smith and Romack get the job of determining who would profit from Miller's death. CAST: Aline Towne; Paul Lees (Ralph Miller); Bartlett Robinson; Don Keefer.

The Quest. (6/26/61) Charlotte Laughlin comes to Denver searching for her mother. The missing matron was quite well known at one time as a dance hall singer. CAST: Ellen Willard (Charlotte Laughlin); John Harmon (Jackie Rouge); Kay Stewart.

Three for One. (7/3/61) Denver City prisoner Ralph Malone is placed in the custody of two deputies named Lucas and Carter, who supposedly take him back to Phoenix for trial. Then a telegram arrives saying the two men were imposters. CAST: Richard Crane (Ralph Malone); Ken Mayer (Lucas); Roscoe Ates; Pamela Duncan; K. L. Smith (Carter); Tom P. Dillon; Claire Meade.

Death at Even Money. (7/10/61) Gambler Frankie Wisdom can't seem to win at ordinary games of chance with Dave Markson, so he proposes a unique wager. He bets Markson can't prevent him from causing Smith's death. CAST: Marc Lawrence (Dave Markston); Robert Lowery (Frankie Wisdom); John Day; Sandy Sanders; Sherwood Price; Herbert C. Lytton.

Hemp Reeger Case. (7/17/61) Smith finally gets outlaw Hemp Reeger locked up in Sheriff Aiken's jail. But Aiken doesn't

Audie Murphy rode his own quarter horse, Joe Queen, in his *Whispering Smith* TV series.

like Smith, and it would please him to no end if he could help Reeger escape. CAST: James Best (Hemp Reeger); Patricia Medina; Edward C. Platt (Sheriff Aiken); John Craven.

The Mortal Coil. (7/24/61) Smith, positive Claude Denton murdered his twin brother Rex, decides to use an amateur production of *Hamlet* as a means to trap the killer. CAST: Henry Brandon (Claude Denton); Hugh Sanders.

Cross Cut. (7/31/61) Smith thinks of April as a sweet young thing spellbound by the charms of an outlaw called Dakota. But April's ambition is to get Dakota and Smith to kill each other in a fight, so she can run off with Dakota's loot. CAST: Audrey Dalton (April); Colin Male (Dakota); Jim Hayward.

Double Edge. (8/7/61) Venetia Molloy and bandit Jim Conley fall madly in love. There is only one thing that might mar their happiness—Venetia's husband. CAST: Myron Healey (Jim Conley); Lori Nelson (Venetia Molloy); Red Morgan.

The Trademark. (8/14/61) When a widow, Maple Gray, offers a large sum of money for revenge on the six men who lynched her husband, ex-convict Fred Gavin sets out to collect it. But what he forgets is that murder makes news, and a newspaper has recorded his trademark. CAST: Marie Windsor (Maple Gray); Forrest Tucker (Fred Gavin); Donald Buka; Andrew Winberg.

The Jodie Tyler Story. (8/21/61) A grocery store owner is murdered and robbed of a large sum of money by Hob Tyler, a notorious gunman. When his sister Jodie pays exactly the same amount to buy the dead man's store, the local citizens become suspicious. CAST: Rachel Foulger (Jodie Tyler); Read Morgan (Hob Tyler); Jimmy Carter.

Poet and Peasant Case. (8/28/61) Lord Hillary, a famous English poet touring America, is robbed and his stagecoach driver murdered. Another Englishman, Carruthers, comes under suspicion. The two men had met previously in a Denver bar, and it was obvious they didn't hit it off. CAST: Alan Mowbray (Lord Hillary); Jack Catron (Carruthers); Yvonne Adrian; Paul Keast; Dean Williams.

Dark Circle. (9/4/61) A lawyer named Philo likes to drink, but he hates Fender, the local saloonkeeper. When Fender is killed, it looks as if Philo had something to do with it, even though the lawyer claims he was dead drunk at the time. CAST: E. J. Andre (Philo); Carleton Young (Fender); Adam Williams.

Swift Justice. (9/11/61) The MacDonalds and the Campbells, always feuding, decide the way to settle which clan is best is to arrange a horse race. The whole town bets on the outcome, but there is something they don't bargain on. When a Campbell steed takes the lead, the rider is shot. CAST: Monte Burkhart; Minerva Urecal; William Tannen.

The Idol. (9/18/61) Ole Brindessen sees swindler Edie Royce commit murder, but refuses to go to the police. His reason is that Ole's girlfriend, Marilyn, is in love with Royce. CAST: Joan O'Brien (Marilyn); Alan Hale Jr. (Ole Brindessen); John Stephenson (Edie Royce); Larry Perron; Marjorie Reynolds.

REMEMBRANCES: *Harry Carey Jr.:* "Audie was really easy to work with. He was self-critical of his acting. He used to put himself down as an actor, he was very modest about it. I didn't think he was as bad as he thought he was. I thought he had kind of a nice quality, actually. The camera loves some people, and it was that way with Audie. When I did *Whispering Smith:* "Safety Valve," I played a nasty sergeant. A really wonderful guy, the singer Guy Mitchell, about the nicest fella I've ever met in my life, was playing Audie's sidekick. I had a fistfight with Guy in this episode. Bobby Herron and Lenny Geer staged this fight, they did the long shot. Then Guy Mitchell said with his glasses off he was blind. But we put on a hell of a fight! The stuntmen said, 'Hell, they don't need us. They're just as good as we were.'

"Audie was most concerned about how I liked his horses. He was very proud of his quarter horses. He knew I'd been around horses. He had Joe Queen. That Queen bunch, there's a sire that was very famous with those Queen horses.

"I learned years later Audie had a problem with gambling. He sure wasn't a drinker. But he was a nice guy to work with. He had a reputation among stunt guys. They said, 'Don't fool with him because he can kill ya.' He had a menace about him. It wasn't frightening but you could see it. A lot of hidden fury."

Bill Catching: "I did some *Whispering Smith* with Audie and the singer, Guy Mitchell — what a funny guy he was! In "Stakeout" John Cliff was the heavy. Joe Yrigoyen was doubling Cliff, and Jack Connors was doubling Guy Mitchell. Chris Nyby was the director. There was a bulldog to be done, one was going north to south and the other, coming east to west, was coming blind into him. Neither one of 'em knew who he was gonna work with 'til they got to work. And they didn't like each other. Nyby explained what he wanted. Yrigoyen for Cliff has his hands tied with ropes in the front, he's escaping. Connors

Singer Guy Mitchell played George Romack, Audie Murphy's partner in **Whispering Smith.**

for Mitchell rode in to cut him off, and when they met, Connors dove in the air and he looped Yrigoyen around the neck with his left arm and jerked him backwards off the horse, and it was the damnedest wreck you ever saw. The horse backed up, didn't step on Joe, stepped over him. When Joe got up, he was mad! [Laughs] We thought there was gonna be a fight, but Nyby got in and stopped it. Audie said that's the wildest bulldog I've ever seen in my life. Now comes Guy Mitchell and John Cliff to do their close-up. Chris says to Guy, 'You saw what they did?' Guy says, 'Yeah, I really liked that.' Chris says, 'Cliff is gonna ride his horse forward, you come running in, with the camera right on you, raise up in the saddle and throw both arms up in the air like you're coming at him.' Well, Nyby didn't tell Guy not to jump! Now Cliff has the real handcuffs on in the real close-up instead of loosely tied. Guy rides into the shot, stood up, dove in the air and did the exact same thing that Connors had done. Looped Cliff around the neck, jerked him backwards off the horse and it duplicated what the stunt guys had done, except the horse didn't step over Cliff, it stepped on him! Audie says, 'I want a copy of that film!' It was the only time I saw him get kinda joking and laughing."

In their book *Feature Players, Vol. 2*, Tom and Jim Goldrup interviewed Richard Devon. They wrote, "Richard did an episode of *Whispering Smith*: "Stakeout," with Audie Murphy and Guy Mitchell. He told us Mitchell was a nice fellow, but Murphy 'was spooky to be around. At the commissary we would sit around the counter and have breakfast in the morning. I was eating and reading *Variety*, and I'm bumped. I said, "Hey, watch it." I look up and here's Murphy reaching over the counter. He gave me a look like you wouldn't believe; the eyes were like totally dead, like he could kill me in a second and it would mean absolutely nothing. That was my introduction to Audie Murphy and now we're going to work on this show together. To begin with, I wasn't too thrilled with him so you get into areas where you do a little deviltry every now and then, something you can slip in and hopefully get away with." In a scene to be filmed that day, Devon and his gang are holed up in a church. He is at the door, opens it a crack, fires his gun and closes it. Murphy is supposed to ride in, jump off and crash into the door, knocking Devon out of the way. They get ready to shoot the scene, they do their business, and when Richard closes the door he deliberately leans against it. 'They told me afterwards Audie came running up and hit the door and popped like a ping pong ball off to the ground. That made him even more furious, so I said, "Gee, I don't understand; the door must have stuck or something." So, you do little things.'"

Bobby Hoy: "I did *Whispering Smith*: "Stakeout" and they never paid me the stunt money, or the combined overtime. I did a hell of a stair fall, wooden steps. Somebody says, 'Hey Bobby, they wanna see you in the production office.' I walked in and there were the three heads of production. They said, 'You held up production.' I said, 'No I didn't! Your first assistant was gone, I went to your second assistant and I asked for an adjustment. He said I can't make a deal.' You make a deal before, not after you do a stunt, especially with Revue in those days! So these guys started naming stuntmen who worked for the cheap money, whatever they pay for the day and they do three, four stunts. I said, 'Hold it. The first guy you mentioned, I know why he's doing it. His mother's in a wheelchair.' Which was a lie. 'The second guy, his son has had a tremendous accident.' Which was all bullshit. 'So they have to do it, I don't.' I said I'm going to labor relations, which means they'd put a seal on the film. I went to Audie, 'What the hell's going on here, Murph? You own a piece of the company?' He said, 'Yeah.' I said, 'Call your money people, they never paid me.' He was there the day I did that fall. He said, 'Bullshit!' The next day I got the money. But I got blackballed for a long time at Universal. Getting the job isn't tough, doing the stunt isn't tough, but getting the money you gotta act like you're Frank James in for Jesse! [Laughs]"

Myron Healey: "Audie was a living, walking hero and a very modest man. He *never* talked about it. One day in the San Fernando Valley he got pulled over by the cops, somebody called and said this guy's carrying guns in his car. So the police pulled him over. 'You got some guns?' He said, 'Sure I have guns.' Audie opened the trunk of his car for them and this guy damn near fell over — it was an armory! He had everything in there. The police said, 'Well, Mr. Murphy, we're gonna have to confiscate this and take you in for questioning.' Audie said, 'Why?' Police said, 'This is illegal. You can't carry guns like that.' Audie said, 'I'm a holder of the Medal of Honor. You wanna question that?' And they backed off. He was a hell of a guy."

Stuntman Dean Smith: "I did some of the *Whispering Smith* episodes. Audie and I talked about Texas a lot. One day I was at [Hollywood tailor] Nudie's and Audie had a pair of Ostrich boots there. I said, 'Boy, I sure like those boots.' And he gave 'em to me. Just said, 'Here.' He just gave me a pair of these really fine orange Ostrich boots. Audie was a nice guy … unfortunately, he went before his time."

Stuntman Walt LaRue: "I remember one time, over at Universal, one of the producers or somebody came out on the set. Audie was up against four or five guys on the street, shooting 'em up. This producer said to the director, 'Jesus Christ, how can this baby face kid … don't you think this is wrong … shooting five guys for Chrissake! How can that look real?' The director says, 'When Audie was in Germany he shot … I forgot how many and brought in a whole bunch of Germans all by himself.' That kinda shut this guy up."

Jan Merlin: "I played basically the same role in *Whispering Smith* as I'd played in *Hell Bent for Leather*. Came out of the desert, hit him with his own gun, rode away. It was the pilot film [Blind Gun]. It was kinda fun … playing the same basic role. I went to Western Costume and they asked what I wanted to wear. I said, 'Give me the same thing I had before.' I wore the same clothes. [Laughs]"

Marc Lawrence: "The camera chooses what it likes or dislikes. In Murphy there were too many hidden qualities that rarely surfaced. The camera failed to give him the dignity he commanded in real life."

NOTES AND COMMENTS: Audie guested on NBC's daytime half-hour celebrity interview show *Here's Hollywood* on May 29, 1961, to promote his new TV series *Whispering Smith*. Dean Miller and Jo-Ann Jordan were co-hosts.

Battle at Bloody Beach

(20TH CENTURY–FOX, JUNE 1961)

CREDITS: *Producer:* Richard Maibaum; *Director:* Herbert Coleman; *Assistant Director:* Francisco Day; *Story:* Richard Maibaum; *Screenplay:* Richard Maibaum, Willard Willingham; *Editor:* Jodie Copelan; *Director of Photography:* Kenneth Peach; *Art Director:* John Mansbridge; *Set Decorator:* Harry Reif; *Wardrobe:* Robert Olivas; *Makeup:* Vincent Romaine; *Sound Recording:* Frank McWhorter; *Sound Editor:* Jack Cornall; *Production Supervisor:* Harold E. Knox; *Music:* Henry Vars. CinemaScope.

CAST: Audie Murphy (Craig Benson);

Audie Murphy in action during the *Battle at Bloody Beach* (1961).

Gary Crosby (Marty Sackler); Dolores Michaels (Ruth Benson); Alejandro Rey (Julio Fontana); Marjorie Stapp (Caroline Pelham); Barry Atwater (Jeff Pelham); E. J. Andre (Dr. Van Bart); Dale Ishimoto (Blanco); Miriam Colon (Nahni); Pilar Seurat (Camota); Lillian Bronson (Delia Ellis); William Mims (McKeever); Ivan Dixon (Tiger Blair); Kevin Brodie (Timmy Thompson); Sara Anderson (Mrs. Thompson); Lloyd Kino (Japanese lieutenant).

RUNNING TIME: 83 minutes

FILMING DATES: January 16, 1961–February 15, 1961

LOCATIONS: Catalina Island, California, and Isthmus of Catalina.

A number of newspaper reports on Murphy's death in 1971 described him as having starred in low-budget westerns and war films. In fact, Murphy made only three war films—*The Red Badge of Courage, To Hell and Back* and *Battle at Bloody Beach*. Possibly the writers concerned were confusing the movie star with the war hero, or more probably they had only heard of one Murphy film, *To Hell and Back*, and drew the conclusion that a war hero would make war movies. Murphy's reluctance to do war films is understandable — he had lived through the real thing, and his studio had difficulty persuading him to film his own biography.

He would have been wise to have backed away from *Beach* as well, and stayed away, since the result was far below the standard he had set with *Hell*, and even his best westerns, and was cruelly revealing in its heightening of his restricted acting range and aging features.

Set during the Japanese occupation of the Philippines in World War II, it had Murphy as a former businessman working

Gary Crosby, Dolores Michaels and Audie Murphy mourn a fallen comrade in *Battle at Bloody Beach*.

with guerrilla fighters and looking for his missing wife. When he finds her, he discovers she is the mistress of a guerrilla leader, but eventually wins her back. Filmed in black-and-white on location at Catalina Island, 26 miles off the California coast, it was generally dull going, apart from the noisy battle scenes. Although Murphy displayed his usual competence in action, he was uncomfortable in the romantic interludes and received little boost from an uninspired supporting cast.

REMEMBRANCES: *Marjorie Stapp:* "I twisted my ankle once — Audie was near and caught me before I hit the ground. He always asked how the ankle was. It was a very nice relationship. I don't understand the stories you hear about Audie Murphy."

NOTES AND COMMENTS: Amusingly, the film underwent a title change for its British and Australian release. In both countries, where the word "bloody" is a swearword more than a descriptive one, it became *Battle on the Beach*.

Producer and screenwriter Richard Maibaum became the chief writer for the James Bond films in the years to follow (*Dr. No, From Russia with Love, Goldfinger, Thunderball,* etc.).

In April 1961 Audie announced plans to film *The Way Back*, a continuation of his life after World War II. The production never came to fruition.

6 Black Horses
(UNIVERSAL-INTERNATIONAL, JUNE 1962)

CREDITS: *Producer:* Gordon Kay; *Executive Producer:* Edward Muhl; *Director:* Harry Keller; *Assistant Director:* Ivan Volkman; *Screenplay:* Burt Kennedy; *Editor:* Aaron Stell; *Director of Photography:* Maury Gertsman; *Art Directors:* Alexander Golitzen, Robert Luthardt; *Set Decorator:* Oliver Emert; *Makeup:* Bud Westmore; *Sound Recording:* Waldon O. Watson, Frank H. Wilkinson; *Hair Stylist:* Larry Germain; *Music Supervisor:* Joseph Gershenson. Eastman Color by Pathé.

CAST: Audie Murphy (Ben Lane); Dan Duryea (Frank Jesse); Joan O'Brien (Miss Kelly); George Wallace (Will Boone); Roy Barcroft (Head mustanger); Bob Steele (Joe); Henry Wills (Coyotero leader); Phil Chambers (Undertaker); Charlita Regis (Mexican girl); Dale Van Sickel (Kelly's hired gun); Richard Pasko (Charlie); Bill Catching (Man at dog fight). Stunts: Jimmy Sheppard, Bobby Herron, Dale Van Sickel, Richard Farnsworth, Bill Catching, Henry Wills, Dave Sharpe.

RUNNING TIME: 80 minutes

FILMING DATES: August 10, 1961–September 5, 1961

LOCATIONS: St. George, Utah area; Snow Canyon, Leeds, Utah; Red Rock Canyon, west of Las Vegas, Nevada; Universal backlot, California.

BUDGET/COST: Approximately $500,000

Canadian-born producer Gordon Kay, whose association with Audie Murphy had begun with *Hell Bent for Leather* and would continue through Audie's final Universal western, put together a strong team of professionals for *6 Black Horses*. The screenplay was by Burt Kennedy, a proven talent through his association with Randolph Scott and Budd Boetticher, and the director was again Harry Keller, who had proved so successful with *Seven Ways from Sundown*. The result, though less appealing than *Sundown*, was nonetheless quite pleasing, with Murphy in good, laconic form, and teamed to good effect with Dan Duryea and singer-actress Joan O'Brien. Duryea's familiar variation on his Waco Johnny/Whitey Kincaid/Whitey Harbin character had by now grown somewhat stale, with the actor tending to overplay at times, but it still proved fairly entertaining and provided the usual contrast to Murphy's more sober treatment. O'Brien, possessed of more abundant physical charms than most Murphy heroines, was decorative without making any particular impact, and minor characters became virtual set dressing in what was essentially a three-actor movie.

Murphy played a wandering cowboy rescued from a lynch mob by the morally ambivalent Duryea. O'Brien subsequently hires both men to transport her across hostile Indian country to join her husband. En route, she tries to kill Duryea, revealing that he is actually her husband's killer. In the final showdown, Murphy reluctantly kills Duryea, and later honors the dead man's wish to have a fancy funeral with *6 Black Horses* pulling the hearse.

The sparse population and thin story line gave the film a somewhat insubstantial feeling, and Burt Kennedy's script, though intelligent and intriguing in its dialogue exchanges, showed similarities to his Randolph Scott work. In fact, one whole sequence, in which a group of Indians try to buy O'Brien, was a direct copy of a similar scene in Scott's *Ride Lonesome* (1959). Kennedy also reused his famous line from Scott's *Tall T* (1957): "Some things a man can't ride around."

Brisk outbursts of action periodically brightened the plodding pace, which made for a stop-start form, but the harsh locations, in the vicinity of St. George, Utah,

Joan O'Brien hires Dan Duryea (left) and Audie Murphy to escort her across hostile Indian territory in *6 Black Horses* (1962).

and Red Rock Canyon, Nevada, provided a spectacular background, and the Eastman Color, though not as crisp as the Technicolor of Murphy's early westerns, produced some interesting effects.

Less pretentious in its aims than *Posse from Hell*, and consequently more successful in achieving them, *6 Black Horses* became an undemanding, easy-to-watch little effort while remaining somewhat flat overall.

Remembrances: *George Wallace* told interviewer Robert Nott: "Audie Murphy was really something. You'd look at this guy who wasn't very big and he had this piercing look in his eye. You'd look at him and say, 'This guy killed 150-some odd Germans all by himself?' It just seemed hard to believe, that his demeanor and his look would warrant that somehow, but he did. You didn't dare knock on his door after he went to sleep until early morning because you didn't know what was gonna come back through the door—it could have been a bullet. If you knocked on his door, you stood to the side.

"He had a funny way of getting acquainted with you because he wasn't an outgoing type of kid—he looked like a kid. When he wanted to get to know me, he came over with a piece of thin rope, like a piece of clothesline, and he always had it with him; he was always tying knots, and he'd look down at that piece of rope and say, 'George? That scene we just rehearsed ... are you going to do it that way during the take?' I'd say, 'Yeah, I guess so, why?' He'd say, 'Nothing, just wanted to know.' He never looked up at me. This was his way of getting acquainted. But he was

Audie Murphy and Dan Duryea await an Indian attack on the desert.

putting me on. Onlookers noticed his face was chortled up with laughter. It was just his way — a strange way — of doing things.

"Audie wasn't an actor. He played himself. I got the feeling he didn't enjoy acting. He was the opposite of Dan Duryea, who I also worked with on *6 Black Horses*. We became the closest of friends; he was a sweetheart of a guy. A wonderful smile and glittering eyes all the time. Dan would just open up, but Audie wouldn't open up. He'd just say 'Yeah' or 'No' or shake his head.

"We were on location and there were Indian reservations up there and [producer Gordon Kay] hired a lot of local Indians for atmosphere, then they had to send back to Hollywood for Hollywood Indians because the Indians they hired couldn't ride horses. They kept falling off bareback. They were fat and out of shape."

Regarding Hollywood's drastic reduction of western films at about this time, Audie stated, "I guess all those westerns on television killed the market. I seem to be the only one left. I'll keep making them until they get wise to me."

Bill Catching: "Audie was a nice guy, very quiet, very reserved while he was working. Very professional on the set. At night he'd go party with ya, have a few drinks, play cards, but he wouldn't stay long. But in the daytime he was all business. He and Willard Willingham were best friends. I played poker with them on a couple of sets.

"The best double Audie had was Jimmy Sheppard. Audie really liked him, and Shep was a good double for Audie. Earlier, Willard was more of a photo-double. Jimmy was a stuntman's stuntman."

NOTES AND COMMENTS: *6 Black Horses* was the only Murphy film adapted into comic book form. Dell issued *6 Black Horses* under their Movie Classics line in late 1962. The basic story was faithfully retold, but lacked the nuances of Kennedy's script. The cover and inside front cover featured several scenes from the film.

Audie Murphy and leading lady Joan O'Brien in *Six Black Horses*.

Showdown
(UNIVERSAL-INTERNATIONAL, MAY 1963)

CREDITS: *Producer:* Gordon Kay; *Executive Producer:* Edward Muhl; *Assistant to Producer:* Willard Willingham; *Director:* R. G. Springsteen; *Assistant Director:* Terence Nelson; *Screenplay:* Bronson Howitzer; *Editor:* Jerome Thomas; *Director of Photography:* Ellis W. Carter; *Art Directors:* Alexander Golitzen, Alfred Sweeney; *Set Decorator:* Oliver Carter; *Costume Designer:* Rosemary Odell; *Makeup:* Bud Westmore; *Sound Recording:* Waldon O. Watson, Frank H. Wilkinson; *Hair Stylist:* Larry Germain; *Music:* Hans J. Salter; *Music Supervision:* Joseph Gershenson.

CAST: Audie Murphy (Chris Foster); Charles Drake (Bert Pickett); Kathleen Crowley (Estelle); Harold J. Stone (Lavalle); Skip Homeier (Caslon); L. Q. Jones (Foray); Strother Martin (Charlie Reeder); Charles Horvath (Hebron); John McKee (Marshal Beaudine); Henry Wills (Chaca); Joe Haworth (Guard); Kevin Brodie (Buster); Carol Thurston (Blacksmith's wife); Dabbs Greer (Express man); William Phipps (Deputy Lloyd); Bob Steele (Poker player); Harry Lauter (Bartender); Bill Henry (Saloon patron); Dale Van Sickel (Bouncer); Norman Leavitt (Feed and grain store operator). Stuntmen: Jimmy Sheppard, Henry Wills, Charles Horvath.

RUNNING TIME: 79 minutes
FILMING DATES: Early September 1962–September 25, 1962
LOCATIONS: Lone Pine, California.
BUDGET/COST: $250,000–$300,000

Murphy's final teaming with Charles Drake fell far below the standard of their earlier screen partnerships, due mainly to the dull direction of R. G. Springsteen and the lack of color, which combined to waste the potential of an offbeat idea. Murphy and Drake played a pair of wandering cowboys mistakenly imprisoned with an outlaw gang and forced to join them in an escape. Drake attempts to buy their freedom

Showdown

Audie Murphy slugs badman Harold J. Stone while both are chained to the "Iron Maypole" prison in a staged publicity shot not actually seen in *Showdown* (1963).

with some stolen securities, but double-crosses the gang by giving the money to his girlfriend. Murphy recovers the money, learning Drake has treated the girl very badly, and ultimately destroys the outlaw gang after Drake has sacrificed his life.

The film's offbeat quality was emphasized by the use of the little-known, but historically accurate, "Iron Maypole" prison—a pole stuck in the ground to which prisoners were chained by iron collars (the film's original title was to have been *Iron Collar*). The casting of powerful actor Harold J. Stone, better known for his tough roles in contemporary dramas, gave it another dimension, but again the potential was wasted, and the characters remained superficial and undefined. Charles Drake, reverting to the moral weakling he had played in such early Universal films as *Winchester 73*, was suitably craven, and Murphy projected a gritty toughness that suited the rugged locations, but neither actor was able to rise above the flatness of the direction and the convoluted plot.

Springsteen, competent but unimaginative, had made many westerns for Republic, with stars like Allan Lane and Monte Hale, and *Showdown* was not really any great improvement on these low-budget quickies. By now Murphy was beginning to show his age, with a noticeable thickening of waist and jawline, but if he was less graceful physically, he still had a natural affinity with the outdoors that carried him through the action sequences with conviction.

REMEMBRANCES: Producer Gordon Kay on why *Showdown* was in black and white when Audie's westerns at U-I had previ-

Audie Murphy and Charles Drake, who got along famously, made several films together, but *Showdown* proved to be their last pairing.

ously all been in color: "The sales department said, let's try black and white. They pulled it like a rabbit out of a hat. Just a thing to see how they'd make out with black and white. I thought it was a terrible mistake. As a matter of fact, the gross on that picture is not appreciably less than the others. But it's a little less, so we did agree the savings weren't all that great, and went back to color. Oh, God, I had an explosion out of Murphy over the lack of color. He was going to quit, leave and go home. He wasn't going to make it. I said, 'Audie, you'd better think twice. Walk off this set, you're going right into suspension. You're not going to like that. In the meantime, call your agent, call your lawyer.' [Laughs] I calmed him down. His lawyer, Mark ... I can't think of his name, was a very intelligent guy. We used to deal together. He tried to get me to persuade Audie to take a percentage, which Audie wouldn't do. It's insane, 'cause he didn't have any money. I told him he wasn't going to get as much. 'You're going to have to take a cut in salary, Audie, but by God, you'll be getting the money forever.' About the third picture, I'd already gotten my first check on *my* percentage. I showed it to him. He said, 'I don't believe it.' I said, 'Dammit, it's a check, it's there, it says what it is.' 'No,' he said, 'I don't want to do that.' He just had to have cash. Cash, cash, cash." [Earlier Kay set up a profit sharing arrangement with Universal, from whom he receives royalties on his pictures to this day.] Suggesting to Kay Audie wanted cash because of his gambling obsession, Kay replied, "Exactly right!"

As to whether Audie had conflicts with his co-stars, such as Stephen McNally, Barry Sullivan, John Saxon, Dan Duryea or others, Kay said, "Dan got along with everybody. Audie liked Dan very much. No, he was very easy to get along with. I mean, the ones you've all mentioned, they were professional. They didn't have to have a brick wall fall on them to realize they had an erratic person here."

As to who primarily doubled Audie, Kay explained, "At the very beginning it was Willard Willingham. Will wanted to write, so I used him to do polish at first [*Posse from Hell, Showdown*]. Gradually, he and his wife, Mary, were writing. Then I had them do a rewrite [*Bullet for a Badman*, from a novel] and finally had them do the whole thing from scratch (*Gunpoint*). Then I told Will, you've either got to be a writer or a double, 'cause he was trying to do both and you shouldn't, just for your own reputation. He agreed, and Jimmy Sheppard took over. Jimmy was a stand-in for Audie, then took over as double. Willard and Mary, very nice people, I was very fond of them. Will was a big help because he had worked with Audie quite a lot. He'd keep whispering in my ear.... 'Don't let this throw you, but...' [Laughs]

"In 1963 Audie started making films at Allied Artists, Columbia and other studios ... at much less salary. It wasn't a question of getting so much less. He was getting so hungry for money he was grabbing all these deals paying him not quite as much as we were. The worst part of it was, they were leaning all over our pictures from the standpoint of action. They were making these sort of stagnant westerns. The theater owner isn't going to look to see if it's a Universal or is it a Columbia or whatever.

Audie Murphy tries to understand why Kathleen Crowley took his friend's money in *Showdown*.

It's an Audie Murphy western. I was upset because I knew damn well what they were doing out there. I knew it was going to kill us. I told Audie, 'You're putting yourself right out of this business.' He said, no, no, no. I said, yes, yes, yes! We went ahead, made the last one, *Gunpoint*. I told Universal, 'I don't think you're going to see any profits,' but I'm happy to say it finally made some profits."

L. Q. Jones: "Audie was like Elvis Presley, who I worked with several times. They would always tear up just working with you, trying to figure out how to do this, how can I help that scene, what can I do over here.... But they didn't always give Audie a chance. Audie was his own man. He had certain scruples, he had his own ideas about what Audie Murphy should be, and he stuck to them."

Harold J. Stone: "Murphy didn't associate with the cast. He was kind of a loner. When we were in Lone Pine, at the end of the day's work he'd shoot off his gun. [Chuckles] He had a .45. He was a loner. The reason a lot of these guys are loners is because of background. What they went through. They never associated with anybody intellectual, college grads or even high school grads. Because he was poor he didn't grow up in an environment where people would sit and talk and discuss things. [Besides that,] I don't think he was adequate enough to be an actor."

NOTES AND COMMENTS: The song Kathleen Crowley sings, "Take Me to Town," had been used in three prior U-I westerns: *Wyoming Mail* (1950), *Take Me to Town* (1953) and *A Day of Fury* (1956).

The screenwriter's name, "Bronson Howitzer," is obviously a pseudonym for someone who wished to remain uncredited, for whatever reason. It is known producer Gordon Kay had Willard Willingham do a "polish" on the finished script. Most of the work may be Willingham's.

Audie, although he couldn't carry a tune, had a good ear for music and a great talent for rhyme. With his friend and song writing partner, Scott Turner, they penned "Shutters and Boards," which was a big hit on the Challenge label for Jerry Wallace in late 1962 and early 1963. Basically, Murphy was the lyricist and Turner the music composer. Between 1962 and 1969, Murphy and Turner (and sometimes singer Guy Mitchell) wrote seventeen songs, but none became as popular as "Shutters and Boards."

War Is Hell
(ALLIED ARTISTS, OCTOBER 1963)

CREDITS: *Producers:* Burt Topper, Ross Hahn; *Director:* Burt Topper; *Screenplay:* Burt Topper; *Editor:* Ace Herman; *Director of Photography:* Jacques Marquette; *Special Effects:* Pat Dinga; *Music:* Ronald Stein.

CAST: Tony Russel (Sgt. Keefer); Baynes Barron (Sgt. Garth); Burt Topper (Lt. Hallen); Judy Dan (Yung Chi Thomas); Tony Rich (Miller); J. J. Dahner (Koller); Wally Campo (Laney); Bobby Byles (Gresler); Michael Bell (Seldon); Russ Prescott (Bender); Robert Howard (Connors); Paul Sherriff (Thurston); Kei Chung (Korean Lieutenant); Audie Murphy (Narrator of Introduction).

RUNNING TIME: 81 minutes

FILMING DATES: Late 1962 or early 1963—10 day schedule

BUDGET/COST: $78,000

During the Korean War, cowardly sergeant Russel stays behind and watches as his men bravely storm a Communist bunker. Most of his men are killed, but the rest succeed in capturing the bunker. The sergeant then takes credit for the attack, expecting a medal and claiming to his superior officers that all the surviving soldiers are cowards. One of the officers suspects the truth, but Russel kills the man to ensure his silence. Russel goes even further to plant his name in military history by leading his men on a slaughter of Communist troops who have honored a cease-fire and disarmed themselves. Eventually, Russel is killed as he attacks unarmed Chinese troops who have surrendered.

REMEMBRANCES: *Burt Topper:* "Audie was friends with two producers from Allied Artists, Samuel Bischoff and David Diamond; one of them was good friends with Audie. When I did the picture independently, Allied Artists bought the picture for the United States rights. One of them was with George D. Burrows, who was head of Allied Artists at the time ... and knew Audie pretty well. So they got Audie to do the intro to the picture. I met him and directed him in that sequence. The opening of the picture starts with Audie; he introduces it. There's some heavy action and he tells you what it is. It's about a two minute intro. That picture was later released in Europe as *War Hero*. I had an out-of-competition award from the Cannes Festival, and then I went to Europe from the picture under contract to Carlo Ponti. Then I came back as head of production at American International.

"Audie was a very nice guy. Very unassuming. Very down to earth kid. His life would be an interesting movie of the week. There was a time when he was making westerns for Universal that he was 'bankable.' You could get about $500,000 for him at the time ... to make a picture."

NOTES AND COMMENTS: *War Is Hell* was one of the films playing at the Texas Theater in Oak Cliff, Texas, on November 22, 1963, where Lee Harvey Oswald was captured by the Dallas police.

On the lobby card advertising, each of the eight cards carried a picture of Audie in the bottom right corner stating the film provided "a dynamic foreword by Audie Murphy, America's most decorated war hero."

Gunfight at Comanche Creek
(ALLIED ARTISTS, NOVEMBER 1963)

CREDITS: *Producer:* Ben Schwalb; *Director:* Frank McDonald; *Assistant Director:* Don Torpin; *Story:* Based on a screenplay by Daniel Ullman; *Screenplay:* Edward Bernds; *Editor:* William Austin; *Director of Photography:* Joseph F. Biroc; *Art Director:* Edward Jewell; *Set Decorator:* Clarence Steenser; *Costume Supervisor:* Eddie Armand; *Makeup:* Wally Westmore; *Sound Recording:* Ralph Butler; *Sound Editor:* Marty Greco; *Hair Stylist:* Nellie Manley; *Music:* Martin Skiles. Panavision. Color by Deluxe.

CAST: Audie Murphy (Bob Gifford); Ben Cooper (Bill Carter); DeForest Kelley (Amos Troop); Colleen Miller (Abbie Stevens); Jan Merlin (Nielson); John Hubbard (Marshal Dan Shearer); Damian O'Flynn (Asa Winton); Susan Seaforth (Janie); Adam Williams (Jess Hayden); Mort Mills (Ben Brady); John Milford (Bill Peters); Michael Mikler (Reno Waller); Tom Browne Henry (Michael Bryant); William Wellman Jr. (Alden); Laurie Mitchell (Tina Neville); Alan Wells (Buck); Tim Graham (Delk); Eddie Quillan (Hotel

Gunfight at Comanche Creek

Clerk); Bill Catching (Shearer's Deputy); Willard Willingham (Will, national agent); Reed Hadley (Narrator). Stunts: Bill Catching, Bobby Herron, Willard Willingham.

RUNNING TIME: 90 minutes

FILMING DATES: March 27, 1963 to mid–April, 1963

LOCATIONS: Iverson Ranch; Paramount Studio western street, California.

BUDGET/COST: Approximately $200,000

This sad little potboiler, made on a shoestring by Allied Artists, the company which had produced a batch of second-feature westerns in the 1950s, did nothing to aid Murphy's now-flagging career. It was not even original, being a fifth remake of a plot that had been used since 1945 by Tex Ritter, Whip Wilson, George Montgomery and Wayne Morris. The story, restricted mainly to a town and a ranch, offered more dialogue than action, resulting in a plodding, static and ultimately dreary picture.

Murphy played a detective posing as a badman in an attempt to trap a gang of outlaws whose method is to free a wanted criminal from jail, use him as a recognizable front man in a series of robberies, then kill him for the reward money. Utilizing a somber voice-over narration in TV police-drama style, the film was neither a successful thriller nor a good western, and Murphy, given only a few action sequences and hampered by endless cliché-ridden dialogue, appeared dull and lifeless, looking old and seedy, and almost as awkward as in his very earliest film roles. Ben Cooper, a good young actor in the Murphy baby-face mold, who'd played kid gunslingers in a number of Republic films of the '50s, provided the only interest as a young gang member trying to go straight. Murphy's

Audie Murphy and his detective pal Jan Merlin (far right) are discovered by badman DeForest Kelley in *Gunfight at Comanche Creek* (1963).

leading lady, who matched him in dullness (but in fairness was given virtually nothing to do), was Colleen Miller, who had brightened a number of Tony Curtis films during Murphy's peak years at Universal. She was here making an ill-advised comeback.

Director Frank McDonald was a veteran of Columbia and Allied Artists B-westerns and had directed a large number of early 30-minute TV westerns. This background was reflected in the total lack of imagination in the handling of *Gunfight at Comanche Creek*. Even the final gunfight looked unexciting, a damp climax to a pathetic piece of hack movie-making that understandably sank without a trace in supporting spots.

REMEMBRANCES: *Jan Merlin:* "Audie didn't take anybody's smart kind of attitude. You didn't monkey around with Audie. He had a trigger temper, but he was a gentleman. He was a gentleman. But he could also be very dangerous if you got his back up. He didn't do [in WWII] what he did because he was the nicest little boy in the Army. He grew into manhood under those circumstances. And afterward he was a changed human being. Your reactions are different, your behavior is different. You really had to *know* the guy to play jokes. You don't fool around. But Audie showed an awfully fine sense of humor, a great sense of humor. He was a sweet man, he really truly was.

"What makes a hero is a guy who does a job that has to be done. Whether he did it in the war, in a movie or among his friends, whatever. When he had things going wrong in his life he pursued whatever he thought was the right thing for him to do. Sometimes it worked, sometimes it didn't."

Ben Cooper (left) and Susan Seaforth are taunted by outlaw Adam Williams (seated) while Audie momentarily holds his temper.

Bobby Herron: "'Shot in the Ass at Comanche Creek,' that was our name for it. Out on location they'd have you situated up on some rocks and call out to you, 'We'd love you to get shot off from the top of that rock.' You'd answer, 'Fine.' Then you'd look around and there were no catchers. What you'd have to do is gather some sagebrush and put a tarp over it. It was all about making the money. You would have to fall into the sagebrush because there was nothing worse than seeing a fall go away. [Laughs]"

Ben Cooper: "I served in the Army with some men who had served with Audie in Europe, and they held him in awe. When they mentioned his name, it was almost with reverential tones.

"Audie and I worked very well together. He was very quiet — a quiet dignity. Somebody said, 'What was his personality like?' Kinda wanna say, 'I looked for it.' He was not a chatter. He didn't chat. I found he didn't really start conversations. And he wasn't funny. I think with all of the hell he'd been through there wasn't any humor left. I have a rather weird, strange and depraved sense of humor [chuckles]. So if I did something silly, his way of laughing was he'd do this [simulates weak smile]. That was about it."

Colleen Miller: "I went on an interview for that, but before I went, my agent wanted to see a still of myself and Tony Curtis in *The Purple Mask* [1955]. Isn't that strange? *Mask* is a period picture, not a western. Frank McDonald, the director, looked at the still and said, 'That's what I want you to look like.' We shot that very quick — in only days! The film wasn't

The *Gunfight at Comanche Creek* is about to begin. Left to right: John Milford, Adam Williams (kneeling), Audie Murphy, De Forest Kelley (with rifle) and Colleen Miller being held by the mysterious outlaw leader.

that good. I think it needed some more script.

"Audie played the guitar and would sing songs to me — and every other woman who was around. I never had any problems with him — or anyone else for that matter. Audie always seemed reserved, though. Once, I did see Audie kick a couple of tin cans viciously. I never socialized with any actor, so I never knew him all that well."

NOTES AND COMMENTS: The nucleus of the story for *Gunfight at Comanche Creek* originated in a Tex Ritter/Dave O'Brien B for PRC, *Flaming Bullets*, in 1945. A gang breaks wanted outlaws out of jail, then kills them to collect a reward. That version was scripted by Harry Fraser. Writer Clint Johnson and producer Vincent Fennelly appropriated the idea for Whip Wilson's *Wanted Dead or Alive* at Monogram in 1951. Producer Fennelly revived the idea in 1953 when Monogram became Allied Artists, and had screenwriter Dan Ullman flesh out the plot a bit for *Star of Texas* with Wayne Morris. A producer tight with a buck, Fennelly had Ullman revise it once again at Allied Artists in 1957 for George Montgomery's *Last of the Badmen*. That brings us up to 1960 and *Gunfight at Comanche Creek*. Producer Ben Schwalb and writer Edward Bernds literally stole Ullman's 1957 screenplay, as this version is a nearly word-for-word recreation. But, I reckon, they figured it was all in-house at Allied Artists.

Shortly after this film's completion Audie sold his A-M Farms property near Romoland, California. (See Notes and Comments in *To Hell and Back*.)

The Quick Gun
(COLUMBIA, APRIL 1964)

CREDITS: *Producers:* Grant Whytock, Edward Small (uncredited); *Director:* Sidney Salkow; *Assistant Director:* Herbert S. Greene; *Story:* Steve Fisher; *Screenplay:* Robert E. Kent; *Editor:* Grant Whytock; *Director of Photography:* Lester Shorr; *Art Director:* Robert Purcell; *Set Decorator:* Frank Tuttle; *Makeup:* Ben Lane; *Sound Supervision:* Charles J. Rice; *Sound:* Josh Westmoreland; *Music:* Richard La Salle. Techniscope, Color by Technicolor.

CAST: Audie Murphy (Clint Cooper); Merry Anders (Helen Reed); James Best (Scotty Grant); Ted De Corsia (Spangler); Walter Sande (Tom Morrison); Rex Holman (Rick Morrison); Charles Meredith (Reverend Staley); Frank Ferguson (Dan Evans); Mort Mills (Cagle); Gregg Palmer (Donovan); Frank Gerstle (George Keely); Stephen Roberts (Dr. Stevens); Paul Bryar (Mitchell); Raymond Hatton (Elderly townsman); William Fawcett (Mike); William Tannen (Jake); Al Wyatt (Lacey); Rick Vallin, Walt LaRue, Fred Krone, John "Bear" Hudkins, Willard Willingham (Outlaws); George DeNormand (Townsman). Stunts: Willard Willingham, Fred Krone, Walt LaRue, John "Bear" Hudkins, Al Wyatt, Boyd "Red" Morgan.

RUNNING TIME: 89 minutes

FILMING DATES: Mid-September, 1963 to October 2, 1963

LOCATIONS: Bell Ranch; Iverson Ranch, California; Columbia Studio.

BUDGET/COST: $250,000–$300,000

The first of four films Murphy made with producer Grant Whytock (and his silent partner Edward Small), *The Quick Gun* was another shoddy remake of an already twice-filmed script. It had previously been seen as *Top Gun*, with Sterling Hayden (1955), and *Noose for a Gunman*, with

Jim Davis (1960). Longtime screen heavy Ted De Corsia actually played the same character in both the Davis and Murphy versions. The plot, not so much well worn as totally exhausted, was the old one about the gunslinger returning to a hostile hometown to save it from an expected outlaw attack. Despite opposition from former friends who frown upon his fast-gun reputation, he saves the town and wins back the love of his former girlfriend.

Murphy appeared heavy-footed and seemingly barely interested, content to rely on his standard personality tricks, which, while they worked with a good script and director, only served to enhance his dramatic deficiencies in something as cheap and slapdash as this. The once light-footed walk was replaced by a dogged plod, and there was something slightly ridiculous about the sight of his chunky figure going through all the old clichés against familiar background locations for scores of poverty-row quickies. Peopled as it was by veterans of cheap westerns, the film had a sort of middle-aged sag about it, the general tiredness of the treatment emphasized by banal dialogue, garishly unreal color and patently false indoor sets.

Sidney Salkow, yet another B-movie recruit, offered strictly mechanical direction, consisting mainly of predictable juxtaposition of two-shot, mid-shot, close-up and wide-shot — a mathematical assemblage of footage with total disregard for the dramatic effects of clever cutting. It was also painfully obvious that Murphy's more acrobatic stunts and fight scenes were doubled by a not-very-look-alike stuntman. James Best was reunited with Murphy in the role of the former friend engaged to his one-time girl, Merry Anders. Although Best was the film's second lead, he was actually a more heroic and appealing figure than Murphy. The role was an amalgamation of the characters played by William Bishop (villian) and James Millican (Sheriff) in *Top Gun*.

The Quick Gun was further evidence of

Audie Murphy, coffee in hand, in deep repose before drawing his *Quick Gun* (1964).

Murphy's declining importance in the film world, and set the standard for his remaining films with producer Whytock's Admiral Pictures Company, although he still had two films to make for Universal, a company which always had the edge on others in the production of low-budget westerns.

REMEMBRANCES: *Merry Anders:* "I ended up underplaying quite a bit, which I tried to do on most of my films 'cause I was scared to death to get too emotional in case I might look stupid on screen. Underplaying it, it makes you stand out." Merry's "underplaying" was never more evident than on Audie Murphy's *Quick Gun*. "I think it was probably because I was supposed to be playing a school teacher, a relatively intelligent, wise person, and I thought that would make me appear more intelligent." Meanwhile, heavies like Ted DeCorsia are chewing up the scenery all around Merry. "He was great though. Just perfect as his character. It helped me in a way because I was supposedly so terrified of him I was speechless ... in the character. [Laughs].

"[Director] Sidney Salkow taught acting classes up at the University State College at Northridge. He was a darling to work with. He was so helpful to me; he'd say, 'I'm going to let you do what you want on this one, but I'd love some tears and sobbing.' He was very encouraging and I trusted him enough to open up emotionally. Sid wanted one-on-one communication; he'd take you aside and give you little keys, and he was very agreeable and helpful.

"How can I be kind…Audie had mood swings. I treaded very quietly. He'd look at you like he could just kill you, and I never knew why. We were doing one scene together in which I had most of the dialogue. Audie kept mumbling, swearing, under his breath. Was he mad at me or just joking around? I talked to Jimmy Best, who had worked with Audie many times. He said, 'He'll forget it tomorrow. Don't lie awake nights over it. The picture's going to be over in another three days.'

"We did have rough filming on that; we went out to location about four o'clock in the afternoon and filmed night for night, until 2:30 and 3:00 in the morning.

"Ann Sothern was scheduled to do a film at Columbia about the same time, and they hired Perc Westmore, of the famous Westmores, to do her make-up. Well, for some reason, Ann walked off the set, so they gave me Perc Westmore for my make-up man, so of course I looked just terrific. It was probably the best make-up job I ever had in movies!"

Gregg Palmer: "Somebody lost their six-shooter. Christ, we had to look for two hours. Property master was going crazy. 'Oh Jeez, I gotta fill out a report and give it to the FBI, and the police department.' They were afraid somebody had stolen it. But we found it."

Bullet for a Badman
(UNIVERSAL, OCTOBER 1964)

CREDITS: *Producer:* Gordon Kay; *Director:* R. G. Springsteen; *Assistant Director:* Phil Bowles; *Based on the Novel Renegade Posse by:* Marion H. Albert; *Screenplay:* Mary and Willard Willingham; *Editor:* Russell Schoengarth; *Director of Photography:* Joseph Broc; *Art Directors:* Alexander Golitzen, Henry Bumstead; *Set Decorator:* Oliver Emert; *Makeup:* Bud Westmore; *Sound Recording:* Waldon O. Watson, Joe Lapis; *Hair Stylist:* Larry Germain; *Music:* Frank Skinner; *Music Supervision:* Joseph Gershenson. Eastman Color by Pathé.

CAST: Audie Murphy (Logan Keliher); Darren McGavin (Sam Ward); Ruta Lee (Lottie); Beverly Owen (Susan Keliher); Skip Homeier (Pink); George Tobias (Diggs); Alan Hale Jr. (Leach); Berkeley Harris (Jeff); Edward C. Platt (Tucker); Kevin Tate (Sammy); Cece Whitney (Goldie); Bob Steele (Sheriff of Griffin); Mort Mills (Ira); Ray Teal (Storekeeper); Buff Brady (Outlaw); George De Normand (Banker). Stunts: Jimmy Sheppard, Buff Brady, Bobby Herron.

RUNNING TIME: 80 minutes.

FILMING DATES: Late October 1963–November 11, 1963

LOCATIONS: St. George, Utah; Universal backlot.

BUDGET/COST: Approximately $300,000

By 1964, the full-time western star had disappeared from the screen—Randolph Scott and Joel McCrea had retired, John Wayne was in the "superstar" bracket, and such familiar faces as Rory Calhoun, George Montgomery and Dale Robertson

Opposite top: Audie Murphy faces two old enemies—Walter Sande and Rex Holman—while bartender William Fawcett moves out of the way of Audie's *Quick Gun*. *Bottom:* Merry Anders is in the middle of a *Quick Gun* argument between Audie Murphy and outlaw Ted DeCorsia.

Audie Murphy and production manager Howard Pine on location near St. George, Utah, for *Bullet for a Badman* (1964).

were more often seen as TV guest stars. Only Murphy, whose one fling at TV stardom in the 1950s had flopped, remained as a full-time star of low-to-medium-budget movies.

Bullet for a Badman took Audie back to his home studio, and, after the disastrous results of his films for Allied Artists and Columbia, was surprisingly good — almost, in fact, a return to form. For once, director R. G. Springsteen seemed inspired to inject some life into the proceedings. The film also benefited from good dialogue, solid performances, spectacular locations, and an unexpected ruthlessness in the action sequences. The plot, with overtones of earlier Murphy films, dealt with the efforts of a farmer, once a Texas Ranger, to apprehend a wanted bandit — a former Ranger colleague. The fugitive, Sam Ward (Darren McGavin), is determined to kill Logan Keliher (Murphy) for marrying Ward's former wife, but the two are forced into an uneasy alliance to fight off marauding Indians, and later a group of corrupt posse-members determined to get their hands on the loot from Ward's most recent bank robbery. Keliher and Ward defeat all opposition, and their former friendship is reaffirmed in the final moments, with Ward dying while protecting Keliher from the last of the possemen.

Wisely cast as a mature man of about his actual age (Murphy was then 40) — a happily married husband and father with the skill, but no longer the desire, to handle firearms—Murphy appeared much more at ease here than as a gunslinger hero-figure. Audie projected a likeable warmth in the scenes with his wife and adopted son, a hard-edged authority in his control of the mutinous posse, and a nice blend of wry humor and tension in his scenes with McGavin. As it had in other films, the presence of a vital and versatile co-star seemed to inspire Murphy to reach beyond his normal placid blandness, and the two actors achieved a rapport equal to that between Murphy and Barry Sullivan in *Seven Ways from Sundown*. McGavin, with a strong New York stage background, having co-starred opposite Frank Sinatra, Jerry Lewis and Bob Hope, and possessing experience as the star of two top-rated TV shows (*Mike Hammer* and *Riverboat*), was an unexpected face in an Audie Murphy western, but his presence gave the film a lift that helped it overcome the somewhat crowded plot.

Apart from the opening sequence, obviously shot on the Universal backlot, the action was filmed on location at St. George, Utah, and proved expansive and exciting, particularly a brush with hostile Indians, which included a vigorous travelling shot of Murphy and his comrades riding at top speed across the rugged terrain. The "running insert," as this shot is known in the western trade, was one of the conventions of the low-budget horse opera that never failed to generate excitement, and was here

Audie Murphy is mounted and cameras are ready to shoot a *Bullet for a Badman* scene in St. George, Utah.

used to striking effect. The sudden, unexpected death of bad-girl heroine Ruta Lee, shot from ambush while in the middle of a conversation, also had great impact; and McGavin's last-gasp reunion with his son was prevented from becoming overly sentimental by McGavin's skillful handling of the scene and Murphy's sympathetic support.

Though sketchy, the minor characters were all sharply drawn by the experienced cast, who brought to the fore the feeling of the toughness of the region and the hardships endured. Like *Posse from Hell* and the later *Gunpoint*, the film cast Murphy in the role of a strong man in charge of a motley group on a dangerous mission, and his authority was never in question, despite the presence of such western veterans as Alan Hale Jr. and Skip Homeier.

The color processing was unsatisfactory, seeming to flatten the images, but this was offset to a degree by the playing of the two leads and the toughness of the action.

REMEMBRANCES: *Ruta Lee:* "It was an hysterical cast! We had Darren McGavin, Alan Hale Jr., that wonderful character actor George Tobias ... one laugh after another. Everybody was fast and quick. I was the only girl on location in St. George, so everyone treated me like a baby doll and we had a wonderful time. Audie was not a laugher and a scratcher. Audie had a strange sense of humor that was strictly his own. He would make a joke and we would

Audie Murphy walks through his next *Bullet for a Badman* scene while technicians await the director's word.

all look at one another and wonder—did that go over our heads? His humor was entirely different. He was on a different level. He didn't mix and mingle with the rest of us. He didn't come out to supper with us. He didn't 'play' with us. When I got to spend a little time with him, on a one-on-one basis, he was very gentle, very humble, very sweet, very much of a gentleman, but either he didn't feel secure or he didn't want to play, so I never *really* got to know him the way I did everybody else in ten minutes."

Cece Whitney (interviewed in the *Audie Murphy Research Foundation* online newsletter): "Audie was a natural actor—and that was a surprise, because many times when celebrities begin to make films they are there because of their celebrity and not because of any talent. Audie was very natural. Maybe because we accepted him as an actor. I remembered, of course, who he was, but to me, when I met him, he was an actor. I remember thinking, 'My word, he is really talented! How does he do it?' I didn't know Audie very well. We just worked together and I met him on the set. My gut reaction to him was, 'What a very nice man, what a gentleman.' Not that that is surprising in films. Many, many really great actors are. The better they act, usually, the more gentlemanly they are. My impression of Audie was that he was very quiet, yet very much his own man.

"There was this scene where Skip Homeier, whose name was Pink in the movie, was Goldie's protector, and Audie comes into Goldie's saloon and immediately Homeier and others begin to whistle. And when Audie orders a sarsaparilla there is a bit of a thing about it. As I came down the stairs, Skip was challenging Audie about the drink someone bought him. So I said, 'Pull in your horns, Pink, he's drinking with me.' Well, we must have done that scene 50 times, because the first time we did it, when I said my line—'Pull in your horns, Pink, he's drinking with me'—there was a big silence and Skip said, 'Pull in my what?' Well, Audie Murphy sprayed sarsaparilla everywhere. He just came unglued. And the whole set just came off and laughed so hard. I almost fell down the stairs laughing. We all thought it was so funny. Audie was taking a sip of this sarsaparilla and it just sprayed all over the place. Anyway, that went on all afternoon, I kept climbing up and down the stairs and every time I said that line the whole set would break up and it would start all over again. It was a fun day. Nowadays that is one of the things they would show on bloopers. Audie just kept laughing, he could not hold a straight face. The whole set was just broken up, but Audie was the one who really triggered it with his spraying.

"I'm sorry I didn't know Audie better. One thing that surprised me, even after I met him, I always thought of him as a big man because he was such a nice guy. He wasn't big in the physical sense, but he was a big man in every other way. I really, thoroughly enjoyed working with Audie."

Apache Rifles

(20TH CENTURY–FOX, NOVEMBER 1964)

CREDITS: *Executive Producer:* Edward Small (uncredited); *Associate Producer:* Grant Whytock; *Director:* William Witney; *Assistant Director:* Herbert S. Greene; *Story:* Kenneth Gamet, Richard Schayer; *Screenplay:* Charles B. Smith; *Editor:* Grant Whytock; *Director of Photography:* Arch R. Dalzell; *Art Director:* Frank Sylos; *Production Manager:* Joseph Small; *Set Decorator:* Morris Hoffman; *Wardrobe:* Alexis

Davidoff; *Makeup:* Vincent Romaine; *Sound Recording:* Lambert Day; *Sound Editor:* James Richards; *Hair Stylist:* Gladys Witten; *Music:* Richard La Salle. Color by De Luxe.

CAST: Audie Murphy (Capt. Jeff Stanton); Michael Dante (Red Hawk); Linda Lawson (Dawn Gillis); L. Q. Jones (Mike Greer); Ken Lynch (Hodges); Joseph A. Vitale (Chief Victorio); J. Pat O'Malley (Capt. "Doc" Thatcher); John Archer (Colonel Nathan Perry); Charles Watts (Crawford Owens); Robert Brubaker (Sgt. Cobb); Eugene Iglesias (Corporal Ramirez); Robert Karnes (Marshal-or-Sheriff George); Peter Hansen (Capt. Green); Howard Wright (Thompson); Sydney Green (General of the Army); Hugh Sanders (Delegate from Arizona); S. John Launer (General Nelson); Robert B. Williams (Miller); Boyd "Red" Morgan (Hogan); Herman Hack (Townsman); Stunts: Fred Krone, Jim Sheppard.

RUNNING TIME: 92 minutes

FILMING DATES: May 12, 1964–May 30, 1964

LOCATIONS: Red Rock Canyon, California; Bronson Cave in Griffith Park.

Murphy's second film for Grant Whytock (and silent partner Edward Small) and their Admiral Pictures was no particular improvement on *The Quick Gun*, but it did have the advantage of pleasing locations that provided a much more satisfactory background than the restricted town setting of the first Whytock-Small-Murphy movie. The B-feature title was an indication of the hackneyed plot, with Murphy as an Indian-hating U.S. Cavalry captain eventually attempting to play fair with Apache warriors in early Arizona, but meeting opposition from settlers, gold-miners and his own superior officers. The film was a remake of Small's *Indian Uprising* (1951), with George Montgomery.

Once again the director was a veteran of the low-budget western, William Witney, who had worked mainly at Republic and was responsible for the bulk of Roy Rogers' movies from 1944 until the early 1950s. Here his style is competent but unexciting, with Murphy giving a standard non-performance, slightly better than in *The Quick Gun* but less impressive than in *Bullet for a Badman*. There was an odd irony in the fact that, despite his Army background, Murphy was never completely convincing in uniform (with the notable exception of *To Hell and Back*). Somehow his stocky figure and still youthful (if thickened) features seemed out of place in the familiar dark blue Cavalry uniform. He still handled the bulk of the action scenes with assurance, but it was obvious his films were receiving scant consideration in budgeting, preparation and production, and virtually no advance promotion. They appeared, hung around in supporting spots at minor-league theaters, then vanished without a trace.

REMEMBRANCES: *Michael Dante:* "Grant [Whytock] did the leg work, but Edward Small was the money man behind the films [and Admiral Productions]. William Witney was an excellent director. *Apache Rifles* I did first, and Witney immediately cast me in *Arizona Raiders*, both starring roles. The first night Audie and I had dinner together at a motel out on the Mojave Desert. Said goodnight, see you in the morning, so forth. I got in bed, I was working on the script, it was kinda late and I went off to sleep. I guess it was about one or two o'clock in the morning and I thought I was having a nightmare. I hear this loud train whistle. Now my bed was facing the window, and here was this train coming closer and closer with this light getting bigger and bigger. Lo and behold — coming right at me! I couldn't believe it. I thought I was having a nightmare. Half asleep. All of a sudden it's picking up speed and the light is coming larger and larger at the window. I jumped up and wow — it went right by! The room I had in this motel was in the back, which was supposed to be more private, but nobody figured out where the train makes a turn ... right by

Audie Murphy is back in uniform protecting Linda Lawson from *Apache Rifles* (1964).

that room. Boy! The next day I got ahold of the assistant director and said, 'Get me another room or you won't have an actor. I didn't get any sleep. I was scared to death!' They all laughed. Even Audie laughed, where he was not accustomed to laughing very easily. He was basically very quiet, a loner. He and I got along just royally. We respected each other's privacy. I don't like to talk and be distracted when I'm working, and he didn't either. We sat there in the Mojave Desert and neither one of us would go into the trailer. The trailer had its air conditioner on and it was cold in there ... to us it was ice cold because it was 115 degrees in the Mojave, and if we went in there and came out we'd have pneumonia in a day. So we'd sit under the canopy outside, side by side, and not have very much conversation, just relax and wait for a set-up to be finished and be called to work, and off we'd go. He was very quiet, didn't like to be distracted. But people were always coming around wanting conversation with him and so forth, but he was a very private person."

As to other actors in *Apache Rifles*, "L. Q. Jones was a hell of a character actor, a great western face. We met again in *Winterhawk*. Linda Lawson I had known prior to the film. It was nice working with her because I knew her as a friend. She was married to an agent at the time. Also very quiet. Another guy I liked in the film was Kenny Lynch. I knew of his work, he had that gravel voice, a terrific voice for a heavy, but we had not worked together before. He was just wonderful to me. In a scene where they were torturing me and so forth, he came over and said to me,

Audie Murphy coerces a confession out of drunken Ken Lynch.

'Michael, continue to do good work ... and your attitude ... and you're gonna go a long way in this business.' It was something I never heard another actor say to me or any other actor. I was fairly young in the business and for him to say that, it was really nice ... in this competitive business."

In author Robert Nott's *Last of the Cowboy Heroes* book, Linda Lawson said she reached into Audie's personal life for the scene in which she's shot. She wanted to know what it was like to be shot. Apparently not appreciating the question, Audie stared at her for a moment, then said — quietly, "You don't feel it at first ... but then you do."

Lawson also told Nott, "We did one overnight locale in the Mojave Desert. We were housed in a kind of U-shaped motel for the night. Murphy had a man with him; an assistant, and the next morning one of the crewmembers said to me, 'Did you hear him last night?' I said, 'No, what?' He said, 'He was screaming. He has terrible nightmares.' I never found out if this man that stayed with him was there to help him through it or what. I don't think anybody could go through what he went through and come out whole. He was very professional. He knew his lines, no histrionics. We had a location shoot in Griffith Park and somebody found a baby rattlesnake and Audie milked it; took the venom out. I thought he would kill it but he said, 'No, no, I'll just disarm him,' and he let it go and it ran off ... or sidled off; whatever they do. We were on location at one of the studio ranches and our driver got lost and I was in the first shot of the day. I had to have costuming, get my hair piece on ...

Audie Murphy and another trooper definitely have Indian chief Michael Dante at a disadvantage in this *Apache Rifles* scene filmed at Red Rock Canyon.

and we arrived late. I went into the trailer to get my hair done and the assistant director came in and began screaming at me because we were late. I said, 'I'm sorry, I wasn't driving the car,' but he continued screaming. He made the hairdresser so nervous that her hand began to shake; she was in tears, and that upset me. I went over to where we were going to shoot and I must have looked awful. Murphy said, 'What's the matter?' I said, 'The assistant director was screaming at us and...' I told him the story. He could see I was upset and he called the guy over. I know this sounds like a 'B' movie thing, but I never saw anything so frightening and cold as the way Murphy spoke to this man: 'If you ever do anything like that again to this woman...' and the guy was terrified. And I was too; not for myself, but just to see this. And yet I know he was doing it out of a sense of chivalry. It was the quietness of it that was terrifying and bizarre. Audie had a wry and dry sense of humor with the guys. He'd hang out with the guys and say something and they'd all laugh. But whatever they were talking about, he wasn't going to let me hear it."

L.Q. Jones: "You learn quickly [in this business] that you better have a good script, but if you don't your only chance to get out of it alice is the director. I've worked with about a hundred directors, and I can count on my right hand the really good ones—the Peckinpahs, the Siegels, the Boettichers. Bill Witney was very close to that group. I think part of the reason Audie did so well in that piece was because of Bill."

NOTES AND COMMENTS: Eugene Iglesias has the same basic role and name, Ramirez, as he does in the original *Indian Uprising* (1951), of which this is a remake. Hugh Sanders was also in the original, in the role essayed here by chubby Charles Watts.

Michael Dante, who plays Indian Red Hawk, found his greatest fame in another Indian role — as Chief Winterhawk in the 1976 feature *Winterhawk*. Although he played many Indian roles, including Crazy Horse on the *Custer* TV series (1967), Dante is first-generation Italian, born and raised in Stanford, Connecticut.

Robert Brubaker irregularly played stage driver Jim Buck on the *Gunsmoke* TV series, and during the last two seasons he played Floyd, the bartender at the Long Branch Saloon after the death of Glenn Strange (as Sam the bartender).

Arizona Raiders
(COLUMBIA, AUGUST 1965)

CREDITS: *Executive Producer:* Edward Small (uncredited); *Associate Producer:* Grant Whytock; *Director:* William Witney; *Assistant Director:* Jack G. Lacey; *Story:* Frank Gruber, Richard Schayer; *Screenplay:* Alex Gottlieb, Mary and Willard Willingham; *Editor:* Grant Whytock; *Director of Photography:* Jacques Marquette; *Art Director:* Paul Sylos Jr.; *Set Decorator:* Harry Reif; *Production Supervisor:* Harold E. Knox; *Makeup:* Don Greenway; *Wardrobe:* Joseph Dimmitt; *Sound Recording:* F. Ryan; *Sound Editor:* Al Bird; *Hair Stylist:* Edith Lindon; *Music:* Richard LaSalle. Techniscope. Color by Technicolor.

CAST: Audie Murphy (Clint Bonner); Michael Dante (Brady); Ben Cooper (Willie Martin); Buster Crabbe (Capt. Tom Andrews); Gloria Talbott (Martina); Ray Stricklyn (Danny Bonner); George Keymas (Montana); Fred Krone (Matt Edwards); Eddie Holloway (Willard Willingham); Boyd "Red" Morgan (Tex); Fred Graham (Quantrill); Neil Summers (Convict/barroom onlooker/cavalryman); Bob Shelton (Cavalryman). Stunts: Jimmy Sheppard, Fred Krone, Boyd Morgan, Neil Summers, Walt LaRue, Fred Graham, Frank Noel.

RUNNING TIME: 88 Minutes (97 Minutes)

FILMING DATES: November 30, 1964–December 12, 1964

LOCATIONS: Old Tucson, Arizona, and desert area.

Murphy was teamed again with producers Grant Whytock, Edward Small and director William Witney for yet another routine action drama, similar in some ways to *Kansas Raiders,* made fifteen years earlier, in which Murphy had played the young Jesse James riding with guerrilla leader Quantrill. This time his character was fictional, his performance functional, the results forgettable. *Arizona Raiders* was a remake of producer Small's *Texas Rangers* (1951), which had starred George Montgomery and Jerome Courtland.

Murphy played Clint Bonner, a former Quantrill rider working with co-star Ben Cooper, as an undercover agent for the Arizona Rangers, to help round up his former colleagues. With the death of Quantrill, the Raiders have headed west, where they terrorize the citizens of Arizona. Murphy rejoins them, enlists the help of Indians, and emerges triumphant.

Sparsely populated (revealing its low budget), the film holds little conviction but is high on ultra-violent excitement, although its characters are one-dimensional. It offers some good desert locations and

In *Arizona Raiders* (1965) Audie Murphy fights side by side with one-time B-western star Buster Crabbe (holding rifle).

valid performances from Ben Cooper, Michael Dante and George Keymas. For nostalgic old-timers there was the presence of Buster Crabbe, the screen's immortal Flash Gordon and star of scores of B-westerns, but even his leathery solidity as the Ranger Captain couldn't lift *Arizona Raiders* above second-feature status, and it went the unsung way of all Murphy's last few films.

REMEMBRANCES: *Michael Dante:* "We shot down in Old Tucson; Bob Shelton owned the place at that time. [Shelton also rode as one of the Cavalrymen extras.] That place was wide open then ... now it's full of houses." However, in the 'pistol-hitting-on-horseback' finale filmed at Bronson Canyon, "Stuntmen were used for the long shots and the close-ups were me and Audie.

"Now as to Audie's sense of humor ... when the still photographer wanted a picture of both of us, he said 'C'mon guys, smile.' So we purposely didn't smile that much. Now here's how feline and subtle he was. He lifted the gun from my holster during that photo and I didn't realize it. He was *the* most feline human being I ever met in my life. Like a cat. I can understand why he was able to stay alive [during WWII] under those extraneous circumstances with the odds so much against him in his war experiences. That's part of the reason he survived and became the hero he was."

As to Audie's quickness with a gun, "I've never seen anybody draw from a holster like him ... at least any other actor I've ever worked with ... he was lightning. He didn't like fooling around with his gun, showing off, drawing — he didn't do any of that. He didn't particularly care for Ben Cooper or anybody else doing anything like that. He avoided Ben because Ben was

Audie Murphy poses with co-star Michael Dante. Unbeknownst to Dante, the "feline" Murphy was quietly lifting Dante's gun from his holster while the photo was being taken.

maybe a little too extroverted, vociferous for him. Audie would walk away, not say anything. He wasn't rude or anything, he would just go about his business ... off he went." As for others in *Arizona Raiders,* "George Keymas was a very good heavy. He did some work over at Warner Bros. also. During the shoot, my motel room was on the first floor, a stone's throw away from the pool. Every morning at six o'clock you would hear 'Splash!' Just on the button, every morning, six o'clock. I'd look out the window, and I'd know who it was— like a fish in water, Buster Crabbe was doing his laps in the pool. He'd go at least a half hour or so. What a wonderful guy he was!"

Ray Stricklyn in his book *Angels and Demons* wrote: "I was cast as Audie Murphy's younger brother, which I'd missed out on being when Burt Lancaster booted me out of *The Unforgiven*. I only had about four scenes, but they were good ones, before I died in Audie's arms. The *Daily Variety* film critic liked the movie a lot. Considering its budget, he said the film had an 'almost epic' look."

George Keymas: "Audie and I got along great. He was very pleasant. Sometimes he could be a little volatile in his temper ... you never knew when he was gonna use his temper for some minor incident, perhaps. When I saw it on the set, we were loading up the vans to come back to town from location. Something about the vans, I don't know exactly what the hell it was, he was standing right outside my window and was tearing into the assistant director. It wasn't a soft-spoken kind of anger ... it was [chuckles], I think he had him nose to nose damn near. He never touched him, never hit him. It was more of an explosive ... now maybe other times other people saw a different side of him where his temper was a smoldering temper. There was one actor that bothered Audie a great deal, he didn't like him at all. Audie and I were sitting in the stretchout coming back from location. I talked Audie out of doing anything. 'Aw, forget it. The man's an asshole for Christ's sake. Why do you want to bother expending your energy on him? He's stupid.' And he was. It was very interesting watching Murphy over the years. He was an unskilled actor. He was not a studied actor, he didn't study acting. But the camera really liked him. He was very believable, but he didn't know any tricks as an actor at all, but when the camera likes you as much as it liked Audie, you don't have to be [a skilled actor]."

Ben Cooper: "On *Arizona Raiders* I saw Audie get angry once. He thought the unit manager had done something that was going to be harmful to a couple of the drivers ... something about tires for a car or truck. He thought the unit manager had cheated one of the drivers or something. And Audie took it upon himself to talk to him about this. But he misunderstood the unit manager. I saw Audie take him and shove him up against a car. I swear to God I saw sparks come out of his eyes! For that moment he was very angry! Then the guy explained, 'No, no it was such and such,' and Audie calmed down immediately and apologized. He wasn't angry at something that had been done to him, he was angry because he thought something had been done to other people who couldn't fight back. I thought, now that's class. Kind of revealing about him as a person. I asked him one time, 'Is it true when you go into a tavern or a bar, people try to pick a fight with you?' He said, 'Oh yeah. That's why I don't go in those places anymore.'"

Neil Summers: "In the summer of 1965 one of the stuntmen on *Arizona Raiders*, Red Morgan, finagled me a simple stunt, as I was not yet a professional. After doing my fall I was told Audie Murphy wished to speak to me. He offered to write for me a letter of recommendation into the Screen Actor's Guild, as long as I had the initiation fee to join. True to his word, he did write the letter and that became the beginning of my Hollywood career as a stuntman. I stayed in touch with Murphy and attended his assault trial in Los Angeles to show my support. When Audie produced his last film, *A Time for Dying*, he and director Budd Boetticher cast me as one of the raiders in the film. There is hardly a day goes by without a thought crossing my mind about Audie. He was a most unassuming man, full of fun and practical jokes, not what one would expect from the nation's most decorated soldier. He was loyal to me and one of the greatest fighting men ever to defend our country."

Fred Krone: "Bill Witney directed. What a gentleman he was. He could spot a phony from 500 yards away. He'd cuss their ass and that would be the end of that. We had a blast on that [film]."

Walt LaRue: "Red Morgan and I rode down the street and dropped Fred Krone. We sat around trying to figure which way to handle that, and drop him, without getting him hurt, but it knocked him colder than hell. Fred was a good guy, I like Krone."

About Audie, *Gloria Talbott* told writer Robert Nott: "I liked him. He was very, very into himself. *Arizona Raiders* was shot at Old Tucson. I remember one day I sat next to the driver on the ride out. I had broken my knee prior to making the film. I had a scar on it and I had my legs up on the dashboard, and Audie's stand-in said, 'Hey, Audie, look at that one'—meaning my scar. And Audie, and this was the first time I saw any interest from him, saw this great big scar that cut through half my knee and gave me a look that said, 'Oh my God, this girl has lived a little.' Audie, I suppose, was scars from head to toe. He was not unkind. He was not kind. He was there to work. He did his job. It was difficult to get eye contact with Audie. Maybe he was so terribly shy that I shocked the hell out of him. He was underrated as an actor. It was sort of an oblique thing [he did], but it was good. I don't think he was comfortable being Audie Murphy. He didn't want the celebrity."

NOTES AND COMMENTS: Originally running 88 minutes, a nine-minute prologue with an actor playing a newspaper editor speaking directly to the audience about the history of Quantrill's Raiders was apparently tacked onto TV prints to pad the running time to 97 minutes, a better length for a two-hour TV time slot. However, the effect of this boring, dull prologue only serves to deaden the start of the film.

Producer Grant Whylock and silent moneyman partner Edward Small planned to co-star Audie and Michael Dante in another film, but Murphy's death in 1971 prevented this project from being produced. Dante recalls, "I had a meeting with Audie.

Stuntman Frank Noel (left) had his picture taken with Audie Murphy during the filming of *Arizona Raiders*.

A script was brought to me by Rod Piffath. It was called at the time *The Perfect Target*. It was so perfect for Audie and myself. It was about a pacifist ... a character who was a corporal in the Salvation Army in St. Louis, circa late 1800s. His uncle dies and leaves him all of his money, sole heir. That corporal is Audie, who has to come and claim the inheritance in Arizona. He tells the Citadel he has to leave and claim this inheritance. When you join the Salvation Army, if you come into any money, usually you donate it to the Citadel. So it's set up for Audie to go to Arizona, claim the will and open his own Citadel there. During his journey there, I save his life. The two-fisted character called Zachary Dollar. The two of us become friends and journey into Arizona to claim the inheritance. There's a Madame there who claims she should have the money as the mistress of Audie's uncle. Also there was a son out of wedlock that she claimed his uncle fathered. The battle goes on as to who should be the rightful claimant. It was a great character for Audie ... nothing like that was ever offered him. I met Audie at his house ... he and his wife were separated at the time ... his two sons were there. Audie loved the script. Eddie Small approved it. Last words as I left his home in Toluca Lake, I said, 'I'll see you in a couple of weeks. We'll forge ahead with the project.' In that two week span he was killed in the plane crash. Piffath was a big fan of us both, and he wrote it specifically for us. Eddie Small's secretary, his right hand man, was a very good friend of Piffath, that's how they contacted me first, then I brought it to Audie. What happened with it ... it wound up at Disney with [English actor] Jim Dale as *Hot Lead and Cold Feet*. Unbelievable, beautiful script and they changed it around. I didn't even do the picture. I sold them the property with the idea they'd cast me as the other character. They changed it around so that Dale played three characters. It was an entirely different film."

Gunpoint
(UNIVERSAL, MAY 1966)

CREDITS: *Producer:* Gordon Kay; *Director:* Earl Bellamy; *Assistant Director:* Phil Bowles; *Story:* Mary and Willard Willingham; *Screenplay:* Mary and Willard Willingham; *Editor:* Russell F. Schoengarth; *Director of Photography:* William Marguiles; *Art Directors:* Alexander Golitzen, Henry Bumstead; *Set Decorators:* John McCarthy, Oliver Emert; *Makeup:* Bud Westmore; *Sound Recording:* Waldon O. Watson, Lyle Cain; *Hair Stylist:* Larry Germain; *Music:* Hans J. Salter; *Music Supervisor:* Joseph Gershenson. Technicolor.

CAST: Audie Murphy (Chad Lucas); Joan Staley (Uvalde — Bonnie Mitchell); Warren Stevens (Nate Harlan); Edgar Buchanan (Bull); Denver Pyle (Cap Hold); David Macklin (Mark Emerson); Nick Dennis (Nicos); Royal Dano (Ode); Morgan Woodward (Drago Leon); Robert Pine (Mitch); John Hoyt (Mayor Osborne); Ford Rainey (Tom Emerson); Roy Barcroft (Dr. Beardsley); Mike Ragan (Zack); Kelly Thorsden (Big Ab); Bill Henry, Dee Cooper (Outlaws); William Bramley (Hoag). Stunts: Jimmy Sheppard, Willard Willingham, Dee Cooper, Walt LaRue.

RUNNING TIME: 86 minutes

FILMING DATES: June 2, 1965–June 17, 1965

LOCATIONS: St. George, Utah; Universal backlot.

BUDGET/COST: $250,000–$300,000

Murphy's final film for Universal was a jumbled hodge-podge of badly faked studio sets (the waterfall sequence), impressive locations, contrived plotting and stock footage from earlier Murphy Universal westerns. Certainly there was merit in much of the location shooting around the familiar stomping ground of St. George, Utah, and Murphy was agreeably in control of yet another rebellious posse, but the plot development was jerky, and the only real interest for moviegoers was probably the guessing game of naming the movie from which the action sequences were lifted. Some of the cast were fond of saying, "A lot of gun and not much point," but one scene — an Indian attack on a derelict desert outpost — was quite excitingly handled by director Earl Bellamy. Unfortunately, most of the other big scenes were lifted from other movies, with consequent changes in color quality and glaring errors in geographical continuity.

The film established its low production values at the outset when Murphy appeared in his *Night Passage* costume, followed by his entire introductory sequence from that earlier film (showing him riding up a hill and jumping onto the top of a moving train), with occasional close-ups inserted. Later came action scenes from *Kid from Texas, Cimarron Kid, Kansas Raiders*, the death of Richard Rober under the horse stampede in *Sierra* (this time used to dispose of villain Denver Pyle), and yet another repeat of the canyon ambush from *Bend of the River*.

Murphy played the sheriff of a tough frontier town (a most unconvincing studio backlot setting) who leads a posse in pursuit of an outlaw gang who have kidnapped

Outlaw Morgan Woodward captures Joan Staley while holding Audie Murphy at *Gunpoint* (1966).

saloon singer Joan Staley after robbing the train of a million dollars. The posse gradually dwindles to three: Murphy, the rescued Staley, and saloon owner Warren Stevens (who wants the robbery loot — and Staley — for himself). Despite recurring fits of blindness from a wound suffered during the Indian attack, Murphy kills Stevens, saves the money and gets the girl.

Warren Stevens, an excellent actor who never had the right role to make him a major star, was a suavely mocking good-bad heavy, but weak scripting prevented the development of any particular rapport between he and Murphy (along the lines of Murphy's earlier encounters with Barry Sullivan and Darren McGavin in similar roles); while Joan Staley was no more nor less effective than the standard Murphy heroine. Though an improvement on the Whytock westerns, *Gunpoint* stands as a sad, second-hand conclusion to Murphy's association with the studio that had made him a star.

REMEMBRANCES: *Earl Bellamy:* "We filmed up at St. George, Utah. Audie hated to get up in the morning. He always had a .45 automatic by his bed, so when the alarm clock would go off in the morning, he'd grab the .45 and blast that alarm clock to smithereens. He finally had to quit it because the landlord where Audie was staying ... it cost him so much money in repairs ... the walls and all; of course, Audie had to pay for 'em, but still it was time out to repair, and do this, do that. Finally Audie quit, a little unhappy, but he went along with it. I got a big kick out of that situation!

"I enjoyed Audie. We had a nice rapport together. There was nothing I asked him to do that he wouldn't do … no pouting or anything like that … he was just an all-around regular guy that was liked by everyone … mainly the crew and very definitely me. He was on time, knew his words and was there to please the audience. Willard Willingham wrote the script, and others, for Audie. No one knew this would be Audie's last film for Universal. Not even me."

Producer Gordon Kay: "*Gunpoint* was my last Murphy film. Earl and I had finished *Fluffy* (1965), and Harry Keller had died suddenly of a heart attack. I'm delighted Earl did it; I wanted him."

Joan Staley told author Robert Nott: "I don't think Audie was an actor, I think Audie was a screen persona who acquitted himself well. He was able to play himself. He was affable, to use an old-fashioned word. He liked to play jokes, more of a little boy–type jokes, in the sense that he might open the door and throw a snake in the room. Not to harm anyone, but just to hear everybody go 'Ahhhh!' and that included the stuntmen too. He put a harmless snake in one of the stuntmen's boots. That wakes you up quickly! But he was a giggler; he was fun. He wanted very much to be liked; he wanted very much to be himself; he didn't want to be a star. He wanted to be one of the guys.

"I got the female sense—call it mother's intuition or whatever—of Audie really fighting to be himself, and people were always telling him who it was that he was, but Audie didn't always necessarily agree with it. He kept looking for himself. I don't want to say an unhappy man, but a man at odds with his situation. Maybe he wasn't doing all he wanted to do, but maybe he didn't know what that other part might have been. A regular guy thrust into an area of earning his livelihood because of an incident of extreme bravery. Again, it was very heady stuff, very nice, paid well, but I often wondered if he might not have been happier doing something else.

"He never gave a sense of knowing [this was his last film at Universal], and usually there is a sense of an actor heading off on his own, moving away from the camaraderie of the crew, but I didn't get any sense of his pulling away."

David Macklin: "I wish I knew then what I know now about Audie Murphy. In my book, *Acting in the Motion Picture Business*, I stress the point actors should learn as much as possible about the people they will be working with before the fact. Of course, we didn't have the wonderful tool the internet then, but I could have at least perused his book *To Hell and Back* and seen that film. This would have given me a better understanding about how and why Audie was who he was, and have given me an opportunity to establish a better rapport with him.

"Audie had a bit of a wicked sense of humor. Once on location in St. George I saw him waving a scorpion … I don't know if it was alive or dead … at some locals who freaked a bit. Audie seemed a bit puzzled and tossed the scorpion off the hill, shrugged and walked away. Perhaps he was just trying to re-live a childhood he never had. He was quoted once, 'I never remember being young once in my life.'

"Doug McClure, who I worked with on *The Virginian*, told me this story: Once when working with Audie [on *The Unforgiven*], Audie put horse crap on Doug's saddle before a take and Doug had to do a scene sitting in shit. To pay Audie back he snuck … I don't remember how or if he told me he got in … I'm sure Audie kept his door locked … into Audie's motel room and tried to put a dead scorpion on Audie's bed. In an instant Doug found himself looking cross-eyed at Audie's gun that Audie had silently and swiftly swept from under his pillow. Lot of that old Indian trick of begging and screaming for mercy. Audie lowered the gun and said, 'Get out of here McClure … I gotta get some sleep.' Doug did not tell me if *he* got any sleep that night or if he had to change his pants.

Edgar Buchanan (middle), Royal Dano (holding pistol) and Kelly Thorsden (obscured by Dano) capture Audie Murphy, Warren Stevens and Joan Staley in a scene shot on the Universal backlot.

"I never saw Audie gamble or, for that matter, socialize with any of his co-workers on location. He never joined in the evening's festivities around the pool or things like that. I don't even know if he went out to dinner with anyone. It seems to me he was always in his room.

"Earl 'No Strain' Bellamy told us all that we would have one rather difficult day of shooting — that being the mountain climbing sequence which began at sunrise and ended at dark. Earl was a wonderful guy ... one of the few non-actor directors that really liked actors. However, his warning about that day was a huge understatement. It began for me when my horse ... that I was dragging up the hill ... got pissed off and whacked me in the head with his. He knocked my hat off, and when I bent over to get it, [he] butted me in the rear and sent me sprawling. I seem to remember these were local horses. This was a low-budget eighteen-day wonder, and I don't think they brought them from Hollywood ... maybe Audie's horse, but I'm not sure. Anyway, these critters got more and more cantankerous, and at one point knocked a second unit camera off the cliff with many hours of footage in it. Earl said, 'No strain. We'll get enough coverage.' Toward the end of the day we were all exhausted and 'burning daylight.'

"Audie and I were in a two-shot talking about the death of my friend and mentor, played by Denver Pyle, who was actually a villain. At the end of the scene I walk out of the shot. The camera was positioned on level ground pointing up at Audie and me. The rehearsal went fine and I walked out of the shot. However, after the rehearsal the cinematographer said we had lost the light and would have to reposition. We moved to another position that still had light and proceeded to do a take with no rehearsal. For whatever reason … real exhaustion perhaps … or maybe I was really into the part … I failed to recognize we were now on the edge of a ten or fifteen foot drop to a ledge below where the camera was positioned, shooting up. At the end of the scene I proceeded to walk out of the shot as before and dropped, zip, straight down out of the shot and landed below, barely missing knocking over the camera. I twisted my ankle badly and started screaming every combination of the f-word imaginable while I heard Audie laughing hysterically above. By the way, if Nick Dennis [who played Audie's sidekick], who was near camera, had not blocked my fall I would have gone farther down the mountain and would have been history. I was checked over and it was determined (unprofessionally … no doctors on set or location in those days) that I had not broken anything, and they got me back up in position and we re-shot the scene. Earl printed that *and* the first take, and I heard later that people literally fell off their chairs viewing this 'out-take' in the rushes. After that shot we went on with the sequence, I in pain but nothing like later. Nick Dennis died in 1980. He was born in 1904, so he was in his 60s when I worked with him. Unbelievable. I would have thought late 40s. The guy had so much energy! Nick was a very funny guy.

"So, with the sore ankle, I went on with the rest of the day. Things got hairier by the moment … Joan Staley, who had kept it together pretty well and was very solicitous as to my injury, was the next to get it. Her horse spooked, she fell off and the horse, in a panic, scrambled up some rocks and got stuck way up on a plateau-like rock. Joan lost it and started crying and screaming. After she calmed down and they got her horse down, we managed a few zombie-like takes and it was a wrap for the day. When we got back to the motel I got a stiff drink and was sitting outside by the pool. Joan insisted I soak my foot in ice for what seemed like hours. I remember I was pretty drunk when I limped to bed. I was grateful to the lovely Miss Staley for her nursing; in fact, I developed kind of a crush on her but the feeling wasn't returned at all. Anyway, the ankle was usable from then on. With my crush on Joan Staley, I flirted with her a bit. I got a kind of 'come on, don't be ridiculous' smile in return and that's it.

"I had worked with Denver Pyle in the pilot for the *Tammy* TV show. Without the beard, Denver looked a hell of a lot like my father. I sort of adopted him as a father figure and would whine to him now and then, and he would non-comittably listen. On *Gunpoint* I was whining about my worries over *Tammy* being picked up. It was taking a long time to be sold, and I had a feeling I was either not being picked up or that my part was going to be shredded. Then I started whining over my feelings about Joan (location makes one a bit crazy and horny). Denver finally had enough and said, 'Screw it Macklin! Why don't you just grow up?' He was right, and I did … for a while.

"Despite his rather mysterious, cool, kind of insular aura, there was something about Audie I liked. I had empathy for him even then, as I said, knowing little about him. I was somewhat fascinated by him and developed a respect for him as an actor. I wish I had had, at the time, the natural instinctive way he had of taking the 'stink' off less than good dialog.

"My death scene, when we were home from location, was on the backlot waterfall set. It's a really neat set. I don't want to say he 'underplayed,' although that would be the 'technique' term. There always seemed to be something going on in those pellucid blue eyes. I concentrated on them in the death scene and they gave me a lot to just go with. He was good to work with as an actor and always seemed to 'be there.' That scene ended up the only good work I did in the flick. If I had asked Audie what he was thinking during the take or his close-up he probably would have said something like Garbo did about a long reaction shot from *Anna Karenina*. 'Thinking? I wasn't thinking. I was just counting to 50.' When the scene was in the can Audie gave me a little nod and walked away. I was told that was a rave from Audie. I had an awful line of dialogue in the movie: 'How could be he so cruel ... to do that to a young girl?' I think Audie could have played that or would have thrown it away or had it re-written or ad-lib it or something. I just did it as written, and it stunk worse than anything I have ever done. I literally cringed the last time I saw it. Gag me with a spoon!

Before the death scene, Audie and I were sitting by the waterfall waiting for the set up. My Uncle Lawrence was on Normandy and was decorated and is a member of some veteran heroes organization. I told Audie about my uncle and asked him if he knew about the organization. Audie looked away and mumbled something unintelligible, so I dropped the subject. I guess he had said all he wanted to say in his book. I don't blame him.

"I had another scene with Audie that was done all in a fifty-fifty two-shot. I was talking about my friend (Denver Pyle) who had died. I didn't think the scene was full enough and I asked Earl for another take, but got the 'No, that was just fine' bit. Well, maybe he meant it, but I know I could have done better. Edgar Buchanan was a joy and inspiration to watch at work. But I don't think I had the opportunity to say a word to him. After a rehearsal or take ... such as one of that rather complicated gambling scene ... he seemed to vanish. Anyway, he and Royal Dano and Kelly Thorsden did a great job on that scene in just a few takes.

"One other dude who stood out among the *Gunpoint* group was stunt coordinator Walt LaRue. He was a lot of fun and told great stories around the campfire. Talk about 'those were the days my friend.' Walt was also a cartoonist and made a cartoon of the 'hairy' day on the mountain and gave it to everyone in the cast. I still have it.

"Warren Stevens was nice but kind of a know-it-all. He once said, when the subject of how we were all working cheap came up, 'I think Audie gets

Audie Murphy rechecks his skill with bow and arrow during a *Gunpoint* filming break. Royal Dano had taught Audie to use a bow and arrow during a previous film they made together.

about $25,000 for these pictures. Enough to keep him for a few weeks at the track.' I don't know. I believe Audie was under contract to Universal and would have been paid weekly whether he worked or not. His movies made money."

Warren Stevens: "The second picture I did with Audie, we were in St. George, Utah, on location. Audie had a rather unusual sense of humor. He put rubber snakes or spiders in the girls' beds and thought that was hilarious. The poor girls were frightened to death. He laughed like hell when they screamed. No one ever retaliated as far as I know. They might have been scared to do it, knowing his background. Thankfully, none of his sense of humor was directed my way!"

Denver Pyle: "On *Gunpoint* we were shooting up on location in St. George. Audie had a girlfriend and she liked to ride horses, so Audie told her, 'If you want to ride a horse....' He was going out to work and it's kind of boring to sit around a set all day if you're not in the picture. So he told her to go out and get herself a horse and go riding. He went to work and she went out to the stable and asked the guy for a company horse. The guy asked, 'Do you ride?' And she said, 'Yeah.' And he said, 'Well I can't let you ride one of these horses. They're motion picture horses.' She said, 'What's the difference? A horse is a horse.' He said, 'Well I can't let you have one.' He was just being a shit-head. So she came out to the set around noon and Audie says, 'How was your ride?' She said, 'I didn't go.' He said, 'Why not?' She said, 'The guy wouldn't let me have a horse.' He looked at her — it was like a western picture — he just looked at her and stood up and asked for his car and went down to the stable and said, 'Why wouldn't you give my girl a horse?' He said, 'These are motion picture horses.' Audie said, 'Bullshit, they're just horses. Let her have one to ride.' The guy said, 'Well I'm gonna have to have permission from somebody besides you.' Audie looked at him, grabbed him and threw him up over the stall into the horseshit on the other side. Before you could imagine it, he had it done. He just grabbed that guy and took a flip on him and threw him over the stall into the horse shit. Then just very much like his character, he saddled up a horse, put a bridle on it, brought it out and gave it to her."

Stuntman Walt LaRue: "Audie was a faithful guy and a good guy. After going through all he'd gone through, he never told any war stories.

"I did some horse falls in *Gunpoint*. Willard Willingham, then Jimmy Sheppard, doubled Audie. Sheppard was a good hand. I wasn't really Audie's double, but I doubled him on a couple when they couldn't get ahold of Shep.

"Audie got me on those last ones. He liked my artwork and music ... we used to have parties over at his house. I think he had me over to encourage his kids to play guitars. [Singer] Jerry Wallace and Guy Mitchell, who had a hit on *Singin' the Blues*, used to come over.

"I don't know any director that was any better, personality-wise, [at getting] the job done without a whole bunch of static; Earl Bellamy could sure do it. It was 'No Strain' with him."

Robert Pine: "*Gunpoint* was the first movie I ever did. The thing I remember about Audie is, he was a very playful guy. He had a snake or a spider on a string tied to a stick. He'd take this thing over somebody's shoulder and put it on 'em. Of course, it'd scare 'em to death. He seemed to like that kind of humor. He seemed to be a very nice guy. Not overly talkative.

"Interestingly enough, a couple of years later I did a war movie at Universal with all the contract players, *The Young Warriors* (1967). The whole reason for doing the picture was, Universal had a lot of extra war footage from *To Hell and Back*. Typical Universal, they didn't want to let that go to waste, so they built this picture around all this footage. It was a pretty crummy picture. It starred James Drury.

"I love Earl Bellamy. I remember very well you'd blow a take and he'd say, 'No Strain.'"

As to Audie's gambling, "It makes sense, really, given what we know about him as the war hero, step out into enemy fire, that's what I call a huge gamble. What intrigued me, I was only 22, was that he was the most decorated hero of WWII. God, he was of mythic proportions in my eyes. But, they're also human beings. You wonder what goes on inside them. Audie still slept with a pistol under his pillow.

"There was a lot going on underneath all his joking. He certainly was friendly to everybody, but there was a distance to him. In retrospect, there was a lot going on in that man's mind. The rest of us will *never* be in a situation where we go to 'those places.' The camera loves mystery. In real life you just couldn't penetrate him. But he did draw your eye to what is going on with this guy? And the camera has always loved that. People that the camera can see right through, let's move on, next. But Audie was an interesting fella to be sure."

NOTES AND COMMENTS: Due to declining profits, Universal released Audie from his contract after the completion of *Gunpoint*.

The Texican
(COLUMBIA, JUNE 1966)

CREDITS: *Executive Producer:* Paul C. Ross; *Producers:* John C. Champion, Bruce Balaban, Audie Murphy (uncredited); *Director:* Lesley Selander, José Luis Espinosa; *Screenplay:* John C. Champion, José A. De La Loma; *Editor:* Teresa Alcocer; *Director of Photography:* Francisco Marin; *Art Director:* John Soler; *Costume Designer:* Ralph Borque, *Makeup:* Rod Gurrucharri; *Special Effects:* Tony Molina; *Music:* Nico Fidenco. Techniscope. Technicolor.

CAST: Audie Murphy (Jess Carlin); Broderick Crawford (Luke Starr); Diana Lorys (Kit O'Neal); Aldo Sambrell (Gil, aka Rio); Luz Marquez (Sandy Adams); Antonio Casas (Frank Brady); Molino Rojo (Harv); Juan Antonio Peral (Eb); Helga Genth (Maria Banta); Jorge Rigaud (Mitch); Luis Induni (U.S. Marshal); Martha May (Elena); Victor Vilanova (Roy Carlin); Carlos Hurtado (Tobe); Victor Israel (Station master); Jose M. Pinillo (Miguel); Cesar Osinaga (Bounty hunter); Gerard Tichy (Thompson); Vicente Soler (Dr. Miller); Juan Carlos Torres (Townsman); Oscar Del Campo (Saloon guitar player); Manuel Quintana (Gunslinger); Carlos Miguel Sola, Angel Lombardi (Poker players); A. Malla (Mexican boy).

RUNNING TIME: 86 minutes

FILMING DATES: September 27, 1965–November 3, 1965

LOCATIONS: Barcelona, Spain, area, and Balcazar Studios in Barcelona.

Filmed in Spain, with Murphy and Broderick Crawford the only non–Europeans in the cast, *The Texican* was a bottom-of-the-barrel rehash of every tired old cliché from the B-western files, with Murphy as a fugitive returning to his home town to avenge the death of his brother and subdue the self-styled boss of the town. Specifically, it was a remake of producer John Champion's excellent *Panhandle* (1948), with Rod Cameron. Made at a time when the European western or swashbuckler was the graveyard of Hollywood has-beens, it was a sad reflection on the fortunes of both stars. Respectability for the European western arrived in the

Title lobby card for Audie's only Euro-western.

shape of Clint Eastwood, and it's interesting to speculate that Murphy might well have emulated Eastwood's success if story and production values had been better. As it was, the film received the treatment it deserved — the lower half of cheap double bills, and almost immediate obscurity.

Murphy trudged tiredly through the motions without any apparent enthusiasm, and Broderick Crawford was embarrassingly gross, overweight and amateurish. The script crammed in runaway buggies, main street shoot-outs, and saloon fights with little logical continuity, and the supporting cast milled around looking like extras in a high school comic opera, their Spanish-spoken dialogue dubbed into cliché-ridden English. Sound effects of galloping hooves, gunshots and thudding fists were obviously post-recorded at ludicrously over-emphasized levels, giving the whole thing a cartoon feeling, with some of the more important supporting players allowed inexcusable excesses in over-acting. The color was poor, the editing slack, and the Techniscope process gave all the performers a curiously elongated look, so that Murphy seemed taller and slimmer than he had ever been.

Director Lesley Selander, a long-time western filmmaker, co-directed with Euro "artsy" filmmaker José Luis Espinosa, giving the film a jumbled look. They made generous use of unfamiliar locations, but apart from one well-shot sequence of Murphy riding a horse bareback, the overall result was dull and shoddy.

REMEMBRANCES: *Aldo Sambrell:* "In my opinion, Audie was an actor who had not been in a school or something like that, he was very realistic. He was himself. He didn't try to be somebody else. He was real.

Audie Murphy ready for action in *The Texican* (1966).

Broderick Crawford was a very nice person to work with, but he was drinking too much. Every single day he was almost drunk. It's a very sad story. One of these days when we have a scene together, suddenly I notice a very strong, awful smell. I go to the director and I say, 'There is something, I don't know what it is, it makes an awful smell.' We look at Crawford and he was shitting on himself, running down under his pants. Terrible. He was a very good actor, but he was under the pressure of booze. If he drank a cup of coffee, he'd drink a glass of brandy, cognac, very strong." [In all fairness, perhaps the circumstances of being in a low budget, Spanish-made western caused him to do so, regretting his current status in the business. That, along with the effect of too much Spanish coffee stronger than in the U.S., caused Crawford's "diarrhea."]

"Audie's son was with him in Spain. They'd go alone together to different places, not with the group."

NOTES AND COMMENTS: *Maverick Guns*, under the same production setup, was planned to lense after *The Texican*. It was also to be shot in Spain, with Les Selander again directing. Co-starring with Audie would be Cesar Romero and Gary Crosby, with a screenplay by Willard and Mary Willingham. For whatever reasons, it was not filmed.

Shortly after this film, Audie filed for bankruptcy. Whether or not the failure of this movie added to his financial woes is unknown. However, he was a silent partner (co-producer) with John C. Champion and publicist Paul C. Ross, hence the MCR (Murphy/Champion/Ross) production credit. Also about this time, Champion was planning a TV series based on

Audie Murphy's leading lady in Spain was Diana Lorys.

Audie's WWII exploits. In addition, a *To Hell and Back* sequel was being discussed.

Through his own independent Terrania production company, Audie planned to produce *Tomorrow the Moon*, dealing with a handful of selected American and Soviet combatants who, though allies in the war, become bitter adversaries in the struggle to find important rocket scientists and spirit them out of Germany. Audie discussed the project (based on a true story) with the Secretary of the Army. Audie stated, "It is obvious the success of the WWII special operation was so far reaching that it has involved to this day not only the security and scientific interests of the nation, but also our ability to pace Russians." The proposed production never went past the planning stage.

Actor Aldo Sambrell, who plays Crawford's right hand man — referred to as both Gil and Rio — was one of the most active performers in European westerns, with some 34 to his credit, including such films as *For a Few Dollars More, Man Called Noon, A Minute to Pray ... A Second to Die, Once Upon a Time in the West* and *Bad Man's River*. Living in Spain, he is writing his autobiography.

Trunk to Cairo
(NOAH FILMS—CCC FILM KUNST/RELEASED BY AMERICAN-INTERNATIONAL, JANUARY 1967)

CREDITS: *Producer:* Menahem Golan; *Associate Producer:* Michael Kaban; *Director:* Menahem Golan; *Screenplay:* Marc Behm, Alexander Ramati; *Editor:* Danny Shik; *Director of Photography:* Mimish Herbst; *Art Director:* Shlomo Zafrir; *Set Decorator:* K. Sander; *Makeup:* Rachel Golan, Daliah Priver; *Sound Recording:* Z. Naghtigal; *Hair Stylist:* R. Rimmel; *Music:* Dov Seltzer; *Song:* "Dangerous Woman" by Jean Raskin. Sung by Ouela Gill. In color.

CAST: Audie Murphy (Mike Merrick); George Sanders (Professor Schlieben); Marianne Koch (Helga Schlieben); Hans Von Borszodi (Hans Klugg); Joseph Yadin (Capt. Gabar); Gila Almagor (Yasmin); Elana Eden (Hadassa); Eitan Priver (Jamil); Zalman (Ephraim); Bomba J. Zur (Ali); Tikva Mor (Christina); Zeev Berlinsky (Benz); Eliezer Young (Dr. Heider); Shlomo Vichinsky (Jacob); Yoel Noyman (Egyptian Colonel); Cesar Suberi (Old Mullah); Shlomo Paz (Joe); Mona Silberstein (Hostess); Anna Shell (Belly dancer); Suzanna Ratoni (Fraulein Bruckner); Menashe Glazier (Mahmud); Karin (Young German girl).

RUNNING TIME: 93 minutes

FILMING DATES: Mid–June 1965 to mid–July, 1965

LOCATIONS: Shot entirely in Israel and Italy.

Audie Murphy was an unlikely choice for the role of a hard-drinking, woman-chasing secret agent in this sub–Bond thriller filmed on locations ranging from Israel to Rome, and it can only be assumed that due to the failing market for low-budget westerns he was prepared to accept any work that came along. The film, with Murphy and Sanders adding dubious box-office status to a cast of mainly German and Israeli players, was backed by American-International, a company notorious for its quick-and-cheap teenage and horror exploitation movies, and came plodding in at the tail end of the frantic spy-movie boom of the early 1960s.

The success of the James Bond films had spawned a rash of inferior imitations, but such was the demand that even the shoddiest European co-production could find a willing market, so *Trunk to Cairo* probably looked like a good idea at the time. By the time it gained a limited release, however, the secret agent bubble had burst, and such tame fare was unlikely to revive any interest. Murphy played a spy intent on destroying nuclear rocket installations near Cairo, with Sanders the scientist in charge of the complex who mistakenly believes he is working towards peaceful ends rather than on a deadly military weapon. The climax, with Murphy escaping from a trunk at Rome airport, was obviously suggested by a similar real-life incident a few years earlier.

The complicated and confusing plot was sluggishly developed and self-conscious in its attempts to copy the action-with-comedy style of Bond, Flint, Matt Helm and the other super-spies of the era. Comprehension and believability were not helped by the dubbing into English of many of the supporting players. Murphy, ill at ease in modern clothes, and awkward during the romantic interludes, was totally miscast as a dashing secret agent. He suggested rather a tired businessman trying his hand at movie acting as a tentative experiment, or, worse still, an over-the-hill cowboy star grabbing at cinematic straws to bolster a fading reputation. George Sanders, as he so often did, seemed bored by the whole thing — and the same could be said for the audience of this slapdash,

Newspaper ad for Audie Murphy's made-in-Israel career low point, *Trunk to Cairo* (1967).

trite effort. German actress Marianne Koch, who'd already flopped in Hollywood as Marianne Cook, was a deadly dull heroine.

Murphy did come into his own in the action sequences, particularly when required to ride a horse over sand dunes, an obvious reference to his western star image (an indication of the standard of the film's "in-jokes"), and managed to supply some wry humor in relation to the various trick weapons he employed. The Murphy-Sanders combination was an oil-and-water one which found no middle ground; and although the film offered a smattering of spoof-type humor in the second half (after it seemed to realize too late it had been taking itself too seriously), it remained a pallid, amateurish imitation of its betters. Its only claim to fame might be that Murphy was the least successful of the Bond imitators—a dubious honor, and one which did nothing to rescue his dying career.

REMBRANCES: *Audie Murphy:* "We didn't have any skilled Hollywood stuntmen on our foreign location. So all of us pitched in and performed most of the action ourselves."

NOTES AND COMMENTS: In screenwriter Jack Lewis' book *White Horse, Black Hat,* he relates the story of how Audie came complaining to Ilse Lahn, Audie's "mother-confessor" at the Paul Kohner talent agency: "'Ilse, you've gotta get me outta this. The damned thing's the worst James Bond parody I've ever read.' Ilse reminded Audie, 'There's a contract. You signed it!' Audie grouched, 'I'll pay them back. I won't do this piece of trash.' Ilse scolded, 'You took their money. And you don't have the money now, do you?'"

40 Guns to Apache Pass
(COLUMBIA, MAY 1967)

CREDITS: *Producer:* Edward Small (uncredited); *Associate Producer:* Grant Whytock; *Director:* William Witney; *Assistant Director:* Jack Berne; *Production Supervisor:* Harold E. Knox; *Screenplay:* Willard and Mary Willingham; *Film Editor:* Grant Whytock; *Director of Photography:* Jacques Marquette; *Art Director:* Paul Sylos; *Set Decorator:* H. E. Reif; *Wardrobe:* Joseph Dimmitt; *Makeup:* Ted Coodley; *Sound Recording:* Herman Lewis; *Sound Editor:* Al Bird; *Music:* Richard LaSalle. Eastmancolor.

CASTS: Audie Murphy (Captain Bruce Coburn); Michael Burns (Doug Malone); Kenneth Tobey (Corporal Bodine); Laraine Stephens (Ellen Malone); Robert Brubaker (Sgt. Walker); Michael Blodgett (Mike Malone); Michael Keep (Cochise); Kay Stewart (Kate Malone); Kenneth MacDonald (Harry Malone); Byron Morrow (Col. Homer Reed); Willard Willingham (Fuller); Ted Gehring (Barrett); James Beck (Higgins); Maurice Hart (Narrator). Stunts: Jimmy Sheppard.

RUNNING TIME: 94 minutes

FILMING DATES: May 17, 1966–May 27, 1966

LOCATIONS: Red Rock Canyon, California; Lake Los Angeles, California.

Even the titles of Murphy's films were now downgraded to the sort of cheap, catchall titles of the lowliest Poverty Row westerns of the 1930s and '40s—titles that could mean anything or nothing. Once again in uniform, and generally lethargic, Murphy remained in command of the many (and mindless) action scenes, and if his age continued to show, his leathery features were again compatible with the ruggedness of the locations. Murphy, a Cavalry captain attempting to escort a shipment of forty new repeating rifles through hostile Apache territory to a fort, is beset by problems and betrayals among his own men, as well as threats from Apache chief Cochise. Faced with a court martial when he loses the guns to deserter Tobey, Audie sets out to retrieve them alone, which he does, winning a pardon and a girl.

The film was again routine, lacking style or imagination, especially given the fact it was in the hands of a pro like Bill Witney. It's virtually a throwback to the quickies made by Columbia fast-movie merchant Sam Katzman in the early 1950s. Murphy's co-star, Kenneth Tobey, a familiar face from the '50s second-feature arena, earns the acting awards, turning in an especially vile and deceptive performance. Unnecessary narration of events throughout the picture only intrude and interfere with the natural flow of the events. Interest was slightly enlivened by the use of several new faces—talented youngster Michael Burns, who would later win roles in more prestigious movies and regular work in top-rated TV shows, such as *Rawhide;* strikingly handsome Michael Blodgett, who later co-starred with Kirk Douglas and Henry Fonda in *There Was a Crooked Man;* and blonde actress Laraine Stephens, who starred in the *Bracken's World* TV series and went on to become a regular guest leading lady in major TV shows. Despite their presence, the film was still just another cheap western, as pedestrian as the three previous Edward Small/Grant Whytock films. Destined to be Murphy's final starring role, it was a sad end to a once-bright career. It would be three years before Murphy made his next, and last, screen appearance.

NOTES AND COMMENTS: A continuity error occurs after Audie has beaten the tar

Top: Audie Murphy's face has taken on a more weathered look for his last starring role, in *40 Guns to Apache Pass* (1967). *Bottom:* Screenwriters Mary and Willard Willingham in 1999 beside the poster of a film they scripted for their good friend Audie Murphy. Willard began as a double for Audie, and, over the years, became Audie's closest friend and confidant. (Photograph by Jan Merlin.)

out of Kenneth Tobey in a fistfight. The next scenes show Tobey with a split lip and brilliant shiner; however, later the same day all signs of the beating have vanished.

Audie's policeman brother, Joe Murphy, was killed in January 1968 when his squad car collided with a grain truck near Celina, Texas.

On May 29, 1968, the trade paper *Variety* announced Audie would host 260 four-and-a-half-minute radio segments on military heroism for Woroner Productions. To be titled *Beyond the Call*, the vignettes would recall the exploits of Medal of Honor winners. The idea never materialized.

A Time for Dying
(FIPCO, JULY 1971)

CREDITS: *Producer:* Audie Murphy; *Associate to the Producer:* Willard Willingham; *Director:* Budd Boetticher; *Assistant Director:* Bob Farfan; *Screenplay:* Budd Boetticher; *Editor:* Harry Knapp; *Director of Photography:* Lucien Ballard; *Art Director:* Les Thomas; *Set Decorator:* Andy Nealis; *Costume Supervisor:* Eddie Armand; *Makeup:* Charles Blackman; *Sound Recording:* John Carter; *Hair Stylist:* Joan Phillips; *Special Effects:* Herman Townsley; *Music:* Harry Betts; *Title Art:* Walt LaRue. Color.

CAST: Richard Lapp (Cass Bunning); Anne Randall (Nellie Winters); Bob Random (Billy Pimple — William C. Coots); Beatrice Kay (Mamie); Victor Jory (Judge Roy Bean); Audie Murphy (Jesse James). In Silver City: Ron Masak (Bartender); Burt Mustin (Ed); Peter Brocco (Seth); Walter Reed (Mayor); Louis Ojena (Blacksmith); Jorge Rado (Banker-George); Walt LaRue (Shotgun guard); Maria Desti, Betty Rowland, Tina Stuart, Joanne Shields, Miki McDonald, Darla Paris, Arlette Thomas, Nancy Lewis, Jo Linn, Athena, Suzette DeCarlo (Mamie's girls); Annette Gorman (Mamie's new girl). In Vinegaroon: Charles Wagenheim (Milton); Ira Augustain (Pepe); Terry Murphy (Sonny); Skip Murphy (Curly); Randy Shields (Cauliflower); Bob Herron (Rankin). Jesse's Men: William Bassett (the Southerner); Willard Willingham (Frank James); J. N. Roberts (Bob Ford); Casey Tibbs, Neil Summers (Outlaws). Billy's Boys: Dick Spangler, Robert Grever. Stunts: Bob Herron, Randy Shields, Neil Summers, Walt LaRue.

RUNNING TIME: 69½ minutes

FILMING DATES: April 29 or 30, 1969– May 19, 1969

LOCATIONS: Apache Junction, Arizona.

Murphy first worked with director-writer Budd Boetticher in 1951 when Boetticher directed *The Cimarron Kid*. At this time, Boetticher was one of Universal's stable of action directors who had made a number of westerns and adventure dramas of good, but not spectacular, quality. In the mid–1950s, however, he teamed with Randolph Scott and producer Harry Joe Brown to direct a series of westerns for their Ranown company, and, on the strength of these, developed a strong cult following, particularly in Europe. In 1960 Boetticher left Hollywood for Mexico to work on a personal project and did not return for eight years, at which time he joined Murphy in a newly formed company with the object of producing low-budget westerns. However, only one movie was made, *A Time for Dying*, shot in Arizona in eighteen days, with Murphy returning to films after a three year absence in a five-minute cameo role as Jesse James.

The plot revolved around the adventures of a young farm boy out to make a career as a bounty hunter. He rescues a girl from a brothel and they travel together, meeting up with infamous "hanging judge" Roy Bean and outlaw Jesse James before the boy finally faces his first challenge, in the shape of another young gunslinger. He is killed, and the girl returns to the brothel.

The film was first released in France in 1971, after Murphy's death, and received excellent reviews, but has otherwise been rarely screened. It received a limited release on videotape in the 1990s.

Boetticher cast unknowns Richard Lapp and Anne Randall as the young hero and heroine. Both were quite bland, and the film did nothing to further their careers. Bob Random, who'd co-starred in Dale Robertson's *Iron Horse* TV series, was the gunman who kills the hero, and veteran actor Victor Jory overacted mightily as Judge Roy Bean. Photographed in color by Lucien Ballard, whose credits include *Ride the High Country*, *Nevada Smith* and *Will Penny*, and written by Boetticher himself, it was an artistic try, if not a commercial success.

Murphy, at 45, was excellent in his brief appearance as Jesse James, instructing the young hero in the finer points of gunmanship.

It seems highly probable that with a director of Boetticher's caliber and a strong, experienced production team, Murphy might have gone on to emulate the excellence of Randolph Scott's Boetticher westerns, but he was killed before filming began on the second planned pro-

Audie Murphy, director Budd Boetticher and noted cinematographer Lucien Ballard discuss the making of *A Time for Dying* (1971) at Apache Junction, Arizona.

duction, tentatively titled *When There's Something to Do*, which would have co-starred Murphy and his elder son Terry.

REMEMBRANCES: *Budd Boetticher*, in his book *When in Disgrace*, explains the making of a pet film project, *Arruza*, in Mexico, and how "Overnight I was besieged by creditors. There were honest debts owed for past work on the picture, but up until now they were debts that had been willingly deferred. Suddenly everyone demanded immediate payment, or, quote, 'You will find yourself in real Mexican Trouble.' Then along came Audie Murphy. I'd directed one of Audie's first pictures and we became friends. But I didn't realize what good friends we were until Audie arrived in Mexico City with blood in those deadly gray eyes. Somehow, up in Hollywood, he'd found out about my current problems. He stayed just one day, looked into the situation, deposited $5,500 in our *Arruza* account, and flew back home. Audie didn't want a 'reasonable hunk' of the picture. He said he'd 'just appreciate a sixteen-millimeter print, one day, if there was ever going to be one handy,' and one day he hoped to produce pictures, and maybe I'd direct one for him. They don't give you the Medal of Honor for bein' jes' an ordinary fella.

"Anyone who ever really knew Audie didn't forget much of anything about him. Well now [a few years later], Audie was in trouble. He didn't drink or smoke, but he'd bet his .45 caliber service revolver and both arms on anything that walked, flew or swam. And everything in Las Vegas was his downfall. He didn't complain. He just stated the fact that he owed the government a quarter of a million dollars, and he needed a movie to produce. Well, there wasn't anything I wouldn't have done for Audie, and I immediately told him he had one, *A Time for Dying*. It was a good script by then, and I had planned to make it with Peter Fonda as the young, ambitious gunslinger who stepped out of his class and would end up very dead before 'the end' title faded onto the screen. Well, Audie said he couldn't raise the money for the type of film I intended to make, but Audie was one hell of a lot more important to me than the budget of my proposed picture, so we worked out a deal to his satisfaction in less than five minutes over the phone. He moved his office into the first floor of the Franklin West Towers, and we went to work polishing the script, casting the actors and setting the crew. Naturally, Lucien Ballard was to be my cameraman. The only distasteful thing about the deal was, I didn't care for Audie's associates and financiers, but I didn't have to spend any time with them, so ... what the hell. And all the characters who surrounded the making of that picture, funny thing about them — the good ones and the bad — they got what they deserved. Only Audie Murphy — one of the really good ones— didn't end up with luck. Our picture together, *A Time for Dying*, saved him for a while, but, in the long run, when you win your country's highest honor at eighteen, maybe life can become pretty dull in the humdrum confines of the movie business. And, always searching for excitement, I'll bet Audie knew, with no regrets just before that plane hit the ground, that his own 'Time for Dying' had arrived."

Walter Reed: "I noticed a mean streak in Audie, you could see it in his eyes. There was no reason to do it, but he shot the head off a snake that wasn't bothering anybody and I could see Murphy really enjoyed it."

Walt LaRue: "Audie was producing, he had some Washington, D.C., backers. I was an artist at that time. Budd [Boetticher] approached me about doing the title credit paintings. He knew about my art, I'd been on a lot of his pictures, drawn cartoons and shown him my fine art.

"They called a wrap but the film came up short on footage. It was 15 minutes or so short. They had a script girl who should have kept things straight. What they did, they went back ... in the interim, the town down there, Apache Junction, burned down. So they figured they'd shoot Audie in a few scenes or something. They put that in there because they didn't have the town.

"One time they had to shoot a snake's head off for a shot ... they had four or five different snakes ... and Audie shot all their heads off. [Chuckles] He was probably ten yards away. A snake moves his head around pretty rapidly, but he was a hell of a shot."

NOTES AND COMMENTS: Audie's monetary problems resulted not only from his passion for gambling, but, according to the *L.A. Times*, from a $260,000 loss on an Algerian oil venture. Residuals from TV showings of his earlier films were taken by the IRS for back taxes. "Once I'm squared away with the tax people and my debts," Audie stated in 1969, "I'll be starting all over again. It's not going to be easy, but I look forward to it. We're looking at some [film] properties. I'll produce them and do some acting in hard-hitting secondary parts."

Audie's company was named First International Planning Company, shortened to Fipco. He and director Budd Boetticher planned another picture, to be shot in Spain, *A Horse for Mr. Barnum*, but it was never made. Even after Murphy's death, Boetticher periodically tried to get that film made, right up until the time of his own death.

Director Don Siegel wanted Audie for the villain in Clint Eastwood's *Dirty Harry* (1971). Audie agreed but had to fly to Virginia first on business. It was the trip that ended his life, leaving a myriad of 'ifs' that still loom before us to this day.

Epilogue

In his last years in Hollywood, with his career and finances in ruins, Murphy expressed bitterness at the treatment he'd received from the movie capital, but refused to give in. "I'm too tough for this damn town," he once said. "After the hell of war, nothing could scare me. It can't break me. Being down and out rekindled my spirit. I had the choice of living or dying — and I found out I wanted to live." But the living was hard — and the dying was swift and unexpected.

It was perhaps a fittingly violent end for a man whose life had seen so much violence, and there would doubtless be many who would condemn Murphy for his instinctive reliance on the law of the gun in times of stress. But it was a sad and inescapable fact that from the time of his boyhood, society put a gun in Audie Murphy's hand, and with it he earned all his rewards. As a barefoot boy in Texas, a bullet meant the difference between his family eating or going hungry, as a soldier he was trained to kill in the cause of freedom and patriotism, as a movie actor he rarely made a film without a gun in his hand — small wonder then, when the pressure was on, his instinct was to resort to violence. Murphy's values were simple and direct — black and white, with few gray shadings — and he always took the direct route to solving any problems. Author-cartoonist Bill Mauldin, Murphy's co-star in *The Red Badge of Courage*, probably summed up the essential Audie Murphy better than anyone else in his moving tribute published in *Life* magazine in 1971: "As he grew older, Murphy wanted the world to stay simple so he could concentrate on tidying up its moral fiber wherever he found himself. But nothing came out right. His country got into wars that heroes couldn't win. Murphy's kind of gallantry faced a buyer's market. He kept walking on the balls of his feet like a wary little bobcat, lonely and angry … most of us accept a certain amount of blending as we go along. We adjust, accept, tolerate, temporize and sometimes compromise. Not Murphy. In him we recognized the straight, raw stuff, uncut and fiery as the day it left the still. Nobody wanted to be in his shoes, but nobody wanted to be unlike him, either."

As an actor, Murphy's career achievements were not particularly formidable, but he nevertheless gave a great deal of genuine pleasure to many moviegoers, and made a great deal of money for Universal-International. An indication of the high standard set by his films, as opposed to that of his contemporaries, can be gauged by a glance through the list of actors and actresses who appeared with him. It's unlikely any other western star can boast as many Academy Award winners among his co-stars.

Epilogue

Despite the casual dismissal of his film career by most obituary writers, the fact remains that in his more than 20 years in movies Audie never took less than star billing (apart from his first two films and his last); was never reduced to playing bit parts, as so many other "forgotten" stars had done; and achieved the remarkable feat of starring in his own biography, without self-glorification and to unanimous world-wide acclaim.

Perhaps if he had been prepared to compromise, to capitalize on his war record, even to play the Hollywood game and pander to the whims and egos of those he labeled "phonies," he might have lived to continue a comfortable second-string career in films and television. But then he would not have been truly his own man, and to Audie Murphy, that was unacceptable.

BIBLIOGRAPHY

Books

Affron, Charles. *Lillian Gish: Her Legend and Life*. Scribner, 2001.

Andreychuk, Ed. *Burt Lancaster: A Filmography and Biography*. Jefferson, NC: McFarland, 2000.

Arness, James. *James Arness: An Autobiography*. Jefferson, NC: McFarland, 2001.

Blottner, Gene. *Universal-International Westerns, 1947–1963*. Jefferson, NC: McFarland, 2000.

Boetticher, Budd. *When in Disgrace*. Neville, 1989.

Coleman, Herbert. *The Hollywood I Knew*. Lannam, MD: Scarecrow, 2003.

Cozad, W. Lee. *Those Magnificent Mountain Movies*. Lake Arrowhead, CA: Rim of the World Historical Society, 2002.

Fitzgerald, Michael, and Boyd Magers. *Ladies of the Western*. Jefferson, NC: McFarland, 2002.

Goldrup, Tom and Jim. *Feature Players Vol. 2*. Self-published, 1992.

_____. *Feature Players Vol. 3*. Self-published, 1997.

_____. *Growing Up on the Set*. Jefferson, NC: McFarland, 2002.

Graham, Don. *No Name on the Bullet*. New York: Viking, 1989.

Lentz, Harris. *Television Westerns Episode Guide*. Jefferson, NC: McFarland, 1997.

Lewis, Jack. *White Horse, Black Hat*. Lannam, MD: Scarecrow, 2002.

Magers, Boyd, and Michael Fitzgerald. *Westerns Women*. Jefferson, NC: McFarland, 1999.

Nott, Robert. *Last of the Cowboy Heroes*. Jefferson, NC: McFarland, 2000.

Simpson, Col. Harold B. *Audie Murphy American Soldier*. Dallas, TX: Alcor, 1982.

Stricklyn, Ray. *Angels and Demons*. Los Angeles: Belle Publishing, 1999.

Whiting, Charles. *Hero: The Life and Death of Audie Murphy*. New York, NY: Jove, 1991.

Periodicals

Audie Murphy Research Foundation newsletter (*Vol. 5, Summer/Fall 1998*) (interview with Jack Elam).

Audie Murphy Research Foundation newsletter (*Vol. 9, 2001*) (interview with Cece Whitney).

Chierichetti, David. *Classic Images #331* (*Jan. 2003*) (interview with Tommy Rall).

Magers, Boyd. *Western Clippings*, various issues (1994–2002).

Swines, Steve. *Starlog #141, 142* (interview with Nathan Juran).

Tibbetts, John C. *Kansas History V. 22, No. 3* (*Autumn 1999*) "Riding with the Devil" article.

INDEX

Aaker, Lee 87, 88
ABC 100
Acapulco 164
Acosta, Rudolph 159, 161
Acting in the Motion Picture Business (book) 203
Actors Studio 22
Adams, Edie 147
Adams, Les vii
Admiral Pictures 185, 192
Affron, Charles 151
The African Queen 54
Agar, John 110
Air Cadet 45
Albert, Eddie 128, 129
Alderson, John 133–135
All About Eve 121
Alland, William 156
Allgood, Sara 40
Allied Artists 26, 30, 110, 178, 179, 180, 181, 182, 184, 188
A-M Farms 95, 184
American International 180, 212
Anders, Merry 185–87
Anderson, "Bloody Bill" 41–42, 44
Anderson, Chuck vii
Anderson, James 82
Andrade, Cisco 99
Andrews, Robert Hardy 32
Angels and Demons (book) 198
Ankrum, Morris 81, 103
Anna Karenina 206
Apache Junction, Arizona 216, 217, 218
Apache Rifles 18, 191–96
Apple Valley, California 68, 69, 70, 73, 77, 80
Aragon, Art 100
Archer, Pamela 10, 13, 19, 57, 60
Arizona Raiders 18, 192, 196–201
Arlen, Richard 41, 45
Arlington National Cemetery 8, 19
Armstrong, R. G. 132, 133, 134

Arness, James 37, 68
Arnold, Eddy 147
Arnold, Jack 16, 131–133, 135–136, 156
Arruza 218
Audie Murphy Company 107
Audie Murphy Research Foundation Newsletter 191
Australian Women's Weekly 90
Autry, Gene 12

Bacall, Lauren 128
Bachelor Father 111
Backus, Jim 137
Bad Boy 10, 11, 26–30, 116
Bad Man's River 211
Bad Men of Missouri 42
Baer, Parley 32
Bakersfield, California 89, 93
Balboa, California 128
Balcazar Studios 208
Balin, Ina 151
Ball, Suzan 76
Ballard, Lucien 217, 218
Ballew, Smith 54
Bancroft, Anne 101–104
Band, Albert 50
Barcelona, Spain 208
Barnes, Rayford 124
Barrett, Claudia 155–156
Barton, Gregg 54, 83
Battle at Apache Pass 59, 102
Battle at Bloody Beach 18, 161, 169–171
Battle on the Beach 171
Baudouim I, King 110
Bean, Roy 217
Bear Canyon, Arizona 101
Beery, Noah, Jr. 37, 56, 58
Bell, James 161
Bell Ranch, California 184
Bellamy, Earl vii, 201–208
Bend of the River 65, 112, 113, 201

Benion, Heber 39
Bennett, Jack vii
Bernds, Edward 184
Best, James 42–43, 56–59, 68, 140–141, 185, 187
Bettger, Lyle 82, 83, 85–86, 88
Beverly Hills, California 97
Beyond Glory 10, 23, 21–24, 163
Beyond the Call 216
Bias, Chet 44
Bickford, Charles 35
Big Bear, California 65, 135
The Big Picture 158
The Big Sky 42
Big Valley 42
Billy the Kid 32, 144
Birch, Paul 80
Biscailuz, Gene 67
Bischoff, Samuel 180
Bishop, California 112
Bishop, William 185
The Black Cat 40
Blackboard Jungle 27
Blanchard, Mari 75, 86–88
Blodgett, Michael 215
Blottner, Gene vii
Blyth, Ann 35
Body and Soul 98
Boetticher, Budd 18–19, 55, 57–59, 172, 195, 199, 216–219
Bogart, Humphrey 128
Bogdanovich, Peter 35
Bonney, William 32
Bonzo Goes to College 68
Boone, Richard 143
Bouchey, Willis 132
Boyle, Charles 59
Bracken's World 215
Bradford, Lane 83
Brady, Mathew 48–49
Brady, Scott 41–44
Brainhead, Utah 36
Brand, Max 85

225

Index

Brando, Marlon 3, 15, 133
Bray, Robert 83
The Breaking Point 128
Breck, Peter 136–137
Breen, Joseph J. 35, 54, 59, 63, 96
Brennan, Walter 58, 82–83
Britton, Barbara 72
Brock, Jimmy 49
The Broken Bridge 158
Bromfield, John 56, 58–59
Bronson, Charles 87
Bronson Canyon 192, 197
Brooks, Geraldine 72
Brooks, Rand 56, 58, 162
Brown, Harry Joe 15, 16, 104, 105, 107, 141, 216
Brown, Johnny Mack 32, 63
Brubaker, Robert 196
Brynner, Yul 15
Buchanan, Edgar 86, 88, 204, 206
Bucko, Roy 44
Buckskin 30
Buffington, Sam 163
Bullet for a Badman 18, 178, 187–192
A Bullet Is Waiting 107
Burns, Michael 215
Burro Flats (California) 77, 82
Burrows, George D. 180
Burson, Polly 146
Burton, Richard 151
Bus Stop 83

Caan, James 135
Cabot, Susan 61–63, 65–66, 67, 77–78, 80, 140
Cagney, Bill 9, 22
Cagney, James 9, 10, 22, 23, 25, 78, 162
Calhoun, Rory 12, 18, 107, 131, 187
Callahan, Mushy 134
Callow, Reggie 50
Cameron, Rod 12, 208
Campanella, Joseph 142–143
Campbell, William 100, 103
Cantor, Eddy 35
Carey, Harry, Jr. 47, 167
Carr, Mary 141
Carr, Paul 159
Carr, Thomas 139, 141
Carroll, John 164
Carson, Johnny 71
Carson, Sunset 139
Caruso, Anthony 80, 102, 103, 104
Cassidy, Hopalong 56, 78
Cast a Long Shadow 17, 138–141, 143
Castle, Mary 66, 67
Castle, Peggy 45
Castle, William 25
Cat Ballou 86
Catalina Island, California 170, 171
Catching, Bill 167–168, 174

Caulfield, Joan 23
CBS 60, 96, 119
Cedar City, Utah 36
Champion 98
Champion, John 208, 210
Chandler, Jeff 13, 131, 143
Chapman, Marguerite 41, 43, 45
Charney, Kim 106
Chase, Borden 112, 113, 117, 125, 127
Chase, Frank 109–10, 117, 126, 127
Checkmate 164
Chevy Show 147
Chierichetti, David vii
The Cimarron Kid 12, 55–60, 68, 201, 216
Cinecitta Studios 121
Civil War 41, 45–48, 53–54, 68, 117, 119
Civilian Service Medal 158
Clark, Fred 108–109
Clark, Gen. Mark 72
Clements, Stanley 28
Cliff, John 167, 168
Clift, Montgomery 3, 123
Clifton, "Dynamite" Dick 60
Clum, John Philip 15, 101, 102, 104
Cochise 214
Coleman, Herbert 161, 163
Coleman, Joseph 164
Colgate Comedy Hour 104
Colgate Variety Hour 104
Collins, Ray 68, 72, 73
Columbia, California 55
Columbia Pictures 15, 18, 19, 104, 107, 117, 178, 182, 184, 187, 188, 196, 208, 214
Column South 13, 67–73, 133
The Comancheros 154
Comes a Horseman 138, 156
Comstock, Ned vii
Conejo Valley, California 27, 131
Confessions of an Opium Eater 110
Congressional Medal of Honor 8, 47, 91, 95
Connors, Chuck 18
Connors, Jack 167, 168
Cook, Marianne 213
Cook, Tommy 116
Coon, Gene L. 132
Cooper, Ben 181–183, 196–197, 198–199
Cooper, Gary 12
Copeland, Bobby vii
Copeland, Joe vii
Copeland, Lance vii
Corday, Mara 83
Coronet 10
Corriganville 62
Courtland, Jerome 196
Cowling, Bruce 92
Cozad, W. Lee 95
Crabbe, Buster 197, 198
Cramer, Slim 83

Crane, Stephen 46, 50
Crawford, Broderick 208, 209, 211
Crawford, Dale vii
Crawford, John 54
Crider, Dorothy 106
Crosby, Bing 107
Crosby, Dee 40
Crosby, Gary 171, 210
Crowley, Kathleen 179
Crowley, Pat 102, 103
Cullen, Bill 96
Curtis, Dick 54
Curtis, Tony 13, 37, 42, 43, 44, 83, 89, 137, 182, 183
Custer 196

Daheim (Day), Johnny 94, 112
Daily Variety 198
Dale, Jim 201
Dallas News 9
Dalton Gang 44, 55, 59, 60
Daniels, Ann 23
The Danny Thomas Show 164
Dano, Peg 53
Dano, Royal 50–54, 159–60, 161, 204, 206
Dante, Michael 192–199
Dauphin, Claude 121
Daves, Delmar 143
Davis, Jim 185
Davison, Col. Paul R. 73
Dawn at Socorro 67
A Day of Fury 179
Dealy, Ted 9
Dean, James 3, 7, 12, 15
De Cordova, Fred 68, 70–73, 133
De Corsia, Ted 185–186
Dee, Sandra 16, 136, 137
Dehner, John 17, 67, 139–141
Dekker, Albert 32, 34, 35
Dell Comics 175
Dennis, Nick 205
Destry 14, 15, 75, 84–88, 89, 105
Destry Rides Again 14, 67, 85, 86
Devon, Richard 168
Dew, Eddie 58
De Wilde, Brandon 113, 117
Diamond, David 180
Dick, Douglas 52, 54
Dierkes, John 50, 52, 54
Dietrich, Marlene 67, 86
The Dinah Shore Chevy Show 147
Dinehart III, Mason Alan 141
Dirty Harry 219
Disney 200
Distinguished Service Cross 3, 47
Dix, Bill 54
Dr. No 171
Domergue, Faith 61–63, 76
Donlevy, Brian 41, 44
Donnell, Jeff 106
Doolin, Bill 55, 59, 60
The Doolins of Oklahoma 56

Doolittle, General James Harold 48
Doran, Ann 141
Double R Ranch 147
Doucette, John 86
Doud, Gil 89, 93, 102
Douglas, Kirk 215
Dow, Peggy 35
Drake, Charles 16, 65–66, 91, 96, 102–104, 132–135, 149, 175–177
Dru, Joanne 136, 137
Drums Across the River 14, 80–84, 117
Drury, James 208
The Duel at Silver Creek 12, 13, 60–63, 65
Dugay, Yvette 56, 57, 59
The Dunninger Show 100
Durango, Colorado 112, 115, 116
Durango, Mexico 148
Durango-Silverton Railroad 112
Durante, Jimmy 35
Duryea, Dan 18, 77, 78, 80, 113, 115, 116, 172, 173, 174, 178

Earp, Wyatt 101, 160
Easton, Robert 47–52
Eastwood, Clint 100, 209, 219
Eaton, Gloria 47
Edwards, Ralph 30
Egan, Richard 42
87th Precinct 164
Eisenhower, Dwight D. 23, 24
Elam, Jack 25, 78–80, 115–116, 129–130
Eldredge, George 67
Elephant Butte, Arizona 101
Elliott, William 107
Emerson, Faye 96
Emerson, Hope 105, 106
Empire 12
Enright, Ray 42, 43
Erdman, Dick 54
Erickson, Leif 56, 58
Espinosa, José Luis 209
Evans, Dale 147
Evans, Joan 68–72, 131–134
Everly, Don 157

The Far Country 112
Farr, Felicia 143, 144, 146
Farrell, Tommy vii
Farrow, John 23
Fawcett, William 186
The F.B.I. 56
Feature Players Vol. 2 34, 168
Fennelly, Vincent 184
Field, Margaret (aka Mahoney, Maggie) 24
Field, Mary 127
First International Planning Company 216, 219
Fitzgerald, Michael vii
Flaming Bullets 184

Flaming Star 154
Flippen, Jay C. 112, 113, 117
Fluffy 203
Flying John 80, 96, 100
Flynn, Errol 41, 42
Fonda, Henry 215
Fonda, Peter 218
For a Few Dollars More 211
Forbidden Valley 37
Ford, Glenn 86
Ford, John 22
Ford, Paul 34
Ford, Wallace 86, 88
Ford Startime: The Man 142–43
Fort Lewis, Washington 89, 95, 96
Fortuna, Carl 113
40 Guns to Apache Pass 19, 214–16
Foster, Dianne 113–15, 117
Foulk, Robert 141
Fox, Norman 117
Fox Century Ranch (California) 139
Francis, Arlene 100
Francis, Connie 147
Francis the Talking Mule 74
Frank, Fred 73
Fraser, Harry 184
Freeman, Mona 35, 72
French Foreign Legion 94
From Russia with Love 171
Fuller, Clem 127
Fuller, Sam 93
Fulton, Rad 144

Gable, Clark 42
Garbo, Greta 206
Garfield, John 98, 128
Garland, Judy 7
Garland, Richard 56
Garner, Jack 44
Garner, James 18
Garralaga, Martin 34
Gaye, Lisa 82, 83
G. E. Theatre: Incident 119
Gebert, Gordon 93
Geer, Lenny 167
Geer, Will 32
General Services Studio 24, 78
Geronimo 101, 102
Gibson, Hoot 135
Gilligan's Island 137
Gilmore, Art 35
Gish, Lillian 148, 151
Gittens, Wyndham 38
Glassberg, Irving 59
Gleason, James 28, 29
The Glenn Miller Story 112
Golden, Robert S. 25
Goldfinger 171
Goldrup, Jim vii, 34, 168
Goldrup, Tom vii, 34, 168
Goldwyn, Samuel 69
Gomberg, Sy 109
Gordon, Leo 127

Graham, Don vii, 156, 157
Grant, Bill 124
Grant, Kathryn 105, 107
Greene, Graham 15, 121
Grey, Virginia 133
Griffith, D. W. 151
Griffith Park 192, 194
The Gun Runners 15, 127–30
Gunfight at Comanche Creek 18, 180–84
Gunpoint 18, 178, 179, 190, 201–8
The Guns of Fort Petticoat 15, 104–107, 139, 141
Gunsmoke 12, 13, 15, 37, 64–67, 68, 74, 85, 127, 139, 140, 196
Guys and Dolls 15

Haggerty, Don 34
Hale, Alan, Jr. 86, 190
Hale, Monte 176
Hall, Barbara vii
Hall, Gita 128, 129
Hamann, G. D. vii
Hardy, Stuart 37
Hargrove, Marion 107, 110
Hart, Tommy 76
Havens, James 116
Hawkins, Jimmy 87
Hawkins, Tim 87
Hawks, Howard 42, 140
Hayden, Sterling 184
Hayes, Richard 100
Hayward, Jim 54
Hayward, Louis 45
Healey, Myron 169
Hecht-Hill-Lancaster 152
Heidt, Horace 96
Hell Bent for Leather 17, 143–47, 160, 163, 172
Hell Bent for Paradise 144
Hello Out There (play) 53
Hemingway, Ernest 15, 128, 129
Hendrix, Wanda 10, 22, 27, 30, 34, 35, 36, 37, 38, 39, 40, 60, 141
Henry Holt and Company 25, 30
Hepburn, Audrey 18, 148, 149, 150, 151, 152
Here Come the Nelsons 68
Here's Hollywood 169
Herron, Bobby 151, 167, 183
Hibbs, Jesse 14, 40, 78, 89, 91, 93, 97, 99, 102, 109, 110, 125, 127
Hickman, Darryl 119
High Chaparral 56
Hitchcock, Alfred 161
Hoboken Dock, New Jersey 97
Hoffman, Herbert 164
Hoffman, Joseph 163
Holliday, Doc 101
Hollywood Actors Laboratory 10
Hollywood Bowl 35
Hollywood Citizen News 24
The Hollywood I Knew (book) 163

Index

Hollywood Square Dancers 147
Holt, Tim 12
Homan, Rex 186
Homeier, Skip 190, 191
Hooker, Joe 73
Hopalong Cassidy Productions 25
Hope, Bob 19, 95, 189
Hopper, Hedda 25, 53, 95, 104, 111
A Horse for Mr. Barnum 219
Hot Lead and Cold Feet 201
Houston, Angelica 52
Howitzer, Bronson 179
Hoy, Bobby 87, 94–95, 96, 138, 168
Hudson, Bill 54
Hudson, John 56, 59
Hudson, Rock 13
Huffaker, Clair 154, 156, 158
Hughes, Billy 162
Hughes, Howard 62, 141
Hughes, Whitey 162
Hunnicutt, Arthur 48
Hunt, Terry 24, 67, 100
Huston, John 11, 12, 18, 46, 47, 48, 49, 50, 51, 52, 54, 80, 141, 148, 149, 150, 151, 152

I Am an American Day 35
Ibsen, Henrik 107
Iglesias, Eugene 61, 104, 195
Imelman, Dr. Stanley 107
Indian Uprising 192, 196
Internal Revenue Service 19
Iron Horse 217
Isthmus of Catalina 170
I've Got a Secret 96
Iverson Ranch, California 62, 181, 184
Ives, Burl 36, 37, 39, 40

J&M Productions 164
Jack Garner Ranch (California) 32, 41, 44
Jagger, Dean 36, 37, 39, 40
James, Frank 42, 44, 169
James, Jesse 41, 42, 44, 169, 196, 216, 217
Jamestown (CA) Roundhouse 55
Janss Ranch (California) 27, 125, 139
Janssen, David 103
Jensen, Larry vii
Joe Butterfly 15, 16, 107–11, 138
Joe Queen 127, 163, 167
John Huston Ranch (California) 46
Johnny Come Lately (book) 71
Johnson, Ben 47, 135
Johnson, Chubby 66
Johnson, Clint 184
Johnson, Russell 68, 71–72, 74, 76, 78, 80
Johnson, Van 35
Johnson Flats (California) 41
Jolley, I. Stanford 54

Jones, Ken vii
Jones, L. Q. 179, 193, 195
Jordan, Jo-Ann 169
Jory, Victor 217
Juaregui Ranch (California) 55, 65
Jubal 143
Juran, Nathan 65, 73, 75, 76, 81, 82, 83–84

Kamb, Karl 32, 35
Kanab, Utah 36, 38, 39
Kansas Raiders 11, 37, 40–45, 68, 137, 196, 201
Katzman, Sam 214
Kay, Gordon 69, 134, 135, 154–156, 160–162, 172, 174, 176, 177, 178, 179, 203
Kazear, Paul 147
Keith, Robert 159, 161
Keller, Harry 154, 155, 156, 172, 203
Kelley, DeForest 181, 183
Kelly, Jack 18, 65, 66, 68, 91, 140
Kelly, Paul 64, 65, 66, 140
The Ken Murray Show 60
Kennedy, Arthur 73, 135
Kennedy, Burt 18, 172, 175
Kernville, California 82
Keymas, George 197, 198
Kid from Left Field 138
The Kid from Texas 1, 11, 31–35, 201
Kido, Caroline 110, 111
King, Wright 141
The King and I 15
Koch, Marianne 213
Kohler, Fred, Jr. 54
Kohner, Paul 214
Kohner, Susan 119, 151
Korean War 125, 179
Kraike, Jessica 40
Kraike, Michael 40
Krone, Fred 199
Kronos 110

Ladd, Alan 10, 18, 22, 23, 128, 132, 138, 163
Laguna Beach, California 130
Lahn, Ilse 214
Lake Los Angeles (California) 214
LaMonte, Steve 40
Lampert, Zohra 159, 160, 161, 162
Lancaster, Burt 18, 148, 149, 150, 151, 152, 198
Lane, Abbe 77, 78, 80
Lane, Allan "Rocky" 144, 160–161, 176
Langton, Paul 92
Lapp, Richard 217
Larkins, Bob vii, 1, 3, 4, 5
Larson, Jack 54
LaRue, Walt 169, 199, 206, 207, 218–219
Lassau, Deidre vii, 1, 4, 5

Last of the Badmen 184
Last of the Cowboy Heroes (book) 194
The Last Picture Show 35
The Last Wagon 143
Law and Order 67
Lawrence, Marc 169
Lawson, Linda 193, 194
Lee, Palmer 56, 68
Lee, Ruta 190–91
Leeds, Utah 172
Legion of Honor 3, 10
Legion of Merit 47
LeMay, Alan 152
Lemmon, Jack 146
Lewis, Gene 43
Lewis, Jack 130, 214
Lewis, Jerry 189
Life 9, 221
Lights Out 24
Lillian Gish, Her Legend and Life (book) 151
Lincoln, Abraham 44
Little, Eddie 127
Livingston, Patricia 106
Lloyd, Suzanne 151, 156
London Daily Mirror 90
Lone Pine, California 112, 143, 146, 158, 159, 175, 179
Long, Richard 42, 45, 117
The Long Gray Line 22
Long John 80
Loper, George 44
Lorys, Diana 211
Los Angeles, California 97
Los Angeles Herald and Express 60
Los Angeles Times 147, 219
Lyden, Pierce 32
Lydon, James 28, 29
Lynch, Ken 193, 194
Lynn, Betty 88
Lynn, Diana 25
Lynn, Emmett 54
Lynn, Rita 139

MacDonald, Jeanette 35
Mack Ranch (Arizona) 111
Macklin, David vii, 203–7
MacLaine, Shirley 86
Maddow, Ben 151
Madison, Guy 25
Magers, Boyd 1, 3, 4, 5
Magers, Donna vii
Magnificent Obsession 68
Mahoney, Jock 24
Maibaum, Richard 171
Maloney, Jock 18
Man Called Noon 211
The Man from Laramie 65
Man in the Shadow 131
Man with the Golden Arm 15
Mankiewicz, Joseph L. 15, 121–123
Mann, Anthony 112, 113, 116

Index

A Man's Country 66
Marshall, George 14, 15, 75, 85, 86, 105
Marshall, Herbert 35
Martin, Dewey 42
Marvin, Lee 61, 62
Masterson, Bat 141
Matthau, Walter 125, 126, 127
Mauldin, Bill 46, 47, 48, 51, 53, 54, 221
Maverick 65
Mayer, Louis B. 50, 54
Mayo, Virginia 35
Mazzola, Eugene 101
MCA 163
McClory, Sean 23, 105–106, 118
McCloud 68
McClure, Doug 148, 149, 151, 152, 203
McClure, Spec 25
McCrea, Joel 12, 18, 42, 94, 135, 141, 143, 187
McDonald, Frank 182, 183
McGavin, Darren 188, 189, 190, 202
McGraw, Charles 108
McIntire, John 99, 153, 154
McLaglen, Victor 94
McMurtry, Larry 35
McNally, Stephen 12, 61, 62, 63, 143, 144, 178
McNeil, Don 96
McQueen, Steve 3
MCR 210
Meadows, Audrey 96
Medal of Honor 169, 216, 218
Melbourne Herald 90
Mell, Joe 66
Mendez, Rafael 147
Meredith, Burgess 108, 109, 110
Meredith, Madge 76
Merlin, Jan vii, 122–23, 143, 144–146, 169, 180, 181, 182, 215
Metro Goldwyn Mayer 11, 45–47, 50, 53, 54
Michaels, Dolores 171
Middleton, Robert 144
The Midnight Story 100
Mike Hammer 189
Milford, John 183
Millan, Victor 103
Miller, Alan "Pinky" 163, 164
Miller, Colleen 182, 183–184
Miller, Dean 169
Millican, James 185
Mills, Mort 124
A Minute to Pray…A Second to Die 211
Mires, Rolla vii, 5
Mirisch, Walter M. 141
Mirror Lake (Utah) 36
Mister Cory 107
Mitchell, Guy 18, 163, 167, 168, 179, 207

Mitchell, Thomas 85, 86, 87, 88
Mitchum, Robert 111
Mohr, Gerald 61, 62
Mojave Desert (California) 193, 194
Moll, Giorgia 120
Monogram Studios 27, 184
Monroe, Marilyn 7, 83
Montgomery, George 181, 184, 187, 192, 196
Montgomery, Robert 24
Moore, Garry 96
Moore, Joanna 87, 127
Moore, John 60
Moore, Terry 72, 140–41
Morgan, Henry 96
Morgan, Lee 84
Morgan, Red 199
Moroth, Inga 151
Morris, Wayne 139, 181, 184
Morris Ranch (California) 32
Morrow, Jeff 83
Morrow, Vic 159
MPAA (Motion Picture Association of America) 35, 54
Murphy, Corinne 8
Murphy, James Shannon (Skipper) 13, 88, 114, 127
Murphy, Joe 216
Murphy, Pamela 73, 114, 117, 157
Murphy, Richard 96
Murphy, Terence (Terry) Michael 10, 67, 73, 88, 114, 117, 127, 218
My Favorite Spy 138
My Three Sons 110

Nader, George 109
Nareau, Greta vii
NBC 100, 104, 118, 142, 147, 162, 164, 169
Needham, Hal 137
Neilson, James 112, 116, 117, 119
Nelson, Lori 74, 75–76, 86–87, 88
Neumann, Kurt 28, 32
Nevada Smith 217
Nevins, Francis vii
New Guinea Gold 3
New York Times 89
New York Times Guide to Movies on TV 89
New Yorker 50
Newcomb, Bitter Creek 60
Newport Bay, California 128
Newslife 84
Nicol, Alex 65
Night Passage 15, 16, 111–118, 119, 125, 201
Night Riders 111
No Name on the Bullet 15, 69, 130–135, 148
No Name on the Bullet (book) 135
Noah Films—CCC Film Kunst 212
Noel, Frank 200
Nolan, Lloyd 27, 28, 29, 30, 35

Noose for a Gunman 184
Nott, Robert vii, 75, 80, 94, 173, 194, 199, 203
Nova, Lou 54
Nudie 169
The Nun and the Sergeant 110
Nyby, Chris 167, 168

O'Brian, Hugh 18, 19, 56, 58, 59, 76, 82, 83, 84, 160
O'Brien, Dave 184
O'Brien, Joan 172, 173, 175
Ojala, Arvo 35, 83
Old Tucson, Arizona 101, 104, 107, 196, 197, 199
Olivier, Laurence 15, 123
Once Upon a Time in the West 211
One Trip Across 128
An Open Book (book) 151
Orschel, Marina 147
O'Sullivan, Maureen 76
Oswald, Lee Harvey 180
Overton, Frank 159, 161
Owens, Patricia 128

Paddlefoot 127
Paget, Debra 82
Palmer, Gregg 58, 68, 70–71, 90, 93, 187
Panhandle 208
Paramount Studios 10, 22, 112, 181
Parry Lodge 40
Parsons, Louella 107
Pate, Michael vii, 3, 5
Peavyhouse, Volney 95, 100
Peckinpah, Sam 195
Peer Gynt 16, 107
The Perfect Target 200
Peters, House, Jr. 47, 54
Petrie, Howard 65
The Petticoat Brigade 104
The Phantom of the Opera 52
Picerni, Paul 94
Pickens, Bill 151
Picture (book) 11, 46
Picturegoer 14, 90, 99, 108
Piffath, Rod 200
Pine, Howard 127, 188
Pine, Robert 207–208
Pine Meadows 32
The Police Story 30
Ponti, Carlo 180
Posse from Hell 18, 53, 154, 156, 158–62, 173, 178, 190
PRC 184
Presley, Elvis 12, 150, 179
Pullen, William 80
The Purple Mask 183
Pyle, Denver 80, 94, 141, 201, 204, 205, 206, 207

Quantez 67
Quantrill, William Clarke 41, 42, 44, 196

Index

Quantrill's Raiders 199
The Quick Gun 18, 184–87, 192
The Quiet American 15, 16, 35, 120–123, 129
Quiz Kids 49

Rafferty, Chips 3, 4, 5
Rall, Tommy 99, 102, 103, 104
Ramsey, Ward 159
Randall, Anne 217
Randall, Stuart 161
Randolph, Donald 65, 66
Random, Bob 217
Ranown 216
Rattlesnake Pass (Arizona) 101
Rawhide 215
Raymond, Jeff vii
Real West Romances #5 (comic book) 35
Rebel Without a Cause 15
Red Badge of Courage 11, 12, 45–54, 55, 80, 121, 141, 148, 170, 221
Red Badge of Courage (novel) 46
Red Canyon 40
Red River 35, 140, 141
Red Rock Canyon (California) 73, 82, 192, 195, 214
Red Rock Canyon (Nevada) 153, 172, 173
Red Sundown 131
Redgrave, Michael 15, 120, 121, 122, 123
Reed, Donna 23
Reed, Walter 218
Reid, Elliott 37
Reinhardt, Gottfried 50, 54
Reinhardt, Max 50
Remington, Frederick 102
Republic Pictures 107, 143, 156, 160, 161, 176, 181, 192
Revue 163, 168
Reynolds, William 56, 59, 64
Richard III 15
Richards, Addison 103
Rickenbacher, Eddie 48
Ride a Crooked Trail 15, 16, 87, 124–127, 129
Ride Clear of Diablo 12, 13, 15, 40, 76–80, 82, 113, 153, 154
Ride Lonesome 172
Ride the High Country 217
Riley, Elaine 23
Rin Tin Tin 87
The Ring 100
Ritter, Tex 181, 184
Ritter, Thelma 142
Riverboat 189
RKO 12
Robards, Jason 138, 156
Rober, Richard 37, 201
Roberts, Lee 54
Roberts, Roy 59
Robertson, Dale 12, 135, 187, 217

Robinson's Ranch (Utah) 36
Rogers, Roy 73, 147, 192
Roland, Gilbert 136, 137
Rome, Italy 121, 123
Romero, Cesar 210
Rondell, Ronnie 44
Rooney, Mickey 158
Rooney, Teddy 158
Roosevelt, Buddy 54
Roseanna McCoy 69
Rosenberg, Aaron 93, 96, 97
Ross, Lillian 11, 46, 50, 51
Ross, Paul C. 210
Roughshod 66
Royce, Frosty 73
The Rudells 147
Rudley, Herbert 144
Rush, Barbara 97, 99
Russell, William vii
Russo, Dr. William vii, 34, 122

Sacramento River (California) 46
Saigon, Viet Nam 121
St. George, Utah 172, 188, 189, 190, 201, 202, 203, 207
Salkow, Sidney 185
Sambrell, Aldo 209–10, 211
Sande, Walter 61, 186
Sanders, George 212, 213
Sanders, Hugh 196
Sanford, Erskine 40
Santiago 128
Saturday Evening Post 33
Savage Horde 107
Saxon, John 149–151, 159, 160, 161, 162, 178
Scala, Gia 125, 127
Schary, Dore 22, 50, 54
Schumacher, Phil 73
Schwalb, Ben 184
Scott, Randolph 12, 17, 18, 42, 56, 57, 94, 104, 172, 187, 217
Screen Actor's Guild 199
Seaforth, Susan 182
The Searchers 152
The Second Greatest Sex 116
See Here, Private Hargrove 110
"See What the Boys in the Backroom Will Have" (song) 67
Selander, Les 209, 210
Sepulveda, Carl 44
Sergeant York 48
Set-Up 98
Seven Arts Productions 127
Seven Brides for Seven Brothers 99
Seven Ways from Sundown 17, 18, 152–158, 172, 189
Sevenson, Venetia 157
Shane 113, 132, 138
Sharpe, Dave 59
Shaw, Tom 151
The Sheepman 86
Shelton, Bob 197
Shepard, Allan 164

Sheppard, Jimmy 87, 138, 156, 157, 174, 178, 207
Sher, Jack 102, 136, 137, 138
Sherman, George 17, 143, 146, 155
Shima, Keiko 110, 111
Shoemaker, Bill 135
Shore, Roberta 38
Short, Paul 27, 30, 32, 33, 35, 36
Showdown 18, 175–79
"Shutters and Boards" (song) 179
Siegel, Don 62, 63, 128, 129, 130, 195, 219
Sierra 11, 36–40, 87, 201
Sierra Nevada Canyon (Colorado) 112
Silva, Henry 124, 125, 127
Silver Star 47
Silvera, Frank 56, 59
Silverheels, Jay 73, 102
Silverstein, Elliott 86
Simpson, Colonel Harold B. 7
Sinatra, Frank 15, 142, 189
Since You Went Away 25
Singh, Sita 45
"Singin' the Blues" (song) 207
6 Black Horses 18, 172–175
Sloane, Everett 128, 129
Small, Edward 184, 192, 196, 200, 215
Smith, Dean 156–57, 169
Smith, Richard, III vii
Snow Canyon (Utah) 172
Soldier Parade 100
Son of Destry 88
Sonora, California 55, 60
Sons of the Pioneers 147
Sorenson, Jim vii
Sothern, Ann 187
Springsteen, R. G. 175, 188
Stack, Jack 40
Stack, Robert 40
Staley, Joan 202, 203, 204, 205
Stanislavsky, Constantin 50
Stapp, Marjorie 171
Star of Texas 184
Stars and Stripes 3
Steele, Bob 68, 71, 72, 83, 144
Stehli, Edgar 132
Stephens, Laraine 215
Sterling, Robert 68, 72
Stevens, Bob 143
Stevens, K. T. 76
Stevens, Mark 82
Stevens, Warren 132, 202, 204, 206, 207
Stevenson, Venetia 154, 156
Stewart, Elaine 112, 113, 116, 117
Stewart, James 14, 15, 58, 65, 85, 86, 109, 112, 113, 114, 116, 117, 118, 135
Stier, Ken vii
Stone, Harold J. 176, 179
Storm, Gale 31, 32, 33, 34, 35
Strange, Glenn 48, 54, 196

Stratton, David 1
Stricklyn, Ray 151, 198
Strudwick, Shepperd 32, 34
Stump Run 58
Sullivan, Barry 18, 154, 155, 178, 189, 202
Sully, Frank 54
Summers, Neil 199
Surfside 6 164
Suspense 143
Suspicion: "The Flight" 118–19
Swenson, Karl 134
The Swift Show Wagon 96

"Take Me to Town" (song) 179
Talbott, Gloria 151, 199
Talent Patrol 100
Tall T 172
Talman, William 32, 33, 35
Tammy 205
Tap Roots 45
Tarzan 76
Taylor, Robert 32
Tea and Sympathy 56
Teahouse of the August Moon 109
Terrania 211
Terrell, Steve 162
Texas, Brooklyn and Heaven 24–26
Texas National Guard 45
The Texican 19, 210, 208–211
Thagard, Chuck vii
That Girl 110
There Was a Crooked Man 215
A Thinker's Damn (book) 34, 122
This Is Your Life 30
Thompson, Marshall 91
Thorsden, Kelly 204, 206
3:10 to Yuma 143
Thunderball 171
Tibbetts, John C. vii
Tibbs, Casey 134, 135, 157
Tilghman, Bill 60
Time 19, 90
A Time for Dying 19, 199, 216–219
The Tin Star 112
Tiomkin, Dmitri 113
To Have and Have Not 128
To Hell and Back 7, 10, 12, 14, 15, 16, 18, 25, 29, 30, 46, 58, 68, 78, 85, 88–96, 97, 99, 100, 102, 104, 112, 148, 149, 170, 184, 192, 203, 207, 211
To Hell and Back (book) 93
Tobey, Kenneth 214, 216
Tobias, George 190
Todd, Eleanor 72
Tomorrow the Moon 211
The Tonight Show 71
Toomey, Regis 84
Top Gun 184, 185
Topper, Burt 180
Travers, Henry 23
Treasure of Sierra Madre 12

"True Love" (song) 67
Trunk to Cairo 19, 212–14
Tucker, Mel 155
Tulsa Jack 60
Tumbleweed 13, 73–76
Turner, Scott 179
TV Guide 119, 163, 164
12 O'Clock High 36
20th Century Fox 37, 42, 110, 140, 158, 161, 169, 191
Tyler, Beverly 56, 57, 58, 59

Ullman, Dan 184
Under Two Flags 94
The Unforgiven 18, 46, 148–52, 198, 203
Union City, New Jersey 97
United Artists 17, 100, 110, 120, 127, 138, 141, 148
United States Military Academy at West Point, New York 22
Universal backlot 32, 41, 52, 55, 62, 65, 66, 68, 73, 77, 79, 82, 85, 88, 89, 97, 101, 112, 125, 127, 131, 132, 135, 143, 153, 163, 172, 189, 201, 204
Universal-International vii, 3, 10, 11, 12, 13, 14, 15, 17, 18, 30, 31, 32, 35, 36, 40, 41, 45, 53, 55, 56, 60, 62, 63, 64, 67, 68, 70, 72, 73, 75, 76, 78, 80, 81, 83, 84, 88, 89, 92, 93, 95, 97, 98, 100, 103, 107, 109, 110, 111, 112, 115, 116, 117, 118, 122, 124, 125, 126, 130, 135, 137, 139, 143, 152, 156, 158, 162, 163, 164, 169, 172, 175, 176, 178, 179, 182, 185, 187, 201, 203, 207, 208, 216, 221
University of Southern California vii
U.S.S. *Los Angeles* 108

Valentino, Rudolph 7
Valley of Fire State Park (Nevada) 153
Van Cleef, Lee 74, 76, 162
Variety 168, 216
Variety Clubs International 27
Vasquez Rocks (California) 62, 63, 73, 74
Vejar, Chico 100
Vickers, Martha 27
Vincent, Sailor 88
The Virginian 38, 203
Voss, Howard 49

Wagner, Robert 54
Wagon Master 47
Waightman, "Red Buck" 60
Walk the Proud Land 15, 16, 100–104, 131
Wallace, George 82, 173–174
Wallace, Jerry 179, 207

Wanted Dead or Alive 184
War Arrow 67
War Hero 180
War Is Hell 179–180
Warner Bros. 41, 198
Warren, Earl 76
Warwick, Robert 35, 104
Watts, Charles 196
The Way Back 171
Wayne, John 12, 35, 41, 152, 187
Weaver, Dennis 68, 73
Weaver, Doodles 96
Weaver, Tom vii
Webb, Del 95
The Well 37
Welles, Orson 131
Wessell, Richard 32
Westcoatt, Rusty 84
Western Costume 169
Western Life Romances #2 (comic book) 35
Westmore, Perc 187
When in Disgrace (book) 218
Whispering Smith 18, 19, 22, 147, 162–169
White, Dan 54
White, Jesse 64, 66
White Horse, Black Hat (book) 214
Whitney, Cece 191
Whytock, Grant 184, 192, 196, 199, 202, 215
Wickes, Mary 86, 88
Wilcox, Frank 32
The Wild and the Innocent 16, 135–138
Wild Bill Hickok 25
The Wild Bunch 32
The Wild Innocents 138
Wilke, Bob 116
Wilkerson, Guy 54
Will Penny 217
Williams, Adam 182, 183
Williams, Guy 73
Williams, Jack vii, 83, 93, 116, 117, 126–127
Williams, Rhys 27, 28
Williams, Tex 35
Williamson, Thames 107
Willingham, Mary 178, 210, 215
Willingham, Willard 35, 71, 83, 87, 116, 122, 126, 145, 156, 162, 163, 164, 174, 178, 179, 203, 207, 210, 215
Wills, Chill 74, 75, 76
Wilson, Whip 139, 181, 184
Winchester 73 65, 112, 113, 176
Winterhawk 193, 196
Winters, Shelly 35
Wiseman, Joseph 150
Witney, William 192, 195, 196, 199, 214
The Woods Colt (novel) 107

Index

Woodward, Morgan 124, 125–126, 202
World in My Corner 15, 96–100, 102, 103, 128, 138
World War I 48, 51
World War II 3, 47, 51, 87, 95, 125, 141, 157, 170, 171, 182, 197, 208, 211

Woroner Productions 216
Writers Guild of America 163, 164
Wyatt, Jane 28, 29
Wyatt Earp 19, 141
Wynn, Keenan 108, 109
Wyoming Mail 179

Yarbrough, Tinsley vii

Young, Alan 35
The Young Warriors 207
Younger, Coleman 44
Younger, James 44
Younger Brothers 42
Yrigoyen, Joe 146, 167, 168

www.ingramcontent.com/pod-product-compliance
Ingram Content Group UK Ltd.
Pitfield, Milton Keynes, MK11 3LW, UK
UKHW050532150426
5217IPUK00026B/1904